RISK
WATCH

RISK WATCH

The Odds of Life

JOHN URQUHART, M.D. AND
KLAUS HEILMANN, M.D.

Facts On File Publications
New York, New York ● Bicester, England

RISK WATCH: The Odds of Life

Copyright © 1984 by Kindler Verlag, GmbH

RISK WATCH is a revised English language version of
KEINE ANGST VOR DER ANGST by Klaus Heilmann, M.D., and
John Urquhart, M.D., published March 1983
by Kindler Verlag, Munich.

Grateful acknowledgment is made to the following for permissions to reprint material in
this book:

Pages ix–x, from THE TURNING POINT by Fritjof Capra, pp. 23–24,
    copyright © 1981 by Fritjof Capra, reprinted
    by permission of Simon & Schuster, Inc.

Page 69, figure titled: Cancer Death Rates by Site United States
    1930–1978, from CANCER FACTS AND FIGURES,
    P. 11, The American Cancer Society, 1983.

Page 93, from "Alcohol as a Social Drug and Health Hazard,"
    LANCET I, pp. 443–444, copyright © 1984 by Alex Comfort,
    reprinted by permission of the author and
    Little, Brown & Company.

Library of Congress Cataloging in Publication Data

Urquhart, John, 1934-
  Risk watch.

    1. Risk-taking (Psychology) 2. Fear 3. Technological innovations. 4. Civilization,
Modern—1950- I. Heilmann, Klaus. II. Title
BF637.R57U77 1985   153.4   84-4046
ISBN 0-87196-984-X

Printed in the United States of America

10 9 8 7 6 5 4 3 2 1

Composition by Western Publishing
Printed by R. R. Donnelley and Sons, Co.

Contents

Acknowledgments

The authors are indebted to many people who helped with this book. Margit Heilmann (Munich) translated into German text originally written in English, and Dr. Alfred Amkraut (Palo Alto) translated into English text originally written in German. Malcolm Urquhart (San Diego) suggested the title of the English version. A number of people, knowing that we were writing this book, provided us with pertinent news items and other publications: Marie Barry, Peter F. Carpenter, Susan Laird, and Rose Wright (Palo Alto); Professor F. E. Yates (Los Angeles); Claude Crescioni (Paris); Karen Russell (London). Helpful criticism of the text was provided by Professor Ernst Barany (Uppsala), Peter Hoof (Frankfurt), Professor Harold Hopfenberg (Raleigh), Dr. Otto May (Ingelheim), Dr. Winfried Schlaffke (Cologne), Professor Max Anliker (Zurich), Dr. Lotte Schenkel (Basel), Dr. Robert L. Cloud (Berkeley), Dr. Allan Wolfe (South Laguna), Professor Harry Struyker-Boudier (Maastricht), and Marie E. Barry, Dr. Virgil Place, Peter F. Carpenter, and Joan C. Urquhart (Palo Alto). Constance Mitchell (Palo Alto), Ed Knappman and Kate Kelly (New York) provided invaluable editorial assistance. The secretarial assistance of Marilyn Wells (Palo Alto) was a sine qua non for the entire effort. Many resources of ALZA Corporation (Palo Alto), including use of word processing software and equipment, greatly facilitated work on this book. The cooperation of Facts On File Publications (New York) and Kindler Verlag (Munich), and the skills of Maria Pelikan (New York) and Britta Lucas (Munich) in bringing these two publishers together, are gratefully acknowledged.

Introduction

Risk-taking and risk-avoiding are intrinsic to life itself. Juxtaposing them serves to emphasize the many paradoxes one encounters in threading between risk-taking and risk-avoidance. As we mature, we veer away from the former toward the latter. The quest for vanished youth during our middle years is often expressed by a shift back toward risk-taking, while extreme risk-aversion is often considered a mark of aging.

Risk and fear are twin themes in life. Fear drives us to shun risk, yet risk accompanies any action, however trivial. To grasp opportunity, one must act, and, in acting, one incurs risk: opportunity and risk cannot be separated, and no goal can be attained without accepting risk. When fear paralyzes action, opportunity fades. To understand risk is to balance fear and opportunity. How we try to balance these—as individuals and as a society—reveals strange paradoxes which show how we misunderstand risk.[1] This misunderstanding underlies some strikingly distorted perceptions of the risks of premature death or disability that we face in contemporary life.

We are bombarded by these distorted perceptions, which achieve a certain credibility through sheer repetition. As an illustration, we can cite the following passage from a currently popular book, *The Turning Point,* by Fritjof Capra: "In addition to air pollution, our health is also threatened by the water we drink and the food we eat, both contaminated by a wide variety of toxic chemicals. In the United States synthetic food additives, pesticides, plastics, and other chemicals are marketed at a rate currently estimated at a thousand new chemical compounds a year. As a result, chemical poisoning has become an increasing part of our affluent life. Moreover, the threats to our health through the pollution of air, water, and food are merely the most obvious, direct effects of human technology on the natural environment.

"The deterioration of our natural environment has been accompanied by a corresponding increase in health problems of individuals. Whereas nutritional and infectious diseases are the greatest killers in the Third World, the industrialized countries are plagued by the chronic and degenerative diseases appropriately called 'diseases of civilization,' the principal killers being heart disease, cancer, and strokes. . . . The rise in violent crimes and suicides by young people is so dramatic that it has been called an epidemic of violent deaths. At the same time, the loss of young lives from accidents, especially motor accidents, is twenty times higher than the death rate from polio when it was at its worst. . . . 'epidemic' is almost too weak a word to describe this situation."[2]

One of the aims of RISK WATCH is to correct the distorted perception that we are beset by risks of unprecedented magnitude, and to show that—the threat of war aside (for we have no means to assess it)—the collective risks we face have fallen to a uniquely *low* value that is without historical precedent. To illustrate and document that conclusion, the book seeks to answer five major questions: (1) how should we measure and express risk to permit distinction between big risks and small ones? (2) how can we relate measured risk to a realistic conception of safety, quantitatively defined, and appropriate for balanced judgments of risk versus benefit in today's world? (3) what are the major risks of premature death in contemporary life? (4) how has the risk of premature death in the technologically developed countries changed within the past three generations, and how can these risks be projected to change in the future? (5) how does "victim-oriented" reporting by the news media distort the public perception of risk, and how could this be effectively changed?

There is a great deal more good news in this book than bad. If that is a surprising statement, it is because of the way perceptions of risk are distorted by victim-oriented reporting and because there is little general understanding of how risks are actually measured—a topic that sounds arcane but is understandable in everyday language.

To illustrate one of the distorted perceptions about risk, we accept with remarkably little comment 50,000 deaths per year in traffic accidents, with half those being attributable to drunk drivers; yet we have expended vast amounts of newsprint, air-time, and individual worry time over nuclear power plants, which have yet to kill anybody in 25 years of operations, during which time a million people died in traffic accidents in the United States, plus another million in all the various industrialized countries that have nuclear power programs. The great tampon-toxic shock scare of a few years ago received much public attention, but the total number of victims scarcely equalled one weekend's traffic fatalities. Cigarette smoking is now proven to be responsible for half a million premature deaths yearly from lung cancer and heart disease in the United States alone. This fact gets a modest amount of coverage in the news media, despite the fact that the number of smoking-related deaths is equivalent to three fully loaded 747 passenger jets crashing every day. Yet when an actual jet crash occurs, it is given frenzied attention. For a brief period, airline travel falls off sharply, as does the airport-based car rental business, while the air travel insurance business surges. After a few days, however, these businesses return to normal.

Indeed, a whole catalog of examples could be cited to illustrate the quirkiness of our responses to taking or avoiding risks to our life and health. Many such examples will be discussed in the pages to come. While much has been written about these paradoxes, it can be distilled into four general observations.

● 1. Sudden, surprising news triggers shock and horror and fear.

We know that "people dislike surprises," but sudden bad news certainly sells newspapers and draws people to their TV screens or radios. The fact that "bad news sells" is nothing new, but what is new in the historical sense is the instantaneous dissemination of news, one of the gifts of modern electronic technology. The quantity and timing of information in today's world can scarcely be faulted, but who can say that it does not play much more to our fears than to our understanding? That we are biased today more toward fear than toward opportunity is in large measure a result of so much of our information reaching us in the journalistic format, geared to what can fit an attention span of a few minutes.

One of the aims of this book is to provide some useful ways to learn the news without being exploited by fearmongering reporting.

> ● 2. People find greater misfortune in an accident which befalls a group than if the same number of individuals suffer the same kind of accident individually.

The larger the group, the worse the accident seems—as illustrated by the way traffic fatalities are reported: if ten people die in individual accidents on a Saturday night, there are a few little notes in the paper, but if all ten die in a single accident, it merits a frontpage headline and gets feature television coverage. Of course, big accidents occur infrequently, and thus are "news." In contrast, ten or so people dying on a Saturday night in individual accidents occurs every Saturday night in most big metropolitan areas, and so is not "news."

> ● 3. In voluntary activities people will accept risk that is 10- to 100-fold higher than what they would in activities or circumstances which are imposed on them without their consent.[3,4]

Vehicles—kiddiecars, bicycles, motorcycles, automobiles, trucks and buses, trains, hang-gliders, small and large planes—are a prominent source of risk in our lives today; yet the opportunity to "go" easily outweighs any countervailing fear of accidental death or injury in going. The universal acceptance of the risk of "going" dwarfs the risks of many other hazards that have excited much fear and controversy. Paradoxical attitudes about drinking and driving also illustrate the point about voluntary and involuntary risks: it is all right if I have a couple of drinks and then drive, but it is not all right for the other person to do the same. When we have succeeded in passing strict laws against drunk driving, they pose big problems in uniform enforcement, because everyone wants the enforcement directed at the other guy. Another illustration of the disproportion in the acceptance of voluntary and involuntary risks is the furor that nonsmokers have begun to raise about the risk of "passive" smoking. The issue is undoubtedly tilted a bit further by the unpleasantness of smelling others' smoke.

Many widely accepted human activities are the very essence of risking life and limb. Spend an afternoon in an orthopedic clinic at the foot of a ski resort if you want to understand something about the risks of skiing. Spend a Saturday night in your local emergency room if you want to understand something about the risks of drinking and driving, drinking and fighting, and drinking and being a pedestrian. Spend a day in your local VD clinic if you want to understand something about the risks of sex with strangers—and sometimes with friends. These adverse outcomes have their origins in self-initiated activities, and they illustrate the principle that people will engage in fairly hair-raising activities on their own initiative, while steadfastly maintaining their right to protest vehemently when forced into something quite tame by comparison.

Understanding how risk is measured, and what those measurements show, can allow people to make choices based on information rather than on imagination or wishful thinking.

- 4. There is clear indication that people want to be informed on the nature and extent of risks which our complex world creates, and that, when so-informed in a straightforward manner, will accept more risk than one might be led to believe from many current controversies which have had their origins in devious and belated public revelations about the real nature of the risks involved.[5,6]

This book brings together a large amount of information about the most important risks of premature death or disability in contemporary life, and how—insofar as it is known—these risks relate to certain choices in life. We have also assembled information on some of the risks that have attracted great attention from the news media, but are small—sometimes surprisingly so—when the facts are presented so as to allow easy comparisons with other risks. The examples, and indeed our focus in the entire book, is almost exclusively limited to the risks that prevail in the United States, Canada, Australia-New Zealand, and the countries of Western Europe.

There is a certain unifying theme running through all four points: learning through the fear-provoking element of surprise compromises our ability to balance risk and opportunity. Given the journalistic value of surprise, the dominance of the news media in what we learn about our technological world has gradually pushed us toward overestimation of risk and underestimation of opportunity.

Technology becomes a whipping boy in this imbalance. The Germans have coined a word for it: "technophobia," and West Germany, a quintessentially technology-based nation, currently contends with a small but highly vocal political party, the Greens, that seeks to turn their nation into an idealized pastoral society. Yet technology is so much a part of everyday life that those who yearn for the simplicity of the "good old days" are, if they are not deceiving themselves, certainly deceiving others about the goodness of the "good old days," as we shall show in Chapter 1. But it is not just a matter of having a better understanding of risks then and now, though that is indeed part of understanding risks in contemporary life: understanding the basic concepts of risk is as important in modern life as is a basic understanding of economics, nutrition, or the workings of the body in health and disease—to pick three important conceptual aspects of modern life which can be costly to ignore.

Information is crucial to such understanding, but the methods of generating the information that we need to assess risk are often uncertain. Moreover, the methods of communicating the information—expressing risk—are often confusing, downright misleading, and emotionally charged.

One of the root problems in public discussions of risk-related matters is that the plight of the victims is always emotionally gripping. This fact, of course, leads to one of the basic tenets of journalism: give most of the space to the victims and a few human interest notes about the survivors in the immediate vicinity of the victims, but don't waste any time or space on the nonvictims who tread the same path as the victims. To understand risk, you must take a big step beyond the journalistic view to perceive the number of victims in relation to the number of people who did just what the victims were doing but managed to emerge unscathed. Looking at risk from this perspective is what insurance companies do. Indeed, they have no choice, for they must collect enough in premiums from the nonvictims to pay claims to the victims (or their beneficiaries) and have some left over to pay administrative costs and other overheads, maintain reserves, and to make a profit.

For four centuries, the insurance industry has been rather successfully making these estimates, pricing their policies, selling them, and turning profits ranging from the reasonable to the unreasonable. Business failures among insurance firms are infrequent, which says something about their ability to drive risk out of the risk business. Yet little of the public discussion of risk in the past several years has acknowledged the success of this giant industry in assessing risk. Indeed, the insurance industry itself has been remarkably reticent, while technologists, governmental officials, university professors, consumer groups, and business groups have ventilated extensively on the subject of risk. This book integrates an insurance perspective into our analyses of the risks of premature death or disability.

The lack of acceptance of a uniform standard for expressing risk is one of the reasons that we haggle a great deal about certain risk-related issues. Such a standard for expressing risks could be a big help in making various hazards comparable. Just as it is only when the Richter Scale is added to the report of an earthquake that we can assess its severity, so we need an analogous risk-scale so that everyone can understand to what extent, for example, a newly discovered hazard affects, or might affect, our already-known health risks. The Richter Scale is almost universally comprehended, even if few understand the complex geophysics upon which it is based. So, we believe, might it be with a well-chosen risk-scale, and it is to that end that we offer one in Chapter 3, with an elaboration of its background in Appendix A.

If the book seems to overemphasize the risks of dying, and to neglect degraded physical capacity or mental function, it only reflects the available information. Our public health mechanisms have been correctly focused as a first priority on compiling accurate records on the occurrence of deaths and their evident causes. As a growing fraction of the population reaches hitherto rarely attainable ages, a looming public health task is to quantify and collate information on degraded physical and mental capacities—but that is for the future. The data we have now mostly concern deaths.

It is important to clarify the meaning of the word "risk." Unfortunately, a number of commentators have burdened this word not only with the notion of the probability that something bad may happen, but also with an implication about the extent of the badness. In this cumbersome and confusing view, the same degree of risk could be a very low probability that something very bad may happen, or a fairly high probability that something merely unpleasant may happen. Conveying the ideas of both probability and badness is a heavy burden for four letters to bear, and it obscures the crucial issue of the probability of occurrence. Throughout this book, the word "risk" means the probability that something bad will happen. This practice differs from past, engineering-oriented usage,[7] but is in keeping with contemporary thinking.[8] What the badness is has to be stated in conjunction with the numerical value of its risk of occurring.

Badness comes in various flavors, all entailing some kind of loss: of life, of a previous ability, of a perceived future opportunity, of something of direct monetary value, or of some other quality of life which has value. Because these various values can assume such widely differing importance to individuals, depending on their age and condition of life, it is only sensible to be explicit about the badness so that people can make their own judgments about what the risk of its occurrence means.

The word "chance," by the same token, usually (but not always) means the probability of something good happening—one's chance of winning the Irish Sweepstakes, for example. One would speak of the "risk" of winning the Irish Sweepstakes only if, through a previous win, one had dissipated health in expensive, riotous living and feared the necessity of having to go through it all once again. To avoid judgment about the goodness or badness of the outcome, one can use the neutral term "probability." The term "chance" is simply too ambiguous for us to use it in this book.

A further semantic note is that, because "risk" is synonymous with "probability," it is expressed as a number and does not mean a hazardous activity, product, or other thing whose use or proximity may cause harm; a good general-purpose synonym for such activities or things is "hazard"—as in "smoking is a hazard."

Our last semantic point is that the word "safety" appears only a very few times in this book without being attended by some kind of modifier, such as "degree of safety." When the word "safety" appears alone, it is usually as a direct or implicit quotation from another source. Without some kind of modification or qualification, "safety" is a very slippery word. It suggests or promises an unattainable absolute. Indeed, "safety" (unmodified) is a word of primitive simplicity that has lost its utility in the face, not just of expanded technology, but of growing knowledge about the sometimes malignant complexities of nature.

"Safety" as an unmodified word persists in American political language—for example our regulations on the development of new drugs require that they be "safe and effective"—and no politician wants to be seen accepting anything less than guaranteed absolute "safety" for his or her constituency in what they eat, drink, take as drugs, etc. However, even staying in bed has its risks, and most people in the technologically advanced countries realize, even if our politicians might like to pretend otherwise, that absolute safety is a myth. It is time, therefore, to abandon use of the unmodified term "safety." The Swedes, for example, have done so, with a term that translates into English as "degree of safety"—thus avoiding the unfulfillable promise of absolute safety. It is one of the themes of this book that we should follow this practice by abandoning use of the term "safety" and using instead "degree of safety" or "safety-degree." Indeed, in Chapter 3 and Appendix A we present a specific set of concepts and terms that formally link measured risk and "safety-degree."

Our society faces a dilemma: on the one side it is paralyzed by the fear that technology may become uncontrollable; on the other side, technology—and the research and development which produces technology—is the basis of our social and economic lives. It is an illusion to believe that we can get along without technology, that we can use technology without consequences, or that we can live without risk. The technological age may not be a paradise, but it need not end in chaos and can be as bearable—indeed, considerably more so—as any other age. The precondition for this is to balance fear and opportunity by understanding risk.

Thomas Jefferson wrote: "I know of no safe depository of the ultimate powers of the society but the people themselves; and if we think them not enlightened enough to exercise their control with a wholesome discretion, the remedy is not to take it from them, but to inform their discretion."[5] This book seeks to "inform your discretion" on the subject of the important risks of premature death or disability that prevail in our lives today—how they came to be what they are and where they seem to be heading.

NOTES TO INTRODUCTION

1. *Risk in a Complex Society—A Marsh & McLennan Public Opinion Survey.* Conducted by Louis Harris and Associates, Inc. Marsh & McLennan, 1980.

2. Capra, F. *The Turning Point—Science, Society, and the Rising Culture.* New York: Bantam, 1982, pp. 23–24.

3. Starr, C. "Benefit-cost studies in socio-technical systems," in *Perspectives on Benefit-Risk Decision Making.* Washington, D.C.: National Academy of Engineering, 1972.

4. Kletz, T.A. "The risk equations—what risks should we run?" *New Scientist,* May 12, 1977, pp. 320–22.

5. Bazelon, D.L. "Risk and responsibility." *Science* 205 (1979): 277–80.

6. Payne, B.J. "Dealing with hazard and risk in planning (1)," and Brough, C.W. "Dealing with hazard and risk in planning (2)," in *Dealing with Risk—The Planning, Management and Acceptability of Technological Risk,* edited by R.F. Griffiths. Manchester: Manchester University Press, 1981.

7. British Standards Institution. "Glossary of terms used in quality assurance (including reliability and maintainability terms)." BS 4778 (1979); U.S. Congress, Office of Technology Assessment. "Assessing the Efficacy and Safety of Medical Technologies." Glossary of Terms. September 1978.

8. Royal Society. *Risk Assessment—Report of a Royal Society Study Group.* London, 1983.

1

Risks Then and Now

Many people believe that life in the modern technological era poses risks of disease, injury, and death of an unprecedented magnitude. We receive daily news of pollution, air crashes, toxic drugs, toxic chemicals being added to our foods, nuclear radiation hazards, and the appearance of mysterious lethal diseases such as Legionnaire's disease, toxic shock syndrome, AIDS, and the like. The "best-sellers" on the list of catastrophes change continuously; at the moment, asbestos is high on the list, but among the big news stories of the recent past were the Spanish cooking oil catastrophe, toxic shock syndrome, Three Mile Island in the United States, Flixborough in Great Britain, Seveso in Italy, and so on. Each has become a code word for technological error, breakdown, or other misadventure— some involving actual harm to people, others only the threat of harm.

These incidents compel us to think back to a simpler time, when life was presumably safe, uncomplicated, and something that an ordinary well-educated person could comprehend. We have—or think we have—a vivid image of such a life, for it has been conveyed to us through the combined artistic forces of many great writers of the 18th and 19th centuries and of the great adapters of the film industry who have brought us such classics as *Tom Jones.* These works present an image of life as it was one or two centuries ago. But this image is an illusion, for few of these works convey anything resembling the full magnitude of the risks to life which prevailed at that time. The purpose of this chapter is to put the risks of the past into perspective in relation to the risks that prevail today.

The contrast could not be more stark between life as we know it now and have known it during the past 40 years or so versus life as it was for all of human history up until about a century ago, when a gradual decline in the risk of premature death commenced. That decline accelerated after 1930 and has continued right up to the present.

Before this historic change began, life was punctuated by capricious, premature death with a frequency that is difficult now to comprehend. The risk of premature death in those days can be sensed by reading the inscriptions on old tombstones. Tables and graphs cannot adequately convey what the risks to life then were like. In any case, many of the available statistics are of uncertain reliability. Indeed, the methodical collection of information on vital statistics is one of the many innovations that, starting about 140 years ago, began to postpone death.

One family's history may serve to convey the sense of life as it was. The family is that of Richard Gough, a prosperous, but not wealthy, English farmer. He wrote a uniquely detailed account of life in his village, *The History of Myddle*,[1] which he completed in 1701. The setting of Myddle is much like that of the motion picture, *Tom Jones.*

Richard Gough was born in 1635 and lived to be 88. He had the benefits of a good classical education from a local schoolmaster, but he did not attend university. Richard married Joan Wood in 1661, and they had eight children in the 15 years between 1663 and 1678. Their oldest child, Richard, died at age 26. Their second son, Baddeley, died of smallpox at age 20. (While Richard describes Baddeley as his second son, he was in fact the second son to be named Baddeley, which was Joan's mother's maiden name.) Richard says: "I have omitted to say anything of two children . . . which died in their childhood," one named William and the other also Baddeley. There was a second William, who died at about age 30. Richard's eldest daughter, Joyce, lived to be 61. His middle daughter, Anne, married at age 24 and is known to have borne a daughter, through whom Richard's remarkable history was passed down to modern times, but we do not know how long she lived, nor the fate of her children. Richard's youngest daughter, Dorothy, died at age 28. Finally, Richard's wife, Joan, died at about age 55. Of "my deare wyfe," he wrote, "too good to live with me; and I, not good enough with her to dye."

Richard's long life—long even by today's standards—thus brought him the pain of having to bury six and possibly seven of his eight children, plus his wife. His oldest daughter outlived him by only two years, so he narrowly missed having to bury his entire family.

Richard's sister, Dorothy, married Andrew Bradoke, and they had two children, both of whom died before either was old enough to marry. Andrew also died a few years after marrying Dorothy. Later, she married Richard Glover, and they had a son and daughter, both of whom grew to adult life. Their son, Richard, became an attorney, but he had not married by the time Richard Gough finished his history. The daughter, Dorothy, married unusually early; Richard wrote: "This couple when they married were so younge that they could not make thirty years betweene them, . . . but they going to school together fell in love with one another, and so married. They live lovingly together, and have many children." Richard Gough tells us no more, but evidently fate treated his niece more kindly than it had either her mother or uncle.

This sketch of Richard Gough's family captures the sense of human history as the story of those few who both survived and achieved in an age of capricious, premature death.[2] Of the 18 people explicitly named in Gough's narrative of his and his sister's families, nine appear to have reached their middle years.

Contrast Richard Gough's times with the situation of those born in 1907, a year for which we have good statistics, and also a year in which many of those born are still alive. Half of those born in Western countries in 1907 could expect, on the basis of risks then prevailing, to reach their fifties, a considerable improvement from Richard Gough's time. In fact, those born in 1907 fared much better than expected, because their lives coincided with technological progress that brought about a continuing reduction in the risks of premature death.[3]

This improvement was only interrupted by the worldwide influenza epidemic of 1918–19, the most recent epidemic of infectious disease with high mortality to hit the Western world. One is tempted to say that it was the "last" such epidemic, but in the brevity of our newly won security from contagious diseases, we should note, as

Richard Gough had occasion to recall, the words of the Roman poet Seneca: "No one has found the gods so gracious that he may promise tomorrow to himself: heaven keeps our mortal affairs in a perpetual ferment." These words clearly weighed more heavily on Richard Gough than they do on us, so far.

As those born in 1907 grew, matured, and aged, some of course died, but the life expectancy of those still living increased continuously, and, if 1 out of 5 of those born in 1907 had already died by age 15, and 1 out of 4 had died by age 35, half of those born in 1907 survived to beyond age 65—in striking contrast to Richard Gough's generation. While we are all beneficiaries of the way in which technological progress of the 20th century has postponed premature death, the survivors among those born in 1907 may feel it especially acutely: had there been no subsequent improvement in the risks prevailing in 1907, only 1 in 5 born that year would still survive, versus the 2 in 5 who do survive. Half of those now living who were born in 1907 would have since died had major technological progress not intersected their lives.

Compared to those born 70 years earlier, those born in 1977 entered the world with a radically improved life expectancy. If today's risks remain unchanged in the future, then those born in 1977 will reach age 60 before 1 in 5 has died, age 65 before 1 in 4 is dead, age 74 before half are dead, and age 80 before two-thirds are dead. These contrasts between those born in 1907 and 1977 are shown in Table 1.

The italicized numbers in Table 1 are actual data; the others "promise tomorrow," for they are projections into the future. Table 1 shows how premature death has been largely excluded from human experience in the Western world over the past 70 years. It also indicates, however, that the longest-lived survivors are not living any longer now than they did in Richard Gough's time. Recall that he lived to age 88—probably only one of many thousands born in 1635 to reach that advanced age. The process of aging does not appear to have been altered in this death-postponing revolution in human life.[4,5]

Many myths surround human longevity. Literature overflows with fountains of youth, and even today certain regions have the reputation for exceptional longevity. Systematic study,[4] however,

TABLE 1

SHOWING HOW DEATH IS EXPECTED TO BE DEFERRED AMONG THOSE BORN IN 1977, VERSUS THOSE BORN IN 1907

% Who Have Died or Who Are Expected
to Have Died after Various Ages

year of birth	10%	20%	30%	50%	67%	80%	90%
1907	*1*	*15*	*55*	*67*	75	82	87
1977	50	59	69	75	80	85	89

Years after Birth

Sources: U.S. Bureau of the Census, *Statistical Abstract of the United States, 1979; Historical Statistics of the United States, Colonial Times to 1970,* Part 1, p. 60

Note: Italicized ages are actual data; all others are projections based on prevailing death rates.

reveals several things: (1) the claims of remarkable longevity all come from areas of high illiteracy, with generally poor record-keeping; (2) the greatest authenticated age on record is 114; (3) in Sweden, where systematic health records are kept of individuals owing to the nature of the health care and social insurance systems, there is no documented instance since the system was started early in this century of anyone surviving past 110. About 1 in 10,000 persons in the Western world lives past age 100. Undoubtedly, of course, an occasional individual will live a few years beyond the current records, which, like all human records, are destined to be broken. However, there is no evidence to suggest that the many death-postponing changes of the past century have altered what seems to be a fundamental biological limit on human longevity.

Thus, no one lives any longer now than the longest-lived persons ever did, but, whereas only a very few, like Richard Gough, used to reach that limit, now a very substantial minority reach their eighties. The long-lived are now largely spared the burden of burying their children, whereas for all but the past few decades of human history, it had been an almost inescapable price of reaching old age to bury most or all of one's children.

What has happened over the past century in the Western world is that the risks of dying in infancy, childhood, and young adulthood have fallen precipitously, and the risk of dying in later years has fallen by about half. To illustrate: in 1907, 1 in about 7 newborns died in their first year of life, whereas in 1977, 1 in 67 died then; between the ages of one and four, 1 in about 17 of those born in 1907 died, whereas 1 in about 360 died among those born in 1977—representing a 21-fold reduction. It is small wonder that the image of the dying child was so prominent in Victorian literature and painting, and small wonder that it seems so mawkish today: it is an exceptional event to lose a child in today's world.

Between the ages of five and 14, 1 in about 30 died among those born in 1907, versus a predicted 1 in 300 among those born in 1977; between the ages of 15 and 24, the difference narrows—1 in 20 for those born in 1907, versus a predicted 1 in 85 for those born in 1977. At older ages, the difference between the actual mortality among those born in 1907 and the predicted mortality for those born in 1977 narrows to about a factor of two.

One can visualize the meaning of these numbers in another way, by recalling another cinematic image from the many films showing 18th or 19th century battles in which a broad front of foot soldiers marches in attack toward the other side's stationary battle line. As the attacking front marches forward, soldiers are hit by enemy fire, and fall. The advancing line pulls together, side-to-side, and continues. As the soldiers draw nearer to the enemy line, both the density and accuracy of enemy fire increases, and men fall from the advancing line at an accelerating pace. The ever more depleted line continues to draw together, side to side, until finally, as it approaches the enemy line, the last few men fall, and the battle is over.

Of course, real battles never quite worked out that way, for there almost always were survivors, no matter how badly things went, and often enough the attacking side succeeded in overwhelming the other side's battle line. But in the analogy we use here, the other side is death, destined never to be overtaken, and the field is marked off not in distance but in years. The field is 110 years "long"—using that as an approximation of the age past which no one lives. Each year's crop of newborns comes up out of their trench, at year zero, and commences marching toward certain death, 110 years hence. With each passing year, some are struck and fall, with the line pulling together, side to side, so that there always seems to be an even line which gives no indication that some—or many—have already fallen.

Pursuing this analogy, one may say that, until about 30 years ago, the newborns stepped promptly into a minefield. Recall that the newborns in 1907 lost about 1 in 7 of their "cohort" in the first year of life. ("Cohort" is a Roman military term, akin to a brigade, that has been adopted by statisticians to signify a group assailed by a common enemy—for example, all infants born in 1907, assailed by the then-prevailing childhood diseases.) That minefield has been largely, but not entirely cleared, such that the 1977 cohort of newborns lost only 1 in 67 in their first year of life. Still, the first year of life is a risky time—the risk of death in that year is not to be equalled until the cohort reaches about age 60 along its march to oblivion by age 110.

It is useful to put this whole matter into pictorial terms, which may be conceived as a series of aerial photos of a battlefield, oriented so that the advancing line appears to be vertical and moves across the pictures of the field from left to right. The line closes its gaps by each survivor's shifting to the right as the others fall. Thus, as the cohort shrinks in size, the position of its upper end descends in the picture. These pictorial relations are illustrated in Figure 1, which plots the march of the cohort of 1907 through its life up to the present.

The vertical scale in Figure 1 is marked off in percent survivors, which is a convenient way to allow this method of graphical representation to be applied to various sized groups of people born in a given year. The horizontal axis is marked off in decades of life, from 0 to 110; alternatively, one could put in the actual year of birth of a cohort, and mark off each decade by actual calendar year. The principle of this graphic representation is that the line falls steeply when the risk has been high, and stays relatively flat when the risk was low. (Note that we use the past tense: one can measure risk only after the fact, after the data have been gathered and analyzed.) A flat portion of the line means that the cohort is marching forward in time with no losses, but, since death never takes a holiday at any age of life, the curve will always have at least a slightly downward course, even at the ages when the risk of death is least. Note that the line

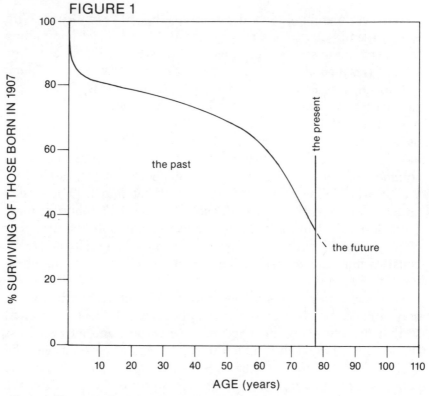

Figure 1. The percentage of survivors among those born in 1907 steadily declined with advancing age. The figure was drawn in 1984, by which time the survivors were 77 years old. Slightly over 40% still survived. Probably the curve will follow the dashed line during the next few years, as discussed in the text.[6]

can never turn upwards, unless in some future time humans discover how to clone themselves, or to reanimate the dead. Children belong to cohorts of their own years of birth, so having children does not add numbers to the parents' cohort. Thus—setting aside the fantasies of cloning and reanimation—the line is destined to run downhill or at best to be almost level; like a river, it cannot run uphill.

In Figure 1, the solid line represents the fate of the cohort of 1907 up to the present, and its extension as a dashed line shows the projection into the future. It is a projection of the future based on the experiences of previous cohorts. For example, in 1984, the cohort of 1907 was in its 77th year of life, and the cohort of 1906 was in its 78th year. Thus, if one wants to make a prediction of the future of the cohort of 1907, one assumes that what happened to the cohort of 1906 during 1984 will be a good approximation of what will happen during 1985 to the cohort of 1907, and that what happened during 1984 to the cohort of 1905 will be a good approximation of what will happen to the 1907 cohort during 1986, and so on to the point of saying that what happened during 1984 to the 110-year-old cohort of 1874 is the best basis we have to predict what will happen to the cohort of 1907 when it reaches age 110 during the year 2017!

As with all predictions, three things are certain: (1) they are almost always in error, by a little or a lot; (2) the farther one extrapolates into the future, the greater is the likelihood of large error; (3) the immediate past usually gives a fairly accurate indication of the immediate future—thus, the effect of 1984 on the 1906 cohort and the effect of 1985 on the 1907 cohort should be very similar.

Let us look in some detail at this last point about how the statistics of the immediate past give a fairly accurate guide to those of the immediate future. Suppose tomorrow a new drug is discovered that cures heart disease. One is tempted to think that there might be an abrupt change in the predicted fate for the 1907 cohort, since heart disease is its biggest cause of death. For many reasons, however, some of which are discussed later in this book, miracle drugs and surgical procedures have their effect only gradually on the kinds of events we are looking at here. Indeed, we can see this point by considering what has happened to the 1907 cohort during its almost eight decades of life: phenomenal progress has occurred in both the prevention and treatment of disease, but, as we shall see shortly, the life curve of the cohort of 1907 has only gradually, although steadily, pulled away from what was predicted would be the case back in 1907, before these changes were even dreamed of. First, let us examine the technological progress that has occurred since 1907 in the medical area.

Table 2 indicates some of the milestones of medical progress which have had a direct bearing on the cohort of 1907. There are other important achievements which could have been listed, but they occurred too late to benefit the 1907 cohort directly. For example, corrective surgery for congenital heart diseases did not become widely available until the 1960's and has improved considerably since then; by that time, the cohort of 1907 was so far along in years that only those with the most minor kinds of congenital heart defects still survived. On the other hand, surgery for rheumatic heart disease

TABLE 2

SOME SPECIFIC, MAJOR TECHNOLOGICAL ADVANCES OF THE 20th CENTURY WHICH CONTRIBUTED TO RISK REDUCTION FOR THE COHORT OF 1907

Year of discovery, recognition, or first use	*technological advance*
1901*	X-rays for diagnosis
1910*	salvarsan: beginning of modern drug therapy
1911*	recognition of vitamins
1921*	discovery of insulin
1936*	liver extract for pernicious anemia
1937*	1st sulfa drug
1944*	introduction of DDT
1945*	penicillin, the 1st antibiotic
1945	1st renal dialysis
1948*	streptomycin, the 1st anti-TB drug
1949	tetracycline, the 1st broad-spectrum antibiotic
1952	1st practical antihypertensive drug
1953**	1st cardiac surgery for rheumatic heart disease
1955*	1st kidney transplant
1960	1st cardiac pacemaker implanted
1962	1st beta blocker drug for circulatory diseases
1970**	coronary artery bypass surgery made practical
1975	parenteral nutrition
1976*	computer assisted tomography

* Nobel Prize for discovery
** Nobel Prize for critical background work

came just in time to benefit some of the cohort of 1907, for they were in their mid- to late forties by the time this surgery had spread from a few pioneering centers to become widely available. Even here, however, those with very severe rheumatic heart disease had died in earlier years, before corrective surgery was even conceivable.

On the other hand, coronary bypass surgery appeared just as the 1907 cohort was reduced to about half its original size, and with coronary artery disease destined to be its foremost cause of death. We can expect that the vigorous application of bypass surgery will tend to flatten the future course of the line in Figure 1 relative to the extrapolation. Only time will tell, however, for the first convincing evidence has just been published showing that coronary bypass surgery has a life-extending effect for patients with certain patterns of coronary artery obstruction.[7] At this time, no one can be sure that these new findings will be: (a) universal; (b) universally accepted; (c) put rapidly or relatively slowly into practice. It will take the participation of the 1907 cohort and the cohorts of both earlier and later years in a multiyear "experiment" before the full effect is known.

This is not to say that the surgical procedure of coronary bypass is itself experimental, for it no longer is in the narrow sense of perfecting the surgical techniques involved. However, the real extent of its impact on mortality in the population as a whole remains to be learned, and it is not yet completely clear how the various distributions of obstructions in the three major coronary arteries influence the outcome of surgery. In this sense, coronary bypass surgery is an experiment, as indeed many things in life are experiments, even though they are not carried out in a laboratory.

Participation in medical-surgical experiments is nothing new for the cohort of 1907. While there is much anxious debate over the ethics of medical experiments involving humans (and animals, too), it must be said that the cohort of 1907 has benefited rather well from having been joined in its march through life by the technological progress listed in Table 2. Indeed, what is listed in Table 2 is but a small part of the technological progress made during the lifetime of those born in 1907. Many of the advances do not have clear-cut dates, because they did not have a precise moment of discovery or introduction into general use. Table 3 lists many of the "undated" technological advances. Some of the things listed—e.g. sewage disposal and central heating—may seem too mundane to characterize as "technological progress"; in fact, however, central heating, sewage disposal, and the provision of safe supplies of drinking water are actually things that rest on a strong base of scientific and engineering knowledge, though in some cases they started to be put in place a century or more ago.

TABLE 3

SOME IMPORTANT RISK-REDUCING ADVANCES DURING THE 20th CENTURY IN TECHNOLOGICALLY ADVANCED COUNTRIES

Safe drinking water
Sanitary sewage disposal
Hygienic food preparation
Pasteurized milk
Refrigeration
Central heating
Scientific principles of nutrition widely applied
Scientific principles of personal hygiene widely applied
Eradication of major parasitic diseases, including malaria
Rodent and insect control
Continually improved prenatal and perinatal care
Continually improved care of babies and infants
Continually improved care of infectious diseases
Continually improved surgical treatment
Continually improved anesthesia and intensive care
Scientific principles of immunization widely applied
Blood transfusion made practical
Organization of intensive care units in hospitals
Continually expanded and improved diagnostic procedures
Continually improved treatment of cancer
Continually improved treatment of occlusive arterial disease
Planned parenthood made feasible and practical
Improved and legalized methods for interrupting pregnancy
Safety in the workplace widely accepted
Safety belts in cars
Continually improved methods for preserving teeth, vision, and hearing
Smoking, obesity, high blood pressure, and sedentary life recognized as damaging to health

While the cohort of 1907 has enjoyed the technological advances listed in Tables 2 and 3, there have been many negative influences on the same group of people. Among these are participation in World War II and, to a lesser extent, the conflict in Korea; environmental pollution, which, whether or not it worsened during the lifetimes of the 1907 cohort, certainly has become a much-discussed topic in recent years; automobile and airplane crashes increased steadily throughout most of their lives; smoking cigarettes became fashionable during their adolescence, for women as well as men; in their forties and fifties both the sedentary life and high-fat diets were fashionable; they were bombarded by a large number of new drugs from the 1930's to the late 1960's which, by today's standards, were hastily and improperly tested before release into the market; they have been liberally treated with powerful antibiotics for minor coughs and colds, a practice that most experts now condemn; they and the foods they ate were liberally sprayed with DDT for about 20 years; they were subjected to a fair amount of surgery later deemed to be unnecessary; Prohibition was repealed when they were in their late twenties, and the consumption of alcohol has been fashionable since, if it was not already so before Repeal; throughout most of their adult lives they have eaten food derived from chemically fertilized and heavily chemically treated agriculture; they are among the first cohorts to spend their entire adult lives under what is often called "the stress of modern life." All in all, it is an impressive list of negatives.

One can judge the net impact of all the negative and positive influences on the 1907 cohort in a very straightforward way: we can compare how these people actually fared—as shown in Figure 1—with how they would have fared *if all the risks of life prevailing in 1907 had continued to prevail throughout the lifetimes of the people born in 1907,* i.e. if there had been no technological progress, with its negatives as well as its positives. Figure 2 shows this important comparison, and also includes, as a sort of reference line, an estimate for people of Richard Gough's time in the latter part of the 17th century.

As you see, there was no difference up to about the 20th year of life between the actual and the predicted curves for survival among the cohort of 1907. But after about age 20, a gap began to develop between the two curves in the direction of fewer premature deaths,

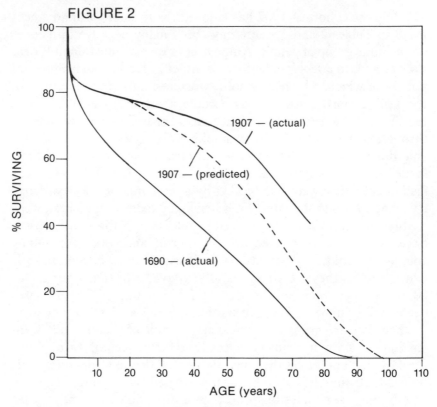

FIGURE 2

Figure 2. The uppermost solid line is the same curve as shown in Figure 1. The dashed line shows the prediction that was made in 1907 for the survival curve of those born in 1907; that prediction was made on the basis of then-prevailing risks. Many improvements since 1907 in methods of preventing and treating disease caused the actual curve to follow a much more favorable course than what had been predicted. The lowermost curve shows the situation for those living in 1690, and is based on data from the city of Breslau, now called Wroclaw, in what is now Poland. Vital statistics were collected much earlier in this city than elsewhere.[6, 8]

such that, as we have already observed, half of today's survivors in the 1907 cohort would be dead if the risks that prevailed in 1907 had not been very substantially reduced in the years between 1907 and the present.

Richard Gough had no expectation through his lifetime that either his or his children's chances of premature death in any way would be improved relative to those his parents faced. In his time, expectations regarding the future were dominated by fears about when the next epidemic would come. His lifetime spanned the recurrence of bubonic plague during the 1660's in England, and it was well-known that the plague had killed about 40% of Europe's population when it struck in the 14th century: some villages in that earlier epidemic lost their entire populations. But fortunately, the reappearance of bubonic plague in Richard Gough's late twenties did not have the force it had had two centuries earlier; smallpox, though, was a recurring nightmare. By 1907, however, that situation had already undergone considerable change, as illustrated by Figure 2 in the difference between the line labelled "1690" and the line labelled "1907-predicted." In 1907, there were already many signs of the favorable impact of technological progress on premature death, and it was already reasonable in 1907 to anticipate that children would face fewer risks than their parents had.

It is also interesting and instructive to compare the risks of the 1977 cohort with those of the 1907 cohort. This comparison is reflected in the life expectancies predicted at the time the 1907 cohort was born, and at the time the 1977 cohort was born. Both predictions are based on the assumption that the then-prevailing risks, as reflected in the death rates measured at that time for each year of life, would continue unchanged into the future. Figure 3 shows this comparison: note that the curve for the 1977 cohort is almost flat until about age 50 and then begins to decline at an increasingly steep rate. Note too that at the beginning of the 1977 curve there is a very much smaller decline than the 1907 curve shows: this is the remnant of infant mortality after 70 years of technological progress against the once-big killers of newborns and infants.

At present, we have only the first few years' data on the cohort of 1977, and we can only guess at what the future will bring for these people. We do know for certain, however, that the cohort of 1977 has successfully negotiated the minefield of its first year of life with losses that are only a little different from those of the immediately preceding years. However, even with newborn and infant mortality so drastically reduced compared to 70 years earlier, it is apparent that progress is continuing.

Table 4 shows how deaths in the first year of life have fallen since 1965. It is very considerable progress, for, with about 3.6 million babies born yearly in recent years in the United States, the change in death risk from 1 in 40 in 1965 to 1 in 84 in 1981 represents a

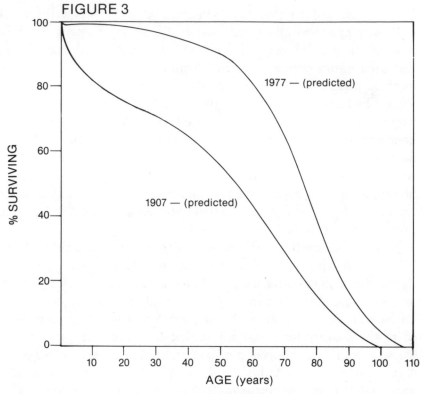

Figure 3. The lower curve is the same as in Figure 2. The upper curve is the prediction for those born in 1977, based on the assumption that the risks prevailing in 1977 will continue unchanged in the future, i.e. that there will be neither progress nor deterioration relative to the present.[6, 9]

decline in deaths from about 90,000 to about 43,000—i.e. an annual saving of about 47,000 lives, which is just about equal to the number of people currently being killed annually in traffic accidents.

We do not yet know if all 47,000 of these salvaged lives can be lived in full, because it is possible that some of these survivors may lack the health and stamina to live a full life. Here again, only time will tell.

As we try to look into the future, it is important to have the perspectives of not just the immediately past few decades—which are only our own life experience—but the distant past as well. In taking this long view, two basic risk patterns can be seen.

One basic pattern is represented by the one we have estimated for Richard Gough's cohort of 1635: it is illustrated by the curve labelled

TABLE 4

RISK OF DEATH IN INFANCY

year	risk of death in first year of life	% dying in first year of life
1965	1 in 40	2.47
1970	1 in 50	2.00
1972	1 in 54	1.85
1973	1 in 56	1.77
1974	1 in 60	1.67
1975	1 in 62	1.61
1976	1 in 66	1.52
1977	1 in 71	1.41
1978	1 in 72	1.39
1979	1 in 72	1.39
1980	1 in 75	1.33
1981	1 in 84	1.19

Sources: U.S. Bureau of the Census, *Statistical Abstract of the United States, 1980;* ibid., Table 114 *Statistical Abstract of the United States, 1982–83,* Table 109

"1690" in Figure 2. This curve has the shape of a slightly distorted triangle. One of the distortions is due to the very high mortality of 1 in 5 during the first year of life in the 17th century; another distortion from a simple triangle is due to the survival of a small minority—to which Richard Gough himself belonged—who survived into advanced years. Let us call this slightly distorted triangle the risk pattern of civilized, pre-technological life—"civilized" because Richard Gough could quote Seneca to us (in Latin) but "pre-technological" because he was essentially defenseless against a barbaric fate that forced him to bury six or seven of his eight children.

The other basic risk pattern, that of technologically modified risk, is exemplified by the predicted survival curve of the 1977 cohort: a slightly distorted rectangle, showing a society in which only a very small percentage of newborns die in the first year, and only a tiny percentage die in successive years, until about the seventieth year of life, after which the risk of death grows rapidly with each succeeding year. The transition to this pattern began to occur about a century and a half ago, gathered force with the discovery of bacteria in the latter years of the 19th century and the implementation of the principles of sanitation and hygiene, and has advanced at a very fast rate since the modern era of drug therapy began after World War II. Figure 4 shows, in the curve marked "1977-actual (???)," an idealized survival curve for the era of technologically modified risk.

In Figure 4, the predicted curve for the 1977 cohort has several noteworthy features. The slight, downward tilt to the line reflects to a considerable extent the toll of accidental deaths—falls, traffic accidents, murder, suicide. After age 70, there appears to be a biological limit to human life that is at once very obvious from the graph, but with respect to its mechanism is not at all understood. The Biblical statement that man is allowed "three score years and ten" seems to be a bit of an underestimate as far as the number of years is concerned. But the Biblical concept that humans are allotted only a finite span is, so to speak, dead on.

It is a pervasive fear of our time to pass the last years of our lives in weakness, pain, and/or mental derangement. Death, which had once been seen "to cut man down, like a flower," or as something that "snatches our precious ones," is feared now for coming in degrees, in a drawn-out period of senescence. Clearly, one of the research priorities for the future is to understand how to compress senescence so as to minimize the period of infirmity before death comes, as come it must.

Part of that effort—indeed one of its first steps—must be to measure and count infirmities, just as we have counted deaths. Infirmities lack the unambiguous finality of death, but it is only by counting and analyzing the resulting tabulations that one can escape from the trap of misleading impressions, rumors, and downright misinformation. And while vital statistics are only so many dry numbers in a table, they can be made to show a great deal of the underlying currents of life, health, and risk in a society. Particularly for the understanding of risks to life and limb, there is no substitute for the facts that are revealed by the most recently available statistics.

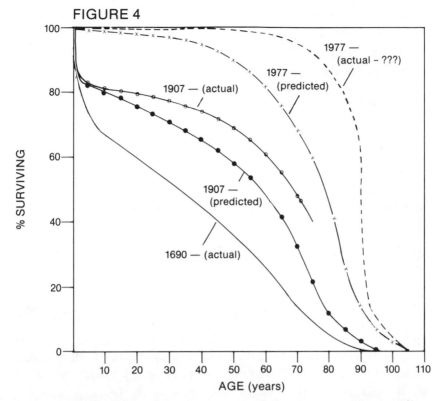

Figure 4. The 1690 (actual), 1907 (predicted), 1907 (actual), and 1977 (predicted) curves are all the same as in previous figures. The curve labelled "1977 (actual — ???)" is only a guess at what the future might bring, assuming: (1) that war, pestilence, or famine — the three traditional scourges of mankind — do not overtake us; (2) that progress continues.

NOTES TO CHAPTER 1

1. Gough, Richard. *The History of Myddle.* First published 1834. Reprinted by Penguin Books, 1981.

2. Wingley, E.A., and R.S. Schofield. *The Population History of England, 1541–1871. A reconstruction.* Cambridge, Mass.: Harvard University Press, 1981.

3. Beeson, P.B. "Changes in medical therapy during the past half-century." *Medicine* 59 (1980): 79–99.

4. Fries, J.F. "Aging, natural death, and the compression of mortality." *New Eng. J. Med.* 303 (1980): 130–35.

5. "Britain's oldest man." *The Times* (London), 29 May 1982.

6. U.S. Bureau of the Census. *Statistical Abstract of the United States, 1981,* Table 107; *Historical Statistics of the United States, Colonial Times to 1970,* Bicentennial Edition, Part 1, Washington, D.C., 1975, p. 60.

7. European Coronary Surgery Study Group. "Long-term results of prospective randomized study of coronary artery bypass surgery in stable angina pectoris." *Lancet* 2 (1982): 1173–80.

8. Doll, H. *Lehrbuch der Lebensversicherungsmedizin.* Karlsruhe: G. Braun, 1959, p. 84.

9. *Statistical Abstract of the United States, 1980.*

2

Progress and Risk

It is clear from the previous chapter that those who have lived since the turn of this century have witnessed dramatic reductions in the risk of premature death. These changes did not occur by accident, but are consequences of prompt and systematic applications of new scientific knowledge to human life. This may seem a remote and mysterious business, viewed from the perspective of today, when so many technically complex matters intersect our lives. It is instructive, therefore, to turn back in history to the beginnings of the changes that have led us to the current era of technologically modified risk, and to examine a time when people far less technically sophisticated than we took the first and—because it was the first—the boldest step to reduce risk.

In order to highlight three important features of risk, this chapter analyzes two very simple but important discoveries made over 200 years ago: one, by Zabdiel Boylston, of an effective but very hazardous procedure of protecting people from smallpox by inoculating them with small amounts of infected material directly from smallpox patients, and the other, by Edward Jenner, of how the simple procedure of vaccination could effectively prevent smallpox with a risk to the recipient so small that it was not even recognized for many years after vaccination was adopted. Implicit in the story of Boylston and Jenner are several important ideas: (1) risks of unknown magnitude had to be taken in this quest for progress; (2) progress was judged by the comparison of risks—vaccination was better than Boylston's inoculation, which in turn was better than contracting smallpox; (3) even in the face of clear evidence of benefit, some risks are nevertheless unacceptable to many, as illustrated by the persistent controversy that surrounded Boylston's inoculation method and its practice by others.

Vaccination against smallpox was the first successful application of science to the prevention of a killing disease. Jenner, an English physician, established the method in 1792. His work had almost immediate effect, for smallpox was a recurring scourge, striking people of all ages and social conditions. In an epidemic, about 1 in 7 of those infected would die, and many of the survivors would be disfigured because of the peculiar scarring left after the skin pustules healed. The familiar mark of vaccination we know today illustrates the kind of scarring left by not one, but a hundred or more skin lesions over the body, usually including the face. Recall that Richard Gough's son, Baddeley, died at age 20 of smallpox—a common event then, but today it is unthinkable that an otherwise healthy 20-year-old should die in a sudden epidemic of infectious disease. In the "good old days," anyone who had reached middle age had almost certainly lived through at least several smallpox epidemics and had almost certainly contracted the disease.

Probably Richard Gough had previously had smallpox, for two notable characteristics of the disease were: (1) those who survived were never re-infected, and (2) during a smallpox epidemic, few of those not previously infected escaped the disease. This latter characteristic made it easy to recognize the success of Jenner's vaccination, without the need for any more statistical analysis than common sense provides to an observant person.

Jenner's discovery in 1792 began the process of eliminating smallpox first from the Western world and ultimately from the entire planet. The World Health Organization, through a ten-year international effort, finally succeeded in breaking the chain of infection in 1979 by isolating the last human smallpox victim in East Africa. The last victim survived, and, with this person's recovery, the last of the virus was gone—except for a few samples stored in WHO laboratories for future reference.

Two basic weapons allowed the unprecedented achievement of

eradicating an infectious disease: (1) methodical application of Jenner's vaccination procedure, little changed in the nearly two centuries since his discovery, combined with (2) meticulous fieldwork to identify and isolate smallpox victims so that they would not infect others. The second weapon depended much on modern transport and telecommunications, permitting men and material to stay one jump ahead of the smallpox virus, even in conditions of human life that make Richard Gough's village of Myddle seem a luxurious, advanced society.

Jenner's discovery had one further consequence. It was abstract, but was in many ways far more important than the triumph over smallpox. He demonstrated for the first time that it was possible to apply the scientific method to combatting human disease. His success, based on abstract reasoning, experimental design, and observation, showed that man could intervene in matters of life and death that had previously been ascribed to the gods, providence, fate, or the miasmas that human imagination had conjured up over the millennia to account for the incessant thievery of young human life. Jenner's discovery accelerated Western mankind's break with fatalism.

Jenner was certainly not the first to apply the scientific method to the physical world. By Jenner's time, the scientific method had already shown its value in providing understanding of some aspects of the physical world. Moreover, it had been applied with astonishing clarity in the early 1600's by William Harvey to demonstrate the circulation of the blood, replacing in a single stroke the orthodox teaching of over 1500 years that blood and spirits ebbed and flowed, to and fro, separately in the arteries and veins.[1] Harvey's demonstration—consummately clear and logical though it was (and it is an astonishingly fresh and lucid work to reread today, 350 years later)—had little practical value to the primitive arts of medicine and surgery as then practiced. It was Jenner who first used the weapon of Galileo, Newton, and Harvey to strike fate a blow utterly without precedent.

If criticism of man's meddling with nature is a familiar theme today, one can look back at Jenner as the first whose meddling had a big impact. Scholarship can of course show that Jenner's work had certain antecedents, but Jenner's discovery gave the first sure light along the path of medical-technological progress. If smallpox could be overcome by rational man, why not other scourges as well?

The most direct antecedent to Jenner's work was that of a Boston physician, Zabdiel Boylston. Seventy-five years before Jenner, Boylston had learned that one could apparently inoculate people with pus from the smallpox lesions of others, produce thereby a mild case of the disease, and thus obtain life-saving immunity in subsequent epidemics. The concept of "immunity" as we know it today was certainly unknown then, but it was understood by all that anyone who had once had smallpox would never contract it again. The idea of inoculation came originally from Turkey, reached England, where it had occasional use, and was brought to North America by Cotton Mather. There it found a receptive audience in Zabdiel Boylston, who was an immune survivor of smallpox. In the face of an appearance of the disease in Boston—brought in by the crew of a visiting ship—he tried inoculation on his son and two others. Each had mild cases of the disease and survived with the precious immunity.

With a growing epidemic in Boston, Boylston proceeded to inoculate 247 others, six of whom died. He did not lack volunteers, because fear of the epidemic drove people to him, and at least one of those who subsequently died was at first rejected by Boylston for being too frail to undergo the inoculation. Boylston's medical colleagues were strongly opposed to this revolutionary practice, and were probably more than a bit put off by Boylston's sudden popularity. The six deaths brought matters to a head. Boylston was seen to have violated two of the ancient injunctions of Hippocrates, whose teachings had guided the ethics of the primitive art of medicine since antiquity: "Above all, do no harm to anyone, nor give advice which may cause his death."

In his boldness, Boylston stood alone among the physicians in Boston, so he had the outrage of his professional colleagues to face, as well as that of much of the community. When the smallpox epidemic had finally run its course, however, a careful count of victims revealed the following: 5759 people had developed smallpox, 844 of whom had died—1 in 7. None of the people previously inoculated by Boylston had been infected in the epidemic, so that 6 in 247, or 1 in 41, died in the inoculated group.[2,3]

This striking reduction in the risk of death exonerated Boylston and demonstrated the principle that smallpox could be prevented by human intervention. In subsequent years, others practiced the inoculation procedure, but always in a limited way, and rarely without controversy.

It was Jenner's genius to recognize that the almost innocuous disease called cowpox provided a safe means to the same end as Boylston's obviously hazardous inoculation. Infection with the cowpox virus had the ability to create immunity to smallpox via an infection that was seen to be trivial. The story goes that Jenner was examining a young woman with a number of broken-out areas on her skin. When Jenner said that one possibility was smallpox, she replied that it could not be smallpox, for she had already had cowpox. Hearing this remark, and recognizing the truth of her folk wisdom, Jenner associated it with Boylston's inoculation method and deduced the idea of inoculating people with the harmless cowpox material.[4]

Jenner's invention illustrates the power of the integrative mind: he combined two previously unassociated facts, neither of which alone had much practical value, but which in combination represented the first great advance in medical science and technology.

Today, in the light of 190 years' experience with Jenner's vaccination, we now know that the procedure is not completely free of risk. Indeed, the risk of death due to ordinary vaccination is on the order of 1 in 100,000. It is an obvious improvement on Boylston's method, which had a risk of death of about 1 in 40—in other words, 2500 times greater. Relative to smallpox itself, with its death-risk of 1 in 7 during an epidemic, the 1 in 100,000 death-risk of vaccination constituted a 14,000-fold dilution of risk.

Fortunately, much time passed after Jenner's discovery before the risk of vaccination became evident, so that Jenner's method did not suffer the same fate as Boylston's. It was only after the disease had been absent among Americans for a number of years that the United States gave up vaccination; the British had done the same thing some years before. These were risky decisions, for, as unvaccinated people grow in numbers, a population of susceptible people develops, making the chance reintroduction of the virus an ever-bigger potential catastrophe. Fortunately, that did not happen before the final eradication of the disease in 1979, although the British had a brief, nasty fright several years later when an accident in a World Health Organization laboratory in England allowed the virus briefly to get loose once again. The laboratory's director committed suicide, and, in that indirect way, might reasonably be counted as the last victim of smallpox.

The story about Boylston is one of long ago, but the dilemma he faced is replayed over and over again in today's world, though fortunately the risks involved in the alternatives today are much, much less than those faced in the 18th century, "when life was simple." For example, the people who had to decide in 1976 whether or not to proceed with the "swine flu" immunization program sat in the same hot seat that Boylston had. They were confronted with incomplete, even sketchy, information which suggested that an epidemic of a particularly virulent strain of influenza virus was coming—one that might rival the 1918–19 epidemic mentioned in Chapter 1. When the ensuing inoculation program turned out to have a small but definite risk of causing a serious neurological condition, there was much furor in the media. And then, when the epidemic failed to materialize, the whole inoculation program was abruptly terminated. It jeopardized the careers of the people involved in the decision to undertake the whole crash program of vaccine development and inoculation: all of them had to leave their positions in the U.S. Public Health Service. In a big bureaucracy, it is always easier to do nothing than to take bold action.

These examples raise the issue of how one logically and rationally goes about avoiding or minimizing risk. They demonstrate that while we show a fairly consistent pattern of behavior intended to minimize needless effort or needless economic cost, we do not practice risk-avoidance in anything resembling a logical and consistent manner; we are frequently penny-wise and pound-foolish. Basic to any program of minimizing risk has to be an understanding of which are the big risks and which are the small. We get most of our information from the news media, including almost all of our information about the risks in our lives, but unfortunately the matters which preoccupy the news media are most often the small risks and least often the big risks.

Perhaps part of the reason is to be found in the fact that we have a fairly direct sense of our effort and a direct measure of economic cost. Moreover, we can anticipate future effort or cost, and, because both are subject to measure, we can take logical steps to minimize either or both. But risk is something else: its measures are those of the statistician—too abstract for everyday use. Perhaps if a readily grasped measure existed, people could budget their risks as they budget their effort, their time, and their spending. It is to the subject of measuring risks that we now turn.

NOTES TO CHAPTER 2

1. Harvey, W. *De Motu Cordis* . . . Frankfurt, 1628. Translated and reprinted by Britannica Great Books, Vol. 28, Chicago, 1952, pp. 265–304.

2. Moore, F.D. "Muddy river and Boylston's 250th." *New Eng. J. Med.* 284 (1971): 1438–39.

3. Moore, F.D. "Therapeutic innovation: ethical boundaries." *Daedalus* (Spring 1969): 502–22.

4. Underwood, E.A. "Edward Jenner: The man and his work." *Brit. Med. J.* 1 (1949): 881–84.

3

Measuring and Comparing Risks

While dying is not the only bad thing that can happen to you—and sometimes not even the worst—it is the natural focus of attention both in charting human progress and in defining priority hazards. Death is inherently newsworthy: most people can count on at least a brief note in the newspaper when they die, no matter how ordinary their lives or how ordinary their deaths. Yet it is a relatively recent development to keep track of the causes of death and the number of people dying from each cause as part of the attempt to improve health and reduce the risk of premature death.

In this chapter, we describe two fundamentals in the understanding of risk: (1) collection and analysis of critical data that define risks and risk factors; (2) how risk can be expressed in simple but quantitative terms, so that the larger hazards in one's life can be distinguished from the smaller.

During the 1840's, a Boston physician, Lemuel Shattuck, first articulated the concept that it was an essential responsibility of government to register both births and deaths, plus the causes of death— the cause of births being taken for granted. Shattuck's analysis of these so-called vital statistics for the city of Boston revealed previously unrecognized major health problems, and his recommendations for doing something about them anticipated many public health measures which were gradually put in place over the succeeding two or three generations. Shattuck had the clarity of vision to recognize that life is a continual "experiment of nature," and that, by compiling and analyzing some of its basic facts, such as the numbers and evident causes of death, one can gain an understanding of the principal hazards of life and seek to minimize the risks they pose. Like many ideas "whose time has come," these ideas simultaneously took hold in England: registration of births and deaths also began there during the 1840's, under the leadership of another foresighted individual, William Farr.

Registration of deaths and their causes proved to be especially valuable during the latter half of the 19th and first half of the 20th centuries, when capriciously occurring, acute diseases were responsible for a substantial fraction of deaths. For example, registration of deaths was already in place at the time of the big cholera epidemics in London in 1849 and 1854, and so provided essential data for John Snow's analysis in 1855 that demonstrated the water-borne transmission of the disease. Snow's work preceded the discovery of bacteria by about three decades, but nevertheless showed conclusively that cholera was spread by water contaminated with a material so small that the water could appear pure to the naked eye. In addition to its practical value, Snow's work became one of the intellectual cornerstones of the scientific discipline of epidemiology,[1] but he could have done little without the registration of deaths and their causes by William Farr.

As the acute infectious diseases and tuberculosis were mastered, chronic diseases have come to be responsible for the majority of deaths. When diseases are chronic, there is often more than one disease present, and that complicates the process of defining the cause of death in the relatively simple terms that have to be used in filling out a death certificate. But for many decades after Shattuck's pioneering work, most of the attention focussed on infectious diseases, because these were then the biggest cause of premature death, and thus the biggest risks to both health and life. That focus, in turn, made sanitation and personal hygiene the top priorities of the day. This is not to say that a century ago people never died of cancer, heart disease, or stroke; some certainly did, but the majority of people died prematurely of communicable diseases, often before they had reached the age where heart disease, cancer, and stroke are prevalent. Shattuck's and others' data collection and analysis showed that the then-leading death-risks came from communicable diseases amenable to control through sanitary measures, quarantine, and improved personal hygiene. However obvious that fact may be today, it was anything but self-evident then, and its acceptance was only gradual: it had to displace the prevailing notion that people died prematurely because they failed to obey what were called "the laws of nature"—a widely held, fatalistic, and very vague concept.

It was a century-long effort to bring about the realization of the principles first taught by Shattuck, Farr, and others. The result is that people in the industrial countries of the world are now well-schooled in the basic principles and practice of sanitation and personal hygiene. With this, plus the many concomitant improvements discussed in Chapter 1, the overall risk of premature death has been drastically reduced, life expectancy has been markedly extended, and a whole new set of death-risks and hazards are now before us. The "when" and the "how" of death have changed; "whether" one dies is unchanged, of course, because the death rate remains, as one of our teachers liked to say, "one per person."

In Shattuck's time as now, the priority hazards are not revealed by what everybody is talking about, but by inspection of what most people are dying of, and by deducing from that and other information what sorts of people are at greatest risk of dying. These questions are the purview of the discipline of epidemiology, which has formally integrated the concept of risk factors into medicine. Epidemiology is responsible for the study of the factors that play causative or supporting roles in disease, how diseases are influenced by the environment, when and why certain groups of people are exposed more or less strongly to various hazards and how these translate into patterns of disease, and, to some extent, how prophylactic and therapeutic measures affect a disease and its course. The shift from acute, communicable to chronic, noncommunicable diseases has beset epidemiology with many complexities, but its fundamental logic remains no less valid than 130 years ago, when John Snow used it to demonstrate the water-borne transmission of cholera.

Because Snow's work illustrates so lucidly the basic principles of epidemiology, and because epidemiology is such an important method in gaining an understanding of risks in contemporary life, it is worth reviewing how Snow was able, working alone, to deduce that cholera was transmitted by water contaminated with microscopic amounts of fecal matter from cholera victims. Cholera is a most virulent form of diarrhea, which would suddenly attack large numbers of people and then gradually disappear from the population until some later time, when it would suddenly reappear. It was a dreaded disease, for over half of those who contracted it died from dehydration due to rapid and overwhelming loss of fluid, via the torrential diarrhea that is the hallmark of the disease. In Snow's time, there were as many theories about the transmission of cholera as there were physicians who tried to treat it. Bad air or accumulated rubbish figured prominently in many of the theories.

Snow conceived the idea that the disease was waterborne after an explosive outbreak of cholera struck the neighborhood of Golden Square in the Soho district of London; in a few days' time it killed over 500 people living within a few blocks' area. He drew a detailed map showing the residence of each victim, and saw that the deaths centered around a public water pump that was much favored in the neighborhood for the taste and clarity of its water. There were a few exceptions to this pattern of distribution, but he pursued these and learned that some peoples' choices of water source were unrelated to the proximity of the pump in question and deviated from the general pattern in ways that were consistent with his theory.

Snow's opportunity to test the theory came when he discovered that a large area in the south of London was served by two competing water companies. The Lambeth Co. drew its water from the Thames River about ten miles upstream from London; the Southwark & Vauxhall Co. also drew its water from the Thames, but from within London, where the water was very dirty, so that it had to be filtered to make it clear. About 20 years before, the two companies had laid their pipes and solicited subscribers, with the result that adjacent houses were served by one firm or the other in a large area in which about 300,000 people lived. It was, in effect, a gigantic "experiment of nature" in which 300,000 people were divided into two groups on the basis of a decision made about 20 years earlier about which water firm to subscribe to. At that time, both firms drew their water from the Thames within London, so there was little to choose between them. It was some years after the initial subscription that Lambeth moved its source 10 miles upstream.

Snow's description is eloquent: "The experiment, too, was on the grandest scale. No fewer than 300,000 people of both sexes, of every age and occupation, and of every rank and station, from gentlefolks down to the very poor, were divided into two groups without their choice, and, in most cases, without their knowledge; one group being supplied with water containing the sewage of London, and, amongst it, whatever might have come from the cholera patients, the other group having water quite free from such impurity."[2]

When cholera struck in the late summer of 1854, Snow monitored the reports gathered by William Farr of cholera deaths within the area served by the two water firms, and simply went to the residence of each victim to learn from which firm their water came. There were 8.5 times as many cholera deaths in the houses served by Southwark & Vauxhall as in the houses served by Lambeth. How else could this huge difference be explained than by Snow's theory of water-borne transmission? Thus the theory was confirmed, with the added insight that the filtering done by Southwark & Vauxhall indicated that the infecting agent had to be of microscopic size—otherwise it would have been caught by the filters used to clarify the water.

Certainly not everyone who drank Lambeth water escaped getting cholera, nor did everyone who drank S&V water get cholera. In fact, only a small minority of those who drank S&V water did get cholera. It remains a mystery why, on an individual basis, only some exposed people contract a disease. The relatively few cholera victims among the Lambeth subscribers must have gotten contaminated liquids or food in other ways. These are minor issues, however, in the face of the large difference in cholera incidence among people who had been divided into two groups on so evidently a random basis. About 30 years later the cholera bacillus was identified, demonstrating the microscopically small agent that Snow's epidemiologically proven theory required. In the intervening 30 years, however, Snow's work showed the practical steps that could be taken to prevent cholera epidemics: isolation of cholera patients, strict personal hygiene, and restricting water sources to those free of contamination by sewage.

Snow's work embodies two intellectual and two practical achievements. The two intellectual ones were: (1) to draw what turned out to be the correct inference that cholera was water-borne, decades before microbiology developed and could provide direct evidence about the actual mechanism; (2) to recognize how he could put the inference to test on a gigantic scale, through the "experiment of nature" created by the two companies' overlapping water service to

300,000 people. His two practical achievements were: (1) to suspend all other activities and devote his full time to gathering the data during the critical few weeks of a major cholera epidemic, and (2) promptly to put the whole story together in a beautifully lucid short book, published in 1855. It is still an inspiration to read how his reasoning cut through the prevailing confusion created by many conflicting, poorly reasoned theories.

Snow's analysis was greatly facilitated by the fact that cholera is an acute disease, occurring within a few days of exposure, developing fully within a few hours of its onset, and with only a few days needed to reveal its outcome of survival or death. He did not have to contend with long periods of incubation or of ambiguous outcome in those who contracted the disease. Since Snow's time, and with rapidly growing force after the discovery of bacteria in the 1880's, the acute bacterial infections have been reduced from leading to minor causes of death. The greatest impact of this change has been practically to banish these infections as causes of death among infants, children, and young adults. This immense achievement has come about through the combined power of epidemiological and microbiological studies, translated into the practice of sanitation and personal hygiene, and reinforced by the more recent advent of the sulfa drugs and antibiotics.

Consequently, our leading causes of death now are chronic diseases, such as coronary heart disease and cancer. Their causes are as unclear as the cause of cholera was in the time of John Snow. The use of the epidemiological method against these chronic diseases is complicated by the long periods of time required for them to develop, and for their outcomes to become known after various measures of prevention or treatment have been taken.

People are surprisingly difficult to keep track of over long periods of time, and in a way which is relevant to the epidemiologic study of chronic disease. We start and stop taking prescribed medicines at odd times; we move, change jobs, change doctors, stop and restart smoking, have episodic binges of eating or drinking, travel to all corners of the earth, change mates and/or sex partners, change diets, change coffee and tea consumption, and so on and on. Very few people write down any of this kind of information on their own initiative, and it is difficult to induce people to do so in a way which gives a reliable record. Anyone who travels on business and has to keep an expense record knows how easy it is to neglect to record a major expense item that is impossible to reconstruct accurately after the fact. Those problems are multiplied many times over in trying to extract useful data in the study of chronic human diseases, not the least because details which turn out later to be critical are often not noted in the first phases of a study.

Despite the problems posed by chronic disease, however, a great triumph of epidemiology in the 1950's was to demonstrate the causal role of cigarette smoking in both lung cancer and coronary heart disease. These studies were based on principles closely analogous to those used by John Snow a century earlier. Just as Snow's theory about the water-borne transmission of cholera did not have the benefit of knowledge about the cholera bacillus, so the studies on the "smoke-borne" cause of lung cancer did not have the benefit of knowledge about the precise nature of potentially cancer-causing chemicals or other factors in cigarette smoke. It is useful to review the nature of the evidence that epidemiology has provided about cigarette smoking, lung cancer, and coronary heart disease.

The inference that smoking causes lung cancer was suggested by the fact that there are very few nonsmokers among lung cancer victims, and that most lung cancer victims are heavy smokers. A big "experiment of nature" was monitored both in England and the United States by asking people to identify themselves as smokers or nonsmokers and then literally to wait and see what they died of. That information came from what was written on the death certificate— following the footsteps of Shattuck and Farr.

Lung cancer turns to be about 15 times more frequent a cause of death among smokers than among nonsmokers, thus confirming the original inference. An unsuspected but important result also emerged from the data, however: deaths from cardiovascular diseases, principally coronary heart disease, were about twice as frequent a cause of death among smokers as among nonsmokers. Coronary heart disease is the leading cause of death in North America and Europe; doubling the already leading cause of death means a very big increase in the risk of premature death. This unexpected finding identified cigarette smoking as the greatest single hazard in contemporary life.

There are other aspects to the risks of cigarette smoking which will be discussed in Chapter 5. The main point in the present context is to understand the nature of the original evidence that was developed in the 1950's, using essentially the same epidemiological principles and methods that John Snow had used in the 1850's, but this time applied to the much more difficult-to-analyze situation of disease conditions that start to develop only after years of exposure to the causative agent and worsen slowly. What Snow was able to accomplish in a few weeks during the late summer of 1854 with drinking water and cholera took a number of years to accomplish during the 1950's with cigarette smoking, lung cancer, and coronary heart disease.

The long duration of epidemiologic studies of chronic diseases is not the only problem confronting the use of this method, however. Another difficulty is that, in some countries—for example, West Germany—there are very strict laws governing the privacy of personal information, indeed so strict that they almost preclude useful epidemiologic studies. As an illustration, even though West Germany was the first country in which thalidomide was marketed and in which probably the largest numbers of children were deformed by this drug, it was never possible for the Germans to establish a central registry of congenital malformations as a data base for subsequent epidemiological studies.

Of course, having public agencies collect data on conditions affecting the living goes a big step beyond what Shattuck and Farr pioneered in the 1840's with registering deaths and their evident causes. Our attention now turns to the mastery of various diseases which themselves are not primary causes of death—Alzheimer's disease, for example—and to do so requires access to data on living people with the disease. If we make it impossible to build such a data base, we are effectively forcing ourselves back to the days before Shattuck and Farr. At the same time, the privacy and confidentiality of sensitive personal health and disability information are precious to today's victims who are being asked to give access to such private and often sensitive information, mostly for the benefit of people in the future. It is a difficult problem to which we shall return at the end of the book.

In the United States, there is an added problem: it has become difficult to guarantee the protection of confidential information gathered in clinical or epidemiological studies. It is one of the unexpected consequences of the Freedom of Information Act, which was intended to give everyone access to the workings of the government. The principle is noble, but the government is involved in so many facets of society that the principle's nobility is not always preserved in practice. For example, it is a matter of current legal controversy whether Procter and Gamble, the producers of the RELY tampon, have the right to learn the names and addresses of the individuals who were included in the epidemiological studies done by the Center for Disease Control on the role of tampons in toxic shock syndrome. Any company in their position in that matter might reasonably want to be able to audit that study, and possibly to challenge the interpretation of the data. Many epidemiologists fear that people will grow increasingly reluctant to participate in such studies if they know that they might be subject to an indefinite future of being pursued for questioning and for potential participation in legal actions arising out of a study.

So, while Germans veer toward one extreme in sometimes over-protecting privacy and Americans veer toward the other extreme with a certain zeal to dispel privacy, the net effect of both is to cloud the prospects for good epidemiological studies at a time when they have become one of our main methods of assessing risks and identifying risk factors in contemporary life. It is as if John Snow had been denied access to the names and addresses of the cholera victims for fear that the water companies might sue, or out of a general concern to protect the privacy of cholera victims and their families. Today we tend to make an issue out of the propriety of giving out names of disease victims so that some mad scientist can, as it were, go knock on their door and ask silly questions, such as "from whom do you buy your water?"

There is another, often-overlooked mechanism for collecting data on the living for subsequent correlation with disease and death. It is provided by the insurance industry, which for decades has developed correlations between information collected at the time of application for insurance and what the firm subsequently is asked to pay in claims. In a sense, this is epidemiology with a financial overlay and is called actuarial prediction. The insurance industry has made a signal contribution to risk reduction by proving and publicizing the risk of premature death associated with high blood pressure. The first big insurance study showing high blood pressure as a risk factor was published in 1959, drawing from the preceding 30 years' actuarial experience among the many major insurance companies that cooperated in assembling the study. Hypertension as a risk factor has been confirmed many times since, in many different ways, but the insurance industry should have the credit for first establishing it, and for doing so conclusively, on the basis of a quantity of data much larger than any medical research study has been able to achieve. The insurance companies have a long-established tradition of protecting confidential information. One hopes that they can maintain this tradition in the transition from paper files to computerized ones.

A recent, innovative step in epidemiological studies has been to sidestep the confidentiality issue, and to ask people to volunteer rather extensive amounts of personal information at intervals over a number of years. The American Cancer Society (ACS) has initiated this approach in their effort to try to define what roles are played in the genesis of cancer by various factors of daily life, such as diet, drinking, work, certain aspects of lifestyle, and, of course, smoking. The ACS has designed a multipage questionnaire and has asked large numbers of people to volunteer to fill it out now as well as again in future years. With this approach, the ACS ought to be able to track hundreds of thousands of people. At least it has begun with that many initial questionnaires. Their ability to re-establish contact with these same people in subsequent years remains to be seen. Obviously, without the follow-up data, the information in the original questionnaire has little value, except as a reflection of contemporary lifestyles. The ACS questionnaire for females is reproduced in Appendix B. There is a separate questionnaire for males, but most of the many questions are the same in both.

The ACS study has been criticized by some as being too much of a "shotgun" approach, in asking too many questions and possibly not the right ones. In this sense, the ACS study differs from Snow's cholera studies and the smoking/lung cancer studies: the ACS study is not a test of a single theory about a cause of cancer. Instead it is a broad net being cast to identify factors in one's life that can be said to increase the risk of developing cancer—"risk factors." The concept of a risk factor is important to understand.

The very idea of a risk factor implies a comparison of risks, as in: "those who smoke cigarettes have a 15 times greater risk of getting lung cancer than those who do not smoke cigarettes." Thus, smoking cigarettes is a risk factor for lung cancer. It is not, in the proper sense of the word, a "cause" of lung cancer: at some time in the future, someone will work out the precise physical, chemical, and biological mechanisms by which cigarette smoking increases the risk of lung cancer, and at that time one could properly speak of what causes lung cancer. In the same manner, we could say that drinking Southwark & Vauxhall water in August 1854 was a risk factor for cholera, and that the subsequently discovered bacterium known as *Cholera vibrio* is the cause of cholera; the biology of this microorganism serves to explain how cholera is water-borne, and current knowledge about the causality of cholera is well-developed, though not complete. There are some residual mysteries: we still do not understand how some people manage not to develop cholera even when they have clearly ingested the bacteria, and we do not have a clear understanding of where the bacteria "hide" in between epidemics or of what causes them to "break out of hiding," as it were, and start up a new series of epidemics. By contrast, our understanding of the causality of lung cancer is very poor. Nevertheless, there is something practical to do based on the proof that cigarette smoking is a big risk factor for premature death—stop smoking cigarettes—just as there were practical sanitary steps to be taken, even before bacteria were discovered, based on Snow's proof that cholera was water-borne.

Thus, the focus of the ACS study on identifying risk factors for cancer can have practical benefits, provided that they are asking the right questions, i.e. those that focus on what will turn out to be actual risk factors. The study is expensive, and some have argued that the money might better be spent on more laboratory studies rather than on this kind of epidemiology. On the positive side, the ACS study pioneers a much-expanded voluntary involvement of people in the elementary fact-gathering that is so obviously essential in identifying risk factors for chronic diseases such as cancer and heart disease. It will take several years to accumulate enough history in the lives of the volunteers on which to base an initial analysis. The study of chronic diseases requires a great deal of patience, and one can only hope that the right questions are being asked and that the volunteers continue their participation.

The foregoing, then, gives an overview of how data collection and the epidemiological method came together over a century ago and of how these have been adapted to some of the big health risk problems of contemporary life—the major chronic diseases that today account for about 90% of deaths among North Americans and Europeans. These chronic diseases consitute the biggest death-risks and so have to be regarded as the highest priority targets of any program of risk-reduction.

Naturally, it is one thing to pick targets, and quite another to do something about them. Here then, are two themes: (1) picking as targets the things that pose the bigger risks, not the smaller ones; (2) picking as targets those about which it is possible to do something. The rest of this book revolves around those two themes, and in the remainder of this chapter we turn to the question of how to distinguish big hazards from small ones.

In order to understand which hazards are bigger than others, we have to have a clear, widely understood index, scale, or measure of risks. Only then would we be able to place them in order of importance and carry on sensible discussions about what measures to take, and at what cost, in order to reduce risks. Just as we have the English and metric units of weights and measures as logical and, indeed, necessary conditions for an orderly and efficient marketplace for products, so we need to have a widely understood and accepted measure of risk. Furthermore, if measured risk is to have broad public understanding, it should relate to a realistic conception of that slippery word "safety." At present, however, there is broad public confusion about which are the large and small hazards in contemporary life, because there is no uniform measure of risk.

Imagine the confusion if there were no uniform measures and weights for the buying of groceries: every market would have its own cups, spoons, or bottles for the measure of volumes, its own metal or stone pieces to determine weights, and sticks or rods for measuring lengths. While one market might offer two "copperweights" of steak for $2.98, another would have a "special" price of three "stoneweights" of steak for $2.49; the buyer would have no way of knowing which was the more favorable unless the relation between "copperweights" and "stoneweights" were known. Among many other problems of this primitive arrangement, the checkout lines would be very long and slow, as each transaction was haggled—as in the village markets one may still see in the developing countries.

This same sort of haggling has characterized much of the past decade's discussions about the risks associated with many industrial and other technological developments. Part of the reason for the haggling is that we do not have a widely understood and accepted scale for measuring risk and comparing hazards.

Experts from the various health- and safety-related disciplines have created scales, which are described in Appendix A, but none has gained wide acceptance in the sense of becoming part of everyday speech and thought. Consider, by way of analogy, the Richter Scale for earthquakes. It is universally recognized, uniformly used in media reporting of earthquakes, and a part of everyday speech. Even though it has a quite complicated physical basis, most people have some knowledge of the different characters of earthquakes at the 3, 4, 5, 6, 7, or 8 levels on the Richter Scale. Because of this understanding, no media story on an earthquake can omit giving the Richter value without compromising its credibility. That is so even though only a small minority of people for whom the Richter Scale is informative can claim to understand logarithms or the geophysical basis of the Scale.

In the absence of a generally recognized risk scale, and for a variety of other good journalistic reasons, the reports we receive in the news media of catastrophes and other untoward events are *victim-oriented,* as in "FOURTEEN DIE OF MYSTERY DISEASE." What does this kind of report tell us, other than that there were 14 victims? In the typical news report of this kind, we do not gain any idea of how many people altogether were in danger, how many may have gotten sick and recovered, how many never even got sick, and so on. This familiar kind of news story is comparable to a supermarket ad for 99-cent steak that neglects to specify how much steak you get for 99 cents. You may find the comparison macabre, because the price of meat is rarely newsworthy, while the death of 14 people in a novel way is always newsworthy. In reality, of course, thousands of Americans die every day of one or another disease, about a thousand a week die in traffic accidents, and about ten thousand a week die of diseases which are induced or accelerated in their course by cigarette smoking. This wholesale mortality rarely gets media attention, because events which occur constantly cease to be newsworthy.

To illustrate the kind of misinformation which victim-oriented reporting can generate, let us analyze the following headline: "411 DIE ON HIGHWAYS DURING LABOR DAY WEEKEND." One's first reaction is: how awful! But let's look behind the headline. Annually, about 50,000 people die in traffic accidents in the United

States—an average of about 137 per day, or 411 in the span of three average days. Since the Labor Day weekend is three days, the 411 total turns out to be right on the average. However, a closer look reveals that the average of 137 is itself misleading, because there is a big difference between weekdays and weekends in traffic accidents and fatalities: Monday through Thursday the average number of traffic deaths in the United States is about 75 per day, while Friday through Sunday it is about 240 per day. In other words, a three-day holiday weekend might be expected to produce $3 \times 240 = 720$ victims. Thus, an alternate headline to the "411 KILLED . . ." could be: "CAREFUL DRIVING ON LABOR DAY WEEKEND—309 LIVES SAVED!"

Our intention in this example is not to rewrite the tenets of journalism, but to indicate that victim-oriented reporting can be very seriously misleading. Victim-oriented reporting tends to leave us with free-floating anxiety and dread about such things as—in no particular order—the bomb, the next earthquake, air pollution, car crashes, jet crashes, lead poisoning, toxic shock syndrome, deformed babies, chemical plant explosions, carcinogens in food, asbestos in drinking water, formaldehyde coming out of the walls of our houses, cancer risk of X-rays, passive smoking, mercury in seafood, dioxin, AIDS, radioactive fallout, and so on.

Basic to putting some kind of order into all these otherwise equally disturbing hazards is to have a scale for risk that integrates information not only on how many victims suffer the adversity in question, but *how many people were at risk and escaped unscathed.* With that information straightforwardly in view, rational people can make rational decisions about which hazards present big risks, which ones present small risks, what corrective actions are worth taking, and how much time, money, and effort to spend to minimize the risk. Of course, no scale for risk can make irrational people rational, but having a well-understood scale for risk as part of our common language can minimize the ability of the irrational members of society to manipulate others by fear mongering, use of misleading statistics, or other forms of disinformation.

We have already cited the Richter Scale as a model for what we are lacking in public discourse on risk. The Richter Scale is useful both to technical experts and the general public. A very important factor in its public acceptance is that the numbers are very simple, going from 1 to 8 with a single decimal place, without tongue-twisting units or physical dimensions. It is a success story in public acceptance and general understanding of something that has a great deal of underlying complexity. Without the Richter Scale, we would have to depend on something like the type size in newspaper headlines as a measure of earthquake force. The need to sell the news has an unfortunate way of magnifying the type size in headlines, which is the news media's equivalent of the butcher's putting his thumb on the scale while weighing the steak.

Britain's Lord Rothschild has suggested a way of expressing risk in terms which are meaningful for the individual and which clearly indicate the relation between the number of people at risk and the number of victims. In a BBC lecture in 1978,[3] he suggested that risks be stated in the straightforward language of 1 harmful event occurring among so many people at risk, during a sensibly selected period of time.

Thus, instead of saying "the death rate from homicide in the United States is 10.4 per 100,000 per year,"[4] one can much more simply say "the risk of one's dying due to homicide in a year's time in the United States is 1 in 9615." These are two equivalent ways of saying the same thing, for the figure of 9615 is the result of dividing 100,000 by 10.4. It is also the result of dividing the total population of the United States by the total number of homicide victims during the year. The important element in Lord Rothschild's suggestion lies in the essential simplicity of the two numbers which are used in his method. Everyone knows what the number "one" means: it means that the event in question happens either to you, or to some*one* else. It is also easy to comprehend the meaning of the other number. It is very much like one's graduating class picture—there you are in the middle of a large number of people who all have something in common. The people in the school picture have in common being in the same class, at the same school. In the "risk picture," as in the class picture, everyone shares participation in some particular activity. It is not a picture of every single person who participates in the activity, but only of the number of people whose participation in the activity will, on the average, produce one victim during a defined time interval.

It is useful to designate this group by a special term: unicohort. It derives from the prefix "uni," meaning "one," and from the term "cohort," which, as we described in Chapter 1, is an old Roman military term, analogous to a battalion, which biostatisticians have adapted to modern use to signify a group of people alike in a sufficient number of respects that they can be judged equally likely to become victims of a hazard to which they are all exposed. The chance of anyone's becoming a victim to the hazard is his or her risk. The bigger the unicohort, the smaller is each individual's risk, and vice versa. Also, the bigger the unicohort, the greater the degree of safety enjoyed by people at risk. Here is where the degree of risk and the degree of safety are linked: the degree of risk is inversely related to the size of the unicohort—a small unicohort means a big risk; the degree of safety is directly related to the size of the unicohort—a small unicohort means a small degree of safety.

The term "unicohort" is new. It represents the idea of taking all the people at risk to a particular hazard—all the airline passengers, all the motorcyclists, all the hang-gliders, all the people with high blood pressure, all the cigarette smokers—and dividing their respective numbers by the total number of individuals who become victims of that hazard within a chosen time interval. The resulting quotient is the unicohort. It is the basis, for example, for making the easily understood statement: "My risk as a passenger of being killed in the crash of a commercial airliner is 1 in 814,000 per trip." Translating a unicohort into a risk statement necessitates that the time interval be stated. In the airline crash example, the time interval is "a trip," which of course can be anything from a few minutes to about 24 hours. Variations in flight length are of secondary importance, however, because most of the problems in flight arise in connection with takeoff and landing. In general, either of two time intervals is used: a year, or an event of usually short duration that is felt to be a special hazard, such as a trip, a surgical operation, being born, giving birth, a parachute jump, and so forth.

The risks of air travel illustrate some of the important points about analyzing risks in general. Look at Table 1, which gives data on fatalities from air travel in the United States in different years between 1960 and 1979.

On the average over these years, about 300 people died per year in commercial air crashes. The exact numbers varied from year to year, and the precise average is 301 per year for the years shown. Within the six most recent years for which the data are tabulated,

TABLE 1

RISK OF FLYING—RECENT HISTORY OF
U.S. SCHEDULED AIRLINES

	1960	*1965*	*1970*	*1974*	*1975*	*1976*	*1977*	*1978*	*1979*
Number of victims	499	261	146	467	124	45	655	163	353
Number of passengers*	62	103	169	208	205	223	240	275	317
Unicohort size*	0.124	0.395	1.16	0.445	1.65	4.96	0.366	1.69	0.89

Source: U.S. Bureau of the Census, *Statistical Abstract of the United States, 1980,* Table 1157

* In millions

there were 1807 victims, and, in the same interval, a total of 1,468,000,000 passengers flew—more or less the equivalent of the entire population of the United States taking one trip every year for six years, though of course everyone knows that some people fly many times per year, some people fly once or twice a year, and many people do not fly at all. The total count is nothing more than the total number of passenger trips. When you divide this total number of passenger trips by the number of victims, you get the unicohort of 814,000, which allows you to say: "My risk of being killed in a commercial air crash is 1 in 814,000 per trip," assuming, of course, that what happens this year will not be fundamentally different from what happened during 1974–79.

If you are a frequent air traveler, and make, say, 100 trips per year, your per-year risk is 100 times greater than that of the per trip risk, and you would say: "My risk of being killed in a commercial air crash is 1 in 8140 per year." This example serves to reinforce the statement that the smaller the unicohort, the smaller the degree of safety, and vice versa.

Looking again at Table 1, you can see that victim-oriented news reporting would make 1977 the worst year. In fact, however, the risk of flying in 1977 was one-third that in 1960. There were one-third more victims, but four times as many passengers in 1977 as in 1960, so the risk of flying in 1977 was *diluted* relative to that in 1960. The size of the unicohort thus can be seen to be like a dilution factor—the larger the unicohort, the more is risk diluted; the smaller the unicohort, the more is risk concentrated. Risk dilution and risk concentration are two perhaps unfamiliar concepts, but they represent a quantitative way to express the old idea of "safety in numbers."

Indeed, we can formally tie risk dilution/concentration together with the concept of degrees of safety. Increasing dilution of risk translates directly into increasing degrees of safety. We can dilute risk ever more greatly, thereby adding corresponding degrees of safety, but we can never dilute risk into nonexistence, nor can we attain absolute safety.

We can now construct a risk scale which is based on unicohort size. It is the first step toward defining the Safety-degree Scale which will allow us to rank-order hazards according to the quantitatively expressed safety-degree status of each. The following pyramid of numbers shows the relation between unicohort size and risk.

1	1 in 1
10	1 in 10
100	1 in 100
1000	1 in 1000
10000	1 in 10000
100000	1 in 100000
1000000	1 in 1000000
10000000	1 in 10000000
100000000	1 in 100000000
UNICOHORT SIZE	RISK

The biggest unicohort that is practical to consider is 100 million. That limit arises because of an inherent limitation in data collection. The United States, with about 220 million people, is the largest country that collects data on a comprehensive basis about many aspects of national life. They are compiled and published yearly, usually with several years' delay for compilation, analysis, and publication, but close enough to the present to give a good approximation of the risks one faces at the present moment. Because of the size of the U.S. population from which all these data are drawn, we can say that the practical upper limit for unicohort size is about half the size of the American population, or 100 million.

Very small unicohorts, approaching 1, arise from exceptionally hazardous actions: if you jump off the Empire State Building or leap in front of a moving train, your risk of death approaches 1 in 1 per jump, because these are virtually certain to be fatal acts. In such circumstances, the degree of safety approaches 0.

THE SAFETY-DEGREE SCALE

The final step in defining the Safety-degree Scale is to compress this big range of unicohort sizes—1 to 100,000,000—down to single numbers. We do so by following a mathematical device employed in the making of the Richter Scale: the logarithm. We utilize the logarithms of unicohort sizes in order to end up with a compressed scale, made up of a single digit from 0 to 8, with a single decimal place. The transformation is illustrated by Figure 1: zero on the Safety-degree Scale stands for a unicohort size of 1, and represents a zero degree of safety. With the increase by each unit of 1 on the Safety-degree Scale, the unicohort size increases by a factor of 10. You can also see that the safety-degree value is the same as the number of zeros in the unicohort size—0 when the unicohort is 1, 1 when the unicohort is 10, 2 when it is 100, 3 when it is 1000, and so on up to 8 when the unicohort is 100,000,000. As risk becomes more dilute, the degree of safety increases, so the ascending numbers on the Scale indicate increasing degrees of safety.

The values on the Safety-degree Scale are measured in "safety-degree units," abbreviated SDU. To become familiar with how the Safety-degree Scale works, it is helpful to see, with the aid of Figure 1, how the different unicohort sizes convert into safety-degree units. When the unicohort size happens to be a number like 10, 100, 1000 . . ., i.e. 1 with some zeros to its right, simply count the zeros; the number of zeros gives the SDU value, as shown in Figure 1. In most instances, however, the unicohort size will be a number like 814,000, which is the unicohort for commercial air travel. Intermediate values give rise to decimal SDU values, in between integers. Appendix A gives the precise way of dealing with decimal SDU values and their relation to unicohort sizes. For the general reader, it suffices to recognize that an SDU value of, say, 3.5 indicates a unicohort that is somewhere between 1000 and 10,000, and that 5.5 indicates a unicohort between 100,000 and 1,000,000.

Table 2 lists an assortment of large and small hazards in contemporary life, with what the available data indicate are their risks, as indicated by both unicohort size and SDU values.

FIGURE 1
SCHEMATIC OVERVIEW OF THE
RELATIONS BETWEEN UNICOHORT SIZE
AND THE SAFETY-DEGREE SCALE.

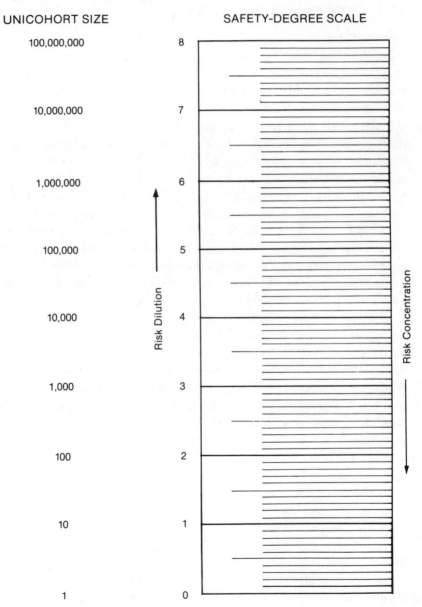

TABLE 2

VARIOUS HAZARDS AND THEIR
PER-YEAR RISKS OF DEATH

hazard	unicohort size (for 1 death per year)	safety-degree status (SDU)
Cigarette smoking (age 35)	600	2.8
Motorcycling (U.S.)	1,000	3.0
Influenza (U.K.)	5,000	3.7
Passenger in motor vehicle (U.S.)	6,000	3.8
Football (U.K.)	6,000	3.8
Oral contraceptive pill (age 25–34)	23,000	4.4
Pedestrian (U.S.)	26,000	4.4
Bicycling (U.S.)	88,000	4.9
Tornadoes (U.S.)	450,000	5.7
Lightning (U.S.)	1,900,000	6.3
Bee sting (U.S.)	5,500,000	6.7
Hit by falling aircraft (U.S.)	10,000,000	7.0
Drowning due to flooding of dikes (Netherlands)	10,000,000	7.0

Sources: Traffic data: U.S. Bureau of the Census, *Statistical Abstract of the United States, 1980,* Tables 412, 1110, 1114; U.S. Department of Transportation, National Highway Traffic Safety Administration, *Fatal Accident Reporting System,* 1980, DOT HS 805 953
Contraceptive data: see Chapter 5
Bee sting and lightning: *Rubenstein, H.S., "Bee-sting diseases: who is at risk? What is the treatment?" Lancet* 1 (1982): 496–99
All others: Note 1, Appendix A

In succeeding chapters, we shall discuss various hazards using both the Safety-degree Scale and the unicohort size, side by side, so as to build familiarity with this way of giving quantitative expression to risk and safety-degree status.

There is no theoretical upper bound on the Safety-degree Scale, the suggested value of 8 being only a practical upper limit set by present methods of data collection. From a conceptual point of view it is useful to note that risk can be diluted ever more greatly but cannot disappear completely; likewise, the degree of safety can increase ever more greatly but cannot attain the ideal of absolute safety.

Recall that the measures of risk and safety-degree status are always based on past human experience. First, one determines or estimates the *total* number of people who participated in the same activity within a fixed time period. Second, one counts the *total* number of people who became victims within the same time period. Third, one divides the number of participants by the number of victims to obtain the unicohort size. Fourth, one takes the logarithm of the unicohort size with a pocket calculator. The SDU figure is the logarithm of the unicohort size.

We believe that there is no simpler way to express risk and safety-degree status, and to communicate them to the public. There are many other ways to express risks, as Appendix A describes, but we know of no simpler way—especially so because of the basic clarity in the connection between risk dilution and degree of safety. Appendix A also shows a very simple way to convert SDU values into an annual or per-event premium you would have to pay to insure yourself for $1 million against the hazard in question. That economic perspective is often very helpful in comparing risks. Appendix A also shows you how advancing age itself increases your overall risk of death from all causes, together with the annual cost to insure your life for $1 million. That information is a helpful baseline against which to judge the risk that is added to your life by specific single hazards.

Because of the urgent need for hazards to be put on a quantitative basis so that they may be compared and made comprehensible, we propose the use of the Safety-degree Scale to the news media and to people involved in communication of health-related issues to the public. It is certainly true that, in some instances, the basic data are not available to allow any reasonable, quantitative estimate of risk and safety-degree status, and it is also certainly true that acceptance of the Safety-degree Scale cannot create data where none exist, or make the available data any more reliable than they already are. But it would also be very helpful if the absence of an SDU value would convey to the public that there are not yet sufficient data to allow a measure or even an estimate of risk and safety-degree status. Then the public would know that judgment has to be suspended until more information is available—an unsatisfactory situation perhaps, but surely preferable to the bombardment of victim-oriented reporting we have now. Systematic use of the Safety-degree Scale would thus improve the character of public debate about the hazards of our technological age.

In the following chapters, we discuss various contemporary hazards, using the Safety-degree Scale where available data warrant doing so. We also give the unicohort size so as to help strengthen understanding at the intuitive level of the Safety-degree Scale.

We suggest that you scan or read Appendix A at some point during your reading of **RISK WATCH**, although Appendix A is not critical for understanding the following chapters.

NOTES TO CHAPTER 3

1. Goldstein, M., and I.F. Goldstein. *How We Know—An Exploration of the Scientific Process.* New York: Plenum, 1978.

2. Ibid., p. 43.

3. Lord Rothschild. "Risk—The Richard Dimbleby Lecture." *The Listener,* 30 November 1978.

4. U.S. Bureau of the Census. *Statistical Abstract of the United States, 1982–83.* Washington, D.C., p. 76.

4

What We Die of: One Way to Look at the Major Risks in Our Lives

The two purposes of this chapter are: (1) to review the diseases and hazards that account for the vast majority of deaths today; (2) to show how these have changed in the years leading up to the present and how they will probably change in the next few years. This is a starting point in understanding the major risks in our lives. Death is not necessarily the worst thing that can happen, because some of the derangements of health leading up to death are themselves so devastating that death is often accepted as a relief. As we have seen, though, there is a long history of collecting and analyzing death-oriented vital statistics, and so it is useful to look first at the major causes of death today and extract what useful information we can, and then, in subsequent chapters, to go more deeply into the options that may influence life, health, and the "when" and "how" of death.

Figure 1 shows how the top ten causes of death have changed since 1900. At the beginning of this century, infectious diseases were the big killers, but, one by one, these have been brought under control: by 1940, tuberculosis, nephritis, diphtheria, and the group called "diarrhea, enteritis, and ulceration of the intestines" had disappeared from the top ten causes of death. Meanwhile, deaths due to diseases of the heart and cancer (called "malignant neoplasms" since 1960) increased and were already in first and second place by 1940. One of the reasons for the increase was that conquering the child-

FIGURE 1

TEN LEADING CAUSES OF DEATH:
DEATH RATES—U.S., 1900, 1940, 1960, 1970, 1979

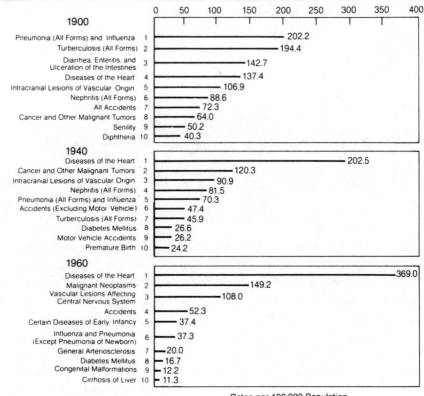

Rates per 100,000 Population

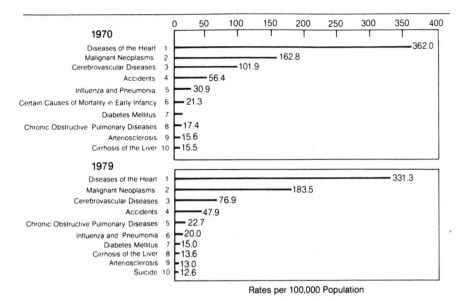

Figure 1. Changes in the leading causes of death from 1900 to 1979, the most recent year for which data are available. Note the sharp growth in heart disease, the less steep growth in cancer, and the decline of everything else. Suicide made its first appearance among the top ten causes of death in 1979, not because the suicide rate is rising, but because the rates of other causes of death fell. (Source: Note 6.)

killing diseases allowed many more people to reach ages beyond 50, which have always been the prime years for heart disease and cancer.

Figure 1 shows that the rate of deaths due to cancer almost tripled between 1900 and 1979, but these numbers are misleading. They have to be adjusted for the concurrent big increase in numbers of people living past 50. The reason for the adjustment relates to the biological fact that the incidence of cancer increases with advancing age, so a population with increasing proportions of older people will also show sizeable increases in the overall incidence of cancer. When adjustments for the aging of the population are made, it is apparent that, with one exception, there have not been dramatic increases in the incidence of any cancer over the years going as far back as one can have confidence in the statistics. The exception is lung cancer, which has risen dramatically in males since 1940 and in females since 1960. The incidence of stomach cancer, however, has fallen dramatically since the early years of this century, and improved diagnosis and treatment have brought about marked improvement in the prospects for disease-free survival of several other cancers, although their incidence has not changed appreciably. Details of these various changes will be discussed later in this chapter.

The main conclusion to be drawn from Figure 1 is that the yet-unconquered chronic and degenerative diseases are the center of attention today for both treatment and research efforts, as reflected by the figures for 1979 in Figure 1: diseases of the heart, cancer (called "malignant neoplasms"), strokes (called "cerebrovascular diseases"), lung diseases (numbers 5 and 6), diabetes, cirrhosis, and arteriosclerosis (which usually is closely related to heart disease and stroke).

Note in Figure 1 that the terms used to describe causes of death have undergone considerable changes since 1900. The "intracranial lesions of vascular origin" in 1900 became the "vascular lesions affecting [the] central nervous system" in 1960, which evolved to "cerebrovascular diseases" in 1970 and 1979. A death doctors would have ascribed to "senility" in 1900 would most likely have been attributed to "general arteriosclerosis" in 1960, and to either "cerebrovascular diseases" or "arteriosclerosis" today. These changes in terminology reflect an increasing but still not fully attained precision in the classification of disease and causes of death.

Accidents have remained high on the list, though their character has changed greatly since 1900 because of the immense growth in the number of motor vehicles. Deaths from motor vehicle accidents were first included in the vital statistics for 1906, when about 150 traffic fatalities occurred.[1] Traffic fatalities now account for about half of the annual toll of 100,000–110,000 accidental deaths.[2] Note, however, that the death rate from all accidents has declined by about one-third, from 72.3[1] to 47.8[3] per 100,000 per year, between 1900 and 1979. To put these population-based rate figures into the more personal terms of the Safety-degree Scale, the per-year risk of accidental death was diluted from 3.1 to 3.3 SDU (1 in 1400 to 1 in 2100).

One can see two opposing technological forces at work in these figures on accidental deaths: the immense growth in motor vehicles created a whole new and steadily growing class of fatal accidents after 1906; on the other hand, many medical and surgical advances since then have improved the care of accident victims. Unless someone wants to make the preposterous claim that people were killed by horse-drawn vehicles in 1900 at a much greater rate than by motor vehicles in 1979, the data can be taken to indicate that the positive effect of advancing medical technology has more than offset the negative effect of advancing automotive technology.

For the first time, suicide has made its appearance among the top ten causes of death, but it is important to note why: it is not due to an increase in suicides, which have occurred at a remarkably constant rate since at least 1900. Other causes of death which used to be among the top ten declined sufficiently to allow suicide to slip into the eighth position merely by staying constant. The overall per-year rate of suicide in the United States is about 1 in 8100 (3.9 SDU).

The most recently compiled data on the currently most-common causes of death today are summarized in Table 1. These are U.S. data from the year 1979 but were not available in final form until during 1983. It used to take about three years before final mortality data were available, but recent federal budget restrictions appear to have lengthened the time. The percentages and terms differ slightly from those for 1979 in Figure 1, which is taken from a 1982 publication of the National Institutes of Health and thus has only the preliminary data for 1979.

Four-year-old data do not give an appreciably distorted view of current mortality patterns. We have already noted that changes in vital statistics occur only gradually, even when revolutionary

TABLE 1

SOME OF THE LEADING CURRENT CAUSES OF DEATH IN THE U.S. (% of total)

Diseases of the heart and circulatory system		50
Heart disease	38	
Stroke	9	
Other	3	
Cancer, all types		21
Accidents, all types		6
Motor vehicle accidents	3	
Other	3	
Chronic obstructive pulmonary disease		3
Pneumonia		2
Diabetes		2
Liver diseases and cirrhosis		2
Suicide		1
Diseases of the newborn		1
Homicide		1
All other		11

Total number of deaths for 1979 = 1,913,800

Source: U.S. Bureau of the Census, *Statistical Abstract of the United States, 1982–83,* Table 113

changes in treatment are taking place. Only war, epidemics, and famine are capable of causing abrupt changes in vital statistics. At least for the time being, those horrors are in abeyance in the technologically advanced countries, and so the data from 1979 can serve to give a reliable indication of mortality patterns today, tomorrow, and for the next several years.

Both Figure 1 and Table 1 show that about half of all deaths are due to heart and circulatory diseases, of which three-quarters are classified as heart disease, and one-quarter can be classed as blood vessel disease. These diseases can claim victims at all ages, but do so at an increasing rate with increasing age. About 80% of what is classified here as "heart disease" has its basis in blood vessel disease that narrows the coronary arteries, which supply the heart itself. Depending on the classification used, this disease process is called "ischemic heart disease" or "coronary heart disease." We shall use the latter, abbreviating it CHD. For some decades, CHD has been the "captain of the men of death," to use a metaphor coined when tuberculosis held that title.

Cancer causes 21% of all deaths. The next eight leading causes together account for about 18% of the total, and the remaining 11% of deaths are caused by all the other 990 entries in the official International Classification of Disease, with no single disease among those 990 accounting for over 1% of the total.

Homicide, at tenth on the list in Table 1, accounted for 22,600 victims in the United States in 1979. Included in the "homicide" category are deaths due to legal intervention. Overall, the per-year risk of homicide in the U.S. population as a whole is 4.0 SDU (1 in 10,000). There is, however, considerable concentration of this risk among black males, whose per-year risk of 3.2 SDU (1 in 1550) is about six times more concentrated than that of the population as a whole. The group with the most dilute risk of homicide is white females, with a per-year risk of 4.5 SDU (1 in 33,300).[4]

In the remainder of this chapter, we discuss salient facts about the major cardiovascular diseases and cancer, because they represent, in an overall sense, the most important risks to life today. There are certain voluntarily accepted risk factors that play a major role in the genesis of both groups of diseases. Those voluntary risk factors will be the subject of later chapters.

CARDIOVASCULAR DISEASE

To begin on a positive note, two things are worthy of mention: (1) deaths due to CHD have, after a long period of yearly increases, begun to decline in the United States and Canada, though they are still rising in some countries, for example, Sweden and West Germany; (2) life expectancy in the United States has increased by almost three years during the past ten years.[5] The decline in CHD is small, but it has continued year by year for about a decade. It is responsible for only part of the extension of life expectancy, which has many factors contributing to it. Overall, however, these two important changes illustrate that a good deal of medical progress is occurring at a time when one is sometimes led to believe that we have come to a halt in progress, or are even slipping backwards. These findings are clearly inconsistent with the often-repeated assertions that we are suffering from either or both mass poisoning due to pollution or a growing epidemic of stress-related diseases.

Two basic factors have contributed to the downturn in deaths due to CHD: (1) improved care of both acute and chronic conditions related to CHD, notably heart attacks and angina; (2) a decline in the number of patients developing CHD-related conditions. So there seems to be both better treatment of CHD and somewhat fewer patients with CHD to treat.[6,7]

The reasons for the decline in the incidence of CHD in the United States and Canada are puzzling, and, as a former Director of the U.S. National Heart, Lung, and Blood Institute remarked, have "too many potential causes, not too few." The factors responsible for the recent decline in CHD in the United States and Canada may change or disappear before we understand the basis for what is happening. One factor which many experts believe important is that more and more adults with hypertension have been brought under control by drug therapy. Hypertension is a well-established risk factor for CHD, which makes that surmise seem plausible. But many other possibly relevant things have also occurred during the past decade, although they are more in the nature of trends, and thus not easily measured: a change in diet away from high-fat content foods, the reduction of smoking, and more adult participation in exercise programs. Another possibility, considerably less Spartan, is described a few paragraphs below.

A skeptic could justifiably say that if we are going to take up jogging in order to impoverish the cardiologists, we ought at least to have good evidence that jogging has as direct a relation to that laudable goal as it does to the enrichment of the orthopedic surgeons. On the other hand, the risk-reducing effect of abandoning smoking is clearly demonstrated, as will be discussed in detail in the next chapter.

The role of diet is ambiguous and is also the subject of a later chapter, but one observation that has attracted special attention to dietary factors is this: the children and grandchildren of Japanese immigrants to the United States have the pattern of CHD characteristic of the United States, not of Japan. Of all countries that collect such data, the United States has one of the highest death rates due to CHD, while Japan has one of the lowest—about one-eighth that of the United States. Thus, it is not a subtle change in the pattern of this disease that occurs in first- and second-generation offspring of Japanese immigrants, relative to their cousins who live in Japan. Certainly it dispels any notion that the Japanese might have some kind of genetically based protection against getting CHD: genetics do not change in one or two generations. It strongly prompts the inference that "it must have been something they ate." Yet diet certainly does not explain the two-fold difference in mortality between males and females. Nor does it account for the strikingly low rate of deaths due to CHD reported in France, given that the character of the French diet is at such marked variance with the much-discussed theory that high-fat diets predispose to CHD. Table 2 shows the four-fold difference in CHD death rates between the United States and France, plus data from five other economically important countries, including Japan.

TABLE 2

ANNUAL DEATH RATES FROM CORONARY HEART DISEASE
(deaths per 100,000 population)

Males	U.S.	Canada	Britain	Sweden	West Germany	France	Japan
1970	320	273	241	225	154	69	49
1975	282	253	249	239	172	78	45
1979	262*	243**	243	245	175*	73**	40
Females							
1970	164	133	101	120	63	29	28
1975	141	118	106	120	75	32	27
1979	133*	113**	101	112	75*	29**	23

Source: U.S. Bureau of the Census, *Statistical Abstract of the United States, 1981*, Table 115

  * 1978 data
** 1977 data

The data in Table 2 show what one might call the interim results of a very large "experiment of nature" involving the populations of seven major countries. The problem is that we do not yet understand the critical variables in the experiment.

Of course, there is always a problem in comparing vital statistics between countries. While there is general agreement on the classification of disease among scientifically trained physicians in all countries, represented by the International Classification of Disease, each national group of physicians does have its unique concepts of what should be written on the death certificate in particular sets of clinical circumstances—for example when elderly patients die after suffering from multiple disease problems. Those national differences tend to color the statistics and may explain some of the differences shown in Table 2. There is widespread agreement, however, that the incidence of CHD in Japan is vastly lower than in North America and Europe; what is not so clear is whether the apparent differences in the incidence of CHD between North America and Germany or France are really as large as the data would indicate.

Nevertheless, these large national differences, taken at face value, are part of the basis for a tantalizing hypothesis about CHD advanced in 1979 by a group of British epidemiologists, St. Leger, Cochrane, and Moore. They called attention to a very strong inverse correlation between national wine consumption and national statistics on CHD mortality.[8] Figure 2, reproduced from their paper in *The Lancet,* shows this inverse correlation—the word "inverse" meaning that CHD appeared to fall as wine consumption rose. The paper elicited a number of critical comments, including questions on the validity of the French data, since France has the lowest reported death rate due to CHD among the 18 countries shown in Figure 2 and shares the lead with Italy in wine consumption. St. Leger and his colleagues indicated, however, that the strength of the inverse correlation was not weakened by omitting the data from France.

An additional dimension can now be added to this theory, however, based on the steady growth of wine production and consumption in the United States during the past 20 years.[9] The rise started during the 1960's, with wine production almost doubling between 1960 and 1980. Growth in wine consumption in the United States preceded by a few years the beginning of the downturn in mortality due to CHD noted above. This is only a qualitative association,

FIGURE 2
RELATIONSHIP BETWEEN I.H.D. MORTALITY RATE
IN MEN AGED 55–64 AND WINE CONSUMPTION.

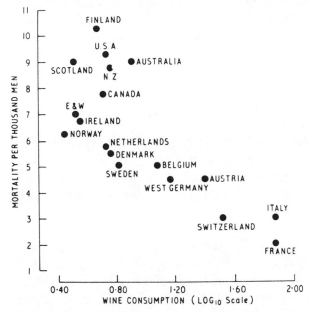

Figure 2. Inverse correlation between per capita wine consumption and the rate of deaths due to coronary heart disease. (Source: Note 8. Reproduced with permission.)

which should be explored quantitatively, but only by an epidemiologist who savors controversy. St. Leger's theory adds an epicurean element to the otherwise unrelentingly Spartan list of injunctions for those who would try to minimize the risk of developing CHD. Judging by the controversy that the wine consumption theory has elicited, however, it is evident that the world is much more predisposed to accept Spartan than epicurean solutions to the CHD problem. With each evening meal, the authors raise a glass to St. Leger, Cochrane, and Moore and pray that some latter-day John Snow will find a way to prove their theory.

Hypertension

High blood pressure is one of the most widely prevailing diseases of our time, involving something like 20% of the adult population over the age of 40 in the United States. There has been a great deal of progress made in drug therapy for hypertension, but only about half of the hypertensives know they have the condition, and only about half of those—a quarter of the total—are properly treated. It is a disease without symptoms, so the diagnosis is usually made as an incidental finding during a medical exam for another purpose or in a screening program.

As with CHD, there are striking national and even regional differences in the incidence of hypertension. Dietary salt intake appears to play a role in hypertension, at least at the extremes: in certain areas where salt consumption is very low, e.g. the Solomon Islands, Greenland, and certain parts of Africa, hypertension occurs infrequently, whereas in other areas where salt consumption is unusually high, 30–40% of those over 50 have hypertension, e.g. in the Japanese province of Akita, where salt consumption averages about 35 gms per day, versus the American figure of 10 gms per day.[10]

Publication of the big insurance study *Blood Pressure and Build, 1959* [11] showed conclusively the risk of even mild degrees of hypertension. Very strong impetus to drug treatment of hypertension came with the publication in 1970 of the results of a large, multicenter study comparing mortality in treated versus untreated hypertensives.[12] That study, and the even larger one which followed it in 1979,[13] have shown unequivocally that drug treatment of hypertension reduces the risk of premature death by reducing the otherwise increased incidence of strokes, heart failure, and kidney failure. In 1979, the insurance industry published a second big study[14] which confirmed the conclusion about the risk of premature death posed by hypertension, and showed that treatment which restored blood pressure to normal also restored risk to the normal level for age and sex. Treatment and its attendant risks are discussed in Chapter 6.

Coronary Heart Disease (CHD)

Because of its prevalence and its leading role among the causes of death, CHD can accurately be described as an epidemic. Three coronary arteries supply blood to the heart muscle itself, and CHD occurs because of the deposition of cholesterol-rich, fatlike material in these arteries, partially or totally obstructing blood flow to heart muscle. When that process reaches the point where the dwindling flow of blood to the heart muscle fails to meet that tissue's requirements for oxygen, pain occurs; if the flow is not maintained at adequate levels for more than a few minutes, there occurs the actual death of heart muscle cells, which is the basis for the "heart attack," or "coronary occlusion," or "coronary attack"—the commonly used synonyms for the medical term, myocardial infarction.

Dying heart muscle can develop uncoordinated electrical activity, leading to life-threatening disturbances in the rhythm of the heart's beat—one of the bases for sudden death. Within a week or two after a coronary occlusion, dead heart muscle is replaced by fibrous tissue, but as this replacement process occurs, there are a few days when the dead tissue is relatively weak and not yet fully replaced by fibrous tissue and so is subject to rupture, which is almost invariably fatal and is another basis for sudden death after a heart attack.

If the heart attack kills too much heart muscle, the heart may be too weak a pump to support a normal range of activity, even after healing is complete: such patients develop congestive heart failure, with breathlessness on even minimal exertion, fluid accumulation about the ankles or in the abdomen, and/or episodes of lung congestion and breathlessness. Some patients, however, recover completely from one, two, and sometimes even three myocardial infarctions without evident disability. It depends on the condition of the heart muscle to begin with, on how much coronary vessel narrowing has occurred in the other two vessels, on the location and size of the dead heart muscle, and so forth. There are about 1.25 million myocardial infarctions per year in the United States; each year, 1 in every 77 people age 35 and over has a heart attack.

Intermediate degrees of narrowing of the coronary arteries can also lead to congestive heart failure and/or to a condition called angina pectoris, which is the clinical term for pain in the chest or arm that occurs related to temporarily inadequate coronary artery blood flow. Angina pains are relieved by the drug called nitroglycerin, taken either as a tablet placed under the tongue at the time of an angina attack or on a continuous, round-the-clock basis as a skin patch. About 1% of the population over age 35 has enough coronary artery obstruction to cause angina; two-thirds of those over 35 have some degree of narrowing in their coronary arteries, but not enough to cause symptoms or changes in an electrocardiogram. (Age 35 is used only as an arbitrary starting age beyond which to keep count; neither angina nor myocardial infarctions are unheard of in people under age 35, but they are distinctly unusual then.) The usually symptom-free process of early coronary artery narrowing can begin during adolescence; for example, one of the surprises to come out of the medical annals of the Korean War was that many young service-men killed in battle turned out on postmortem examination to have a quite distinct narrowing of their coronary arteries. Yet, as with rusty water pipes, narrowing has to be marked before flow falls and causes symptoms.

Stroke

Mortality due to stroke has declined by about one-third in the past decade. Behind this statistic lies a parallel reduction in the incidence of nonfatal strokes, with their often-debilitating consequences of deteriorated brain function: paralysis, speech disabilities, and behavioral derangements.

Strokes arise for either of two reasons: (1) rupture of a cerebral artery, with hemorrhage into the surrounding brain tissue, causing damage because of both interrupted blood flow and compression from the force of leaking blood; or (2) obstruction of a cerebral artery, with consequent death of brain cells due to lack of oxygen in the region previously served by the artery. Distinguishing between hemorrhage and obstruction is important, for their treatment differs, and application of the wrong treatment usually makes matters worse. A big advance during the 1970's was the introduction of the so-called CAT-scanner ("CAT" is an acronym for "computer-assisted tomography"); the CAT-scanner vastly improved the ability to distinguish a ruptured artery from an obstructed one. Probably the biggest factor responsible for the decline in incidence of strokes is the fact that more and more people with hypertension are being successfully treated. Hypertension is a major risk factor for stroke, as will be discussed later.

Heart Diseases in Infants and Children

Surgical correction of most congenital heart defects became possible with the development and widespread availability of open heart surgery during the 1960's and 1970's. While only a few centers did open heart surgery in the 1960's, by the end of the 1970's it was being done in one or more hospitals in virtually every major North American and West European city.

Preventive measures are also important and in the long run have the greatest influence. Understanding the role of German measles (rubella) infections during early pregnancy in the formation of congenital heart defects has had a big effect, for this otherwise harmless viral infection has been one of the leading causes of congenital heart defects in the past. This information came from careful epidemiologic studies in Australia.[15] As a result, careful surveillance is now routine for German measles during early pregnancy, and there is also a vaccine against the rubella virus. Furthermore, knowledge has increased about the potential dangers of various drugs, notably alcohol, for fetal development, and currently much attention is being paid to defining what the adverse effects of maternal smoking may be on fetal development.

Similar developments in both surgical treatment and prevention have served to transform rheumatic fever from a major, often fatal childhood disease to one that is exceptionally unusual today. Also, it used to be that many children who survived rheumatic fever developed fatal deformities of the heart valves 20–30 years later. Most of these valve deformities have been surgically correctable for the last 25–30 years.

Thus, for reasons of both better treatment and better prevention, heart disease in infants and children has disappeared from the top ten causes of death.

CANCER

Many people believe that we are experiencing a cancer epidemic. However, the situation is not quite so simple, not only for the reasons already noted, but for others as well. An overriding consideration is that cancer is not one disease, but many, for "cancer" is a blanket term that includes many diseases of quite different nature and risk.

Each type of cancer has its own biology, influenced by such things as: (1) typical age of onset, (2) antecedent risk factors, (3) rate of growth, (4) pattern of spread, (5) response to various modes of treatment. A good overview of what has been happening to the rates of death from each of the major types of cancer over the past five decades is given by Figure 3. There has been a steady increase of more than ten-fold in the rate of deaths from lung cancer since 1930. During the same half-century, there was a steady drop in the rate of deaths from stomach cancer, not because treatment improved very much (which it hasn't), but because incidence had fallen by 1978 to about one-quarter of what it had been in 1930. No one knows why. Also during this same period, there was a steady drop in the rate of deaths from cancer of the uterus, not because its incidence changed very much, but because both early diagnosis and treatment improved so much that the rate of deaths due to uterine cancer fell to about one-quarter what it had been in 1930. Alongside these big changes in cancers of the lung, stomach, and uterus, death rates from the other major cancers have not changed very much, at least since about 1950.

Note that the rates in Figure 3 are age-adjusted. This process is done in order to distinguish two different ways by which the overall deaths due to cancer might increase. One way is simply due to the aging of the population, because cancer incidence is higher in older people than in younger people, as discussed further below. Today, we have many more older people than ever before, and consequently there are more cancer deaths. The next logical question is, have the death rates due to cancer among people of each of the various ages increased over the years? The answer is that they have not, and that fact is reflected by Figure 3, showing the essential constancy of age-adjusted death rates due to cancer, aside from the big, smoking-related rise in deaths due to lung cancer and the big decreases in deaths due to stomach and uterine cancers. The data in Figure 3 are from the United States, but they are reflective of the situation in most of the technologically advanced countries, which show overall incidence figures for cancer that are within ±15% of one another.[16] Some exceptions will be noted, however.

Table 3 shows how age and sex influence the rate of death from all cancers. In order to make valid comparisons in cancer incidence or mortality among nations or regions, it is necessary to make some

FIGURE 3

CANCER DEATH RATES BY SITE—UNITED STATES, 1930-1978

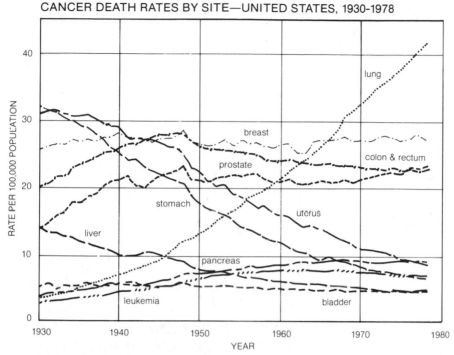

Rate for the population standardized for age on the 1970 U.S. population.

Sources of Data: National Center for Health Statistics and Bureau of the Census, United States.

Note: Rates are for both sexes combined except breast and uterus female population only and prostate male population only.

Figure 3. Changes in death rates from the various major types of cancer in the United States from 1930 to 1978. (Source: American Cancer Society, *Cancer Facts & Figures*, 1983. Reproduced with permission.)

adjustment for different proportions of people of various ages in the countries being compared. You can readily see from Table 3 why the aging of the population tends to produce a rise in the overall death rate from cancer.

Part of the difference in cancer death rates between the sexes is related to the preponderance of lung cancer in males. The big rise in lung cancer occurring during the past 50 years is a delayed consequence of the growth in the popularity of cigarette smoking that started in the second and third decades of this century. Females took longer than males to adopt cigarettes, a fact reflected in Table 4, which shows death rates from cancers of the respiratory system (which includes not only lung cancer, but cancers of the larynx and

TABLE 3

DEATH RATES FROM CANCER AMONG AMERICANS, BY AGE AND SEX, 1975 (deaths per 100,000)

age	male	female
25–44	34	33
45–54	184	177
55–64	512	358
65 and older	1221	725

Source: U.S. Bureau of the Census, *Statistical Abstract of the United States, 1981,* Table 117

of the nasal passages) for males and females between 55 and 64 from 1940 to 1978, the latest year for which data are compiled.

TABLE 4

DEATH RATES FROM CANCERS OF THE RESPIRATORY SYSTEM AMONG AMERICANS AGED 55–64, 1940–1978

(deaths per 100,000 per year)

year	male	female
1940	46	13
1950	94	15
1960	150	17
1970	202	39
1978	224	69

Source: U.S. Bureau of the Census, *Statistical Abstract of the United States, 1981,* Table 117

The numbers in Table 4 bring to mind a cigarette advertisement from the late 1920's that is often included in compilations of famous ads: a young couple, dressed in evening clothes, sit on a rock overlooking the moonlit sea; he is gazing thoughtfully at the sea as the smoke from his cigarette coils slowly in the motionless air; she is looking soulfully at him, and the caption has her saying: "Blow some my way." Women began to blow their own smoke at an increasing pace through the 1930's and 1940's, as discussed in Chapter 5, with one of the results now being reflected in Table 4.

In contrast to this steeply increasing toll from smoking-induced lung and other respiratory system cancers, there has been a steady decline over the same period in deaths from cancer of the stomach, as already noted. There is no generally accepted explanation for why this decline has occurred, but a similarly big drop in incidence of stomach cancer has occurred in most technologically advanced countries except Japan, where cancer of the stomach has had a strikingly high incidence, for unknown reasons, and has been one of the leading causes of death there. It appears that the incidence of stomach cancer in Japan is now beginning to show a small decline, too.

One theory for the North American and European decline in stomach cancers is based on an assumption that eating large amounts of smoked or pickled foods carries with it an added risk of inducing stomach cancers. This idea is not proven, but it is qualitatively in agreement with national differences in the incidence of gastrointestinal cancers and their changes over time. The advent of home refrigeration early in this century, and its subsequent universal adoption, has had the effect of gradually displacing smoked and pickled food from most people's diets. Smoking and pickling are, in effect, pre-refrigeration technologies for preserving foods. There is an interesting correlation here, but no proof of causality.

We have already noted in Figure 2 the striking fall in the death rate due to cancer of the uterus. Unlike cancer of the stomach, whose death rate declined due to a decline in incidence, the decline in the rate of deaths due to cancer of the uterus is related to better methods of early detection and treatment. These have included: (1) the widespread adoption of annual gynecological examination; (2) the development of cytologic techniques for finding the early states of malignant change; (3) a much-advanced understanding of the stages of uterine cancer; and (4) the development of reliable methods of treating uterine cancers at the various stages at which they are identified. The best-known aspect of all this technology for treating these cancers is the discovery and development, by Dr. George Papanicolaou, of cytologic techniques for sampling and analyzing cells from vaginal secretions. This technique, widely known as the Pap smear, has not only facilitated diagnosis of early malignant changes, but has also served as an important guide to recognition of the cellular changes leading up to frankly malignant cell growth.

That information, in turn, has led to effective methods of treatment, appropriate for the stage of the disease. For example, there is an early, not-yet invasive stage of malignant transformation in the cells covering the uterine cervix—so-called cancer in situ. This condition can be effectively treated by surgically removing a cone-shaped wedge from the cervix. It does not require more extensive surgery, such as hysterectomy. Matching the treatment to the stage of the disease is fundamentally important, since one of the consequences of cancerphobia tends to be overly radical treatment methods.

In contrast to the marked improvements in diagnosis and treatment of uterine cancers, breast cancer has yet to yield to substantial improvements. The death rate has crept upwards over time, as Table 5 shows.

TABLE 5

DEATHS PER 100,000 FROM CANCER OF THE BREAST AMONG AMERICAN WOMEN, 1940–1978

year	aged 45–54	aged 55–64
1940	48	75
1950	47	70
1960	51	71
1970	53	78
1978	51	83

Source: U.S. Bureau of the Census, *Statistical Abstract of the United States, 1981,* Table 117

During the last 15 years, however, it has been learned that the long-practiced surgical procedure of radical mastectomy offers no advantage in treatment of any but the most advanced breast cancers. Recognition of this fact has allowed women with breast cancer to undergo far less extensive and thus less risky and less mutilating surgery when the disease is recognized.

Since 1960, the combined use of surgery, X-rays, and chemotherapy has brought about small improvements in five-year survival after various cancers are diagnosed. Table 6 summarizes the latest information for seven of the leading cancers.

TABLE 6

FIVE-YEAR SURVIVAL RATES FOR CANCERS OF SEVEN DIFFERENT SITES

site	diagnosis made 1960–63	diagnosis made 1970–73
	% survivors 5 years after diagnosis	
endometrium	73	81
breast	63	68
cervix	58	64
bladder	53	61
prostate	50	63
colon	43	49
rectum	38	45

Source: National Cancer Institute, *Decade of Discovery*, NIH Pub. 81-2323, 1981

One area of striking improvement, however, is that of the various childhood tumors. Figure 4 shows how two-year survival has improved since 1940. Wilms' tumor and Hodgkin's disease, for example, now can be cured in about 90% of patients. Figure 4 nevertheless indicates that there is still a great deal to be accomplished, but it represents progress that was unthinkable at midcentury.

CANCERPHOBIA VS CORONARYPHOBIA

Cancerphobia is well-known. The facts about cancer are fairly complex, as the foregoing shows. Thus, it is easy to manipulate these complex facts, play on cancerphobia, and mislead people into thinking that we are having a epidemic of all cancers due to "pollutions" of various kinds. As the facts just reviewed show, we are indeed having an epidemic of lung cancer, but it has a very clear basis in

FIGURE 4

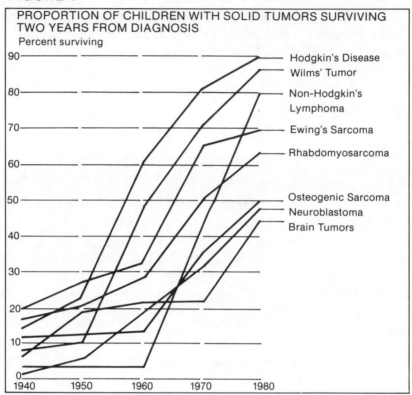

Figure 4. Big improvements in the effectiveness of treating various childhood tumors between 1940 and the present. (Source: National Cancer Institute, *Decade of Discovery,* NIH Pub. 81-2323, 1981, p. 9.)

cigarette smoking, without which lung cancer would be a very minor cause of death; instead it is still growing in males and has started to grow appreciably in females. We seem to be recovering from an epidemic of stomach cancer, but we don't know why, although it may be related to a technological advance called refrigeration. We have made big strides in early recognition and treatment of uterine cancers, though they cannot be said to be mastered, and several of the childhood cancers plus Hodgkin's disease and certain lymphomas are now also curable in a considerable majority of cases. The other kinds of cancer do not seem to be changing very much, although the results of treatment are a bit better than they were in the early 1960's.

Why is there not a coronaryphobia to match or even exceed the cancerphobia? There are about twice as many deaths from CHD as from cancer. Surely the air hunger which comes with the shortness of breath in chronic heart failure can be as gripping as the suffering of terminal cancer, and the body surely wastes away in the terminal stages of heart disease as well as of cancer. While many people with cardiovascular diseases die either suddenly or after only a few days following a heart attack or stroke, about the same number die after progressively more severe, restricting, and wasting heart failure as with cancer in all its forms. In sheer numbers and potential for ugliness, cancer and heart disease are more or less at a draw.

It is well to recall that "the death rate is still one per person—the only questions are when and how." The choice between cancer and heart disease, or any other mode of nonsudden death, is similar to that between being bitten by a cobra or a rabid dog. Balancing realistic concerns about cancer with those about other common fatal conditions will enhance the rationality of public discussions and actions aimed at further reducing risk and improving the quality of peoples' lives.

NOTES TO CHAPTER 4

1. U.S. Bureau of the Census. *Historical Statistics of the United States, Colonial Times to 1970. Bicentennial Edition, Part 1.* Washington, D.C., 1975, p. 58.

2. U.S. Bureau of the Census. *Statistical Abstract of the United States, 1982–83.* Washington, D.C., Table 113.

3. Ibid. Table 119.

4. Ibid. Table 118.

5. Ibid. Table 105.

6. Levy, R.I., and J. Moskowitz. "Cardiovascular research: decades of progress, a decade of promise," *Science* 217 (1982): 121–29.

7. Gillum, R.F., et al. "Sudden death in a metropolitan area, 1970–1980. The Minnesota Heart Survey." *New England J. Med.* 309 (1983): 1353–58.

8. St. Leger, A.S., A.L. Cochrane, and F. Moore. "Factors associated with cardiac mortality in developed countries with particular reference to the consumption of wine." *Lancet* 1 (1979): 1017–20.

9. *Statistical Abstract of the United States, 1982–83.* Table 1402.

10. Heilmann, K., and J. Urquhart. *Keine Angst vor der Angst. Risiko: Element unseres Leben und Motor des Fortschritts.* Munchen: Kindler, 1983; Van, J. "Mystery hypertension is linked to use of salt." *Chicago Tribune,* Jan. 29, 1984.

11. Society of Actuaries. *Build and Blood Pressure Study, 1959.* Chicago, 1959.

12. Veterans Administration Cooperative Study on Antihypertensive Agents. "Effects of treatment on morbidity in hypertension, II." *JAMA,* 213 (1970): 1143–52. "Effects of treatment on morbidity in hypertension, III." *Circulation* 45 (1972): 991–1004.

13. Hypertension Detection and Follow-up Program Cooperative Group. "Five-year findings of the hypertension detection and follow-up program, I." *JAMA* 242 (1979): 2562–71.

14. Society of Actuaries, *Build and Blood Pressure Study, 1979.* Chicago, 1979.

15. Gregg, N.M. "Congenital cataract following German measles in the mother." *Tr. Ophth. Soc. Australia* 3 (1941): 35.

16. *Statistical Abstract of the United States, 1982.* Table 115.

5

Prominent Voluntary Hazards In Everyday Life

This chapter discusses four prominent, voluntary hazards in everyday life. Almost everyone partakes of one, and many partake of all four. Each adds to life an element of risk that has been reasonably or very well-measured. The level of risk associated with each is accepted by practically everyone involved with little current controversy—certainly little in comparison to controversies over nuclear power, for example, or certain pharmaceuticals. Each provides a useful reference point with which to keep in perspective news reports about new hazards. The four hazards we discuss here are: (1) motor vehicles; (2) cigarette smoking; (3) alcoholic beverages; and (4) oral contraceptives. A logical fifth hazard to discuss is food, but this is a big and especially vexatious subject, needing a whole chapter, if not a book, of its own.

Motor Vehicles

Of all the technological changes that have occurred during the 20th century, probably none has had greater effect on our lives than the automobile. Whole cities have been reshaped to accommodate the needs of both traffic flow and parking space. Architectural and other monuments of the past seem literally to be dissolving in automobile exhaust fumes. Yet, automobiles give convenience and freedom, probably their two most attractive features, for which people are willing to pay large fractions of their incomes and to accept with little controversy levels of risk that have driven other kinds of products from the market.

With great expenditure of public monies, highways have been widened, freeways built, and bridges, tunnels, overpasses and underpasses constructed. These are the large public monuments of the 20th century, vastly exceeding in scope those of even the most extravagant monarchs of earlier centuries, and paid for by a public which until recently agitated for their construction, accepting the financial burden without complaint. Even today, when resistance to further growth of freeways has become substantial in many places, it remains politically dangerous to interfere with the intimate love affair between humans and their automobiles. It has required much time and great social and political will, for example, to begin to restrict people's "right" to drink and drive with impunity.

That automobiles injure and kill is no secret, because there are daily reminders of the steady death toll on the roads. Two surprising things about the automobile as a hazard are: (1) the curious passivity with which the risk of automobile use is accepted by practically everyone; (2) the considerable inertia that impedes the utilization of things readily at hand to reduce the risks of automobile use.[1]

It is paradoxical that a number of very small technological risks receive overwhelming attention, while the sizable risk posed by the automobile is relatively neglected and excites so little action. For example, while America's participation in the Vietnam War prompted widespread protests against the killing, there were no demonstrations against death on the roads, even though, during those same years, more Americans died on U.S. roads than in Vietnam. We kill about 50,000 people annually in road accidents, half in accidents in which at least one driver is drunk.[2]

Similar passivity is found in the introduction of measures which demonstrably dilute the risk of driving, e.g. the use of seatbelts and strict control of driving under the influence of alcohol. The Scandinavian countries have pioneered in demonstrating the risk-diluting benefits of these measures. For example, in 1975, the Finns made use of safety belts obligatory, and drastically increased the penalty for drunken driving; at the same time, they instituted strict speed controls according to the various classes of road. During the next five years, they reduced their traffic fatalities to half what they had been in the years prior to the new laws. During those same five years, only small changes in traffic fatalities occurred in Germany and Britain, for example, so the improvement in Finland cannot be readily ascribed to "energy consciousness" or some spontaneous epidemic of defensive driving.[3]

The separation of alcohol consumption and driving has proved to be very difficult to enforce. For example, in 1968 the British enacted a very severe law against drunk driving, with strict limits on blood alcohol levels for drivers. A legal "loophole" was discovered in the law, however, creating a tremendous amount of litigation relating to the procedures used by the police in the roadside conduct of the breath test. As a consequence, the law not only failed to realize the intent that motivated its enactment, but the public disillusionment and controversy provoked by the inequities of the 1968 law have added to the difficulty of marshaling the political will to enact a new, properly written law.

Meanwhile, in the United States, a group called Mothers Against Drunk Drivers (MADD) appears finally to have caught the public's interest and has focussed sufficient political pressure to create stricter laws in a number of states. For example, California has enacted a much stricter law, which went into effect at the beginning of 1982; arrests for drunken driving were reportedly substantially lower during the first year, but this is an ambiguous indicator: were there fewer drunken drivers, or did the stringency of the new penalties make the police more reluctant to arrest? It will become evident when traffic fatalities and data on blood alcohol levels of people involved in fatal accidents are definitively tabulated, a process which will take several years. The new law was promptly challenged in the courts, and for a time it looked as if the law might not stand up. Almost two years after its passage, however, the California Supreme Court ruled unanimously in favor of the legality of the new law. It will probably be five years before there are enough data on road accidents and blood alcohol levels among victims and other participants in the accidents to judge the impact of the new law.

The clear success which the Finns have had in diluting the risk of automobile use has also been achieved by the Swedes, with similar laws on seatbelt use and drunk driving. Yet what works so well in one country can be a complete failure elsewhere. There are astonishing national differences in the risks of automobile use, as illustrated by the fatalities data in Table 1. Anyone who has driven in a

TABLE 1

NATIONAL DIFFERENCES IN TRAFFIC FATALITY
RATE

country	deaths per 100,000 vehicles per year
Turkey	729
France	70
Germany	56
Japan	48
United States	42
United Kingdom	40
Sweden	29

Source: *Le Monde,* 13 Feb. 1982

number of countries is aware that each country has its special style of driving. It is particularly striking in countries where the automobile has only recently made its appearance in a major way in the local society: in such countries, standards of driving invariably seem to be appallingly bad. It seems as if a society requires a certain amount of time—and victims—before a social consensus develops on an appropriate degree of self-discipline in automobile use. Until that self-discipline develops, it is as if the entire population of drivers was made up of the most flamboyantly reckless teenage drivers that one sees in the industrial countries, where the automobile has been an integral part of society for three generations.

For example, in Britain in 1931, there were about 6700 fatalities due to road accidents, when there were only 2.2 million automobiles.[4] In 1979, there were 6352 traffic fatalities, but 18.6 million vehicles on the road—nine times as many vehicles as in 1931, but essentially the same number of traffic deaths. Thus, the automobile-associated risk has been diluted by a factor of about 10, with a 1.0 SDU rise in the degree of safety of automobile use. Another way of looking at the available data is to relate the number of fatalities to the number of miles driven throughout the entire nation. For Great Britain, the data go back only to 1937 and show that the total mileage driven increased six-fold between then and 1979, while the number of traffic fatalities stayed almost the same. Those data indicate a six-fold dilution of risk, or a 0.8 SDU increase in the degree of safety. Similar changes occurred during the same years in the United States, Germany, and other industrialized nations.

What has changed to dilute automobile-related risk during these years? Certainly streets and roads have been improved in many ways, as has the design of automobiles. The general level of driving skills has probably improved also. Medical and surgical treatment of accident victims has greatly improved, so that many people who previously would have died are today listed only among the injured. One can only guess about the relative importance of these various factors, but they and perhaps other factors appear to have increased the degree of safety of automobile use by 0.8–1.0 SDU compared to its value a half century ago.

The risk of automobile use is strongly dependent on age and sex. Males have a traffic fatality rate which is two to three times greater than that for females. In the United States, 8.4% of the licensed drivers are under 20 but are involved in twice that proportion (16.9%) of fatal accidents. Those age 20–24 account for 13.4% of licensed drivers but are involved in 21.6% of the fatal accidents. In contrast, drivers over 65 constitute 10.2% of licensed drivers but are involved in only 6.2% of fatal accidents.[5]

The risk of automobile use is also influenced very strongly by both time of day and day of the week: there are more fatal accidents at night than in the day, and there are many more accidents during Friday through Sunday than Monday through Thursday, as noted in Chapter 3. Figure 1 illustrates these points and more: if you look at Figure 1 with the daily rhythm of traffic flows in mind, you can see that large masses of cars move to work during the morning rush hours coincident with the daily minimum in fatal accidents; about twice as many fatalities appear to occur during the evening commute as during the morning one. Most accidents occur when there are relatively few cars on the road, visibility is limited, and the opportunities for and social approval of alcohol consumption are greatest.

All in all, the car is an important risk factor in modern life. In the United States, one's risk of being killed within a year's time in a road

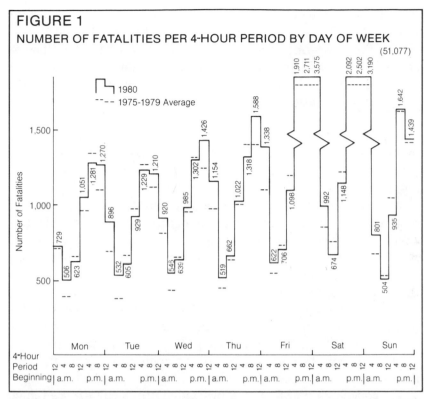

FIGURE 1

NUMBER OF FATALITIES PER 4-HOUR PERIOD BY DAY OF WEEK

Figure 1. Average number of traffic fatalities during four-hour intervals of each day of the week during 1980 in the United States. (Source: U.S. Department of Transportation, National Highway Traffic Safety Administration, *Fatal Accident Reporting System, 1980*, DOT HS 805 953, October 1981, figure 8.)

accident is about 1 in 4200, corresponding to a relatively low safety-degree index of 3.6 SDU. The figure can be refined to say that the safety-degree status of males is 3.4 SDU (1 death per year in 2500), and in females 3.9 SDU (1 in 8000). In Germany, auto-risk is more concentrated, for the safety-degree status is 3.1 SDU (1 in 1300) overall, with a similar difference of 0.5 SDU (three-fold) between males and females, in the latters' favor. In the industrial countries, auto accidents account for about half of all accidental deaths.

The motorcycle warrants consideration, because it has the reputation of being so very hazardous. U.S. data for 1978, for example, show that during the year, 1 car in 5, versus 1 motorcycle in 10, was involved in some kind of accident—not necessarily fatal.[6] When an accident did occur involving a motorcycle, however, it was more likely to result in the cyclist's death: there was 1 motorcyclist or rider killed per 1056 registered cycles during the same year in which there was 1 automobile occupant killed per 4022 registered motor vehicles, exclusive of cycles. These figures support the contention of many motorcyclists that they do indeed exercise greater care than automobile drivers; however, the motorcyclist or passenger is at a relative disadvantage when an accident does occur.

When one takes into account the fact that the vast majority of motorcyclists are males aged 25 or younger and compares the fatality data for that group between motorcycles and cars, it is apparent that there is a much smaller concentration of risk among motorcyclists than is generally supposed—the degree of safety is 0.2–0.3 SDU less than that of automobile use, i.e. 1.5–2 times more concentrated risk of death among the motorcyclists, who lack the protective shield of metal which the automobile provides its driver and passengers. For motorcyclists, the risk-concentrating absence of a protective metal shield is largely but not completely compensated for by the risk-diluting factor of defensive driving.

The concept of the amount of protection provided by one's vehicle can be seen in comparing insurance payments for injuries in relation to the size of the vehicle. For example, U.S. insurance data show that during 1977–78 there was 1 accident per year for every 6 trucks and buses on the road, with insurance payments for personal injury amounting to about $50 for each truck or bus per year. In contrast, there was 1 accident per year for every 4.7 cars and an insurance payment per car for accidental injuries of $110 per year.[7] Intuitively, one can understand that, all other things being equal, one would rather be in a large truck or bus in an accident than in the smallest car or motorcycle. These personal injury payment figures put that intuition on a cash basis.

Recently, an American insurance company published information on accident rates for a wide range of automobile makes and models.[8] The comparisons were properly adjusted for the age of the driver to correct for the obvious fact that drivers of large, expensive cars tend to be in their middle or older years (though of course they may have teenage sons who use the car sometimes), whereas certain makes and models are designed to appeal to a younger age group. When the age factor was corrected for, there was a safety-degree difference of 0.5 SDU for death or injury between the cars with the best accident records and those with the worst—in other words, a factor of 3 difference from the best to the worst, related to automobile design. It is probably not just a matter of relative degrees of protection in various crash situations. There are also elements in the design of some automobiles that inspire aggressive driving.

The most reasonable advice pertaining to automobile-related risk seems to be—and it is much easier to say than to do—buy whatever car suits your means, use your seatbelt conscientiously, do not drive after you have consumed any alcohol, and, probably most importantly, drive defensively, not offensively.

Cigarette Smoking

There has been a tremendous amount of commentary and debate since the original reports during the 1950's from England and the United States on the risks of cigarette smoking. Initial attention focussed on the markedly increased risk of lung cancer in cigarette smokers, but subsequent work showed that cigarette smokers had a considerably greater risk of developing coronary heart disease (CHD) than did nonsmokers. All this information, amounting to about 2000 publications, was assembled in 1964 by the U.S. Surgeon General in a landmark report called "Smoking and Health."[9]

Publication of "Smoking and Health" triggered much debate. Those biased toward smoking—mainly smokers, tobacco growers, manufacturers of tobacco products, and the industry's political allies —stoutly claimed that the "association" between smoking and increased risk of premature death and lung cancer was "only statistical." The tobacco industry established a "Committee on Tobacco and Health," which sponsored a good deal of public comment on various inconsistencies and deficiencies in the Surgeon General's report and the various studies on which it was based. At the same time, however, the tobacco industries began gradually diversifying into nontobacco products. Shortly after the publication of "Smoking and Health," one life insurance company began offering a special life insurance policy for nonsmokers, with premiums about 20% lower than the standard for age and sex.

In 1979, a second Surgeon General's report was published, also called "Smoking and Health."[10] This report reviewed the vast amount of research in the intervening 15 years. Its summary conclusions were:

1. Cigarette smokers are subject to a risk of dying which is 1.7 times greater than that of nonsmokers.
2. This adverse effect of smoking increases as the number of cigarettes consumed per day rises, or as the duration of smoking increases.
3. After one gives up smoking, the risk of dying gradually declines to the nonsmoker's level.

To illustrate various aspects of the meaning of these conclusions, the average life expectancy of a 30- to 35-year-old male two-pack-a-day smoker is 8–9 years less than that of a nonsmoker of the same age and sex. (Recall that life expectancy is the time projected to pass until half those born in a given year have died.) Another perhaps more graphic way to look at it is that each minute spent in smoking diminishes life expectancy by about one minute. For a two-pack-a-day smoker, this amounts to a loss of about 100 days per year of average life expectancy.

Despite all the evidence presented in the two Surgeon General's reports, and despite all the publicity that the evidence received, cigarette smoking did not promptly fade away. There have, however, been some changes in smoking habits, with rather striking differences between males and females. Among males, smokers decreased between 1955 and 1975 from 52.6% to 39.3% of the adult male population; at the same time, the percentage of ex-smokers increased three-fold, from 10.9% to 29.2%. During this time, the adult male population increased from 82 million to 104 million, and the number of males who had ever smoked increased from 52 million to 71 million—so smoking has remained something which a substantial majority of males try, at least for a time.

Among women, smokers increased from 24.5% in 1955 to an interim peak of 33.7% of the adult female population, and then declined a bit to 28.9% by 1975. The actual number of female smokers rose from about 20 million in 1955 to 31.5 million in 1975, and the number of women who had ever smoked doubled.

During this same period, both the production of tobacco and the per capita consumption of cigarettes in the United States have fallen gradually, year by year, signifying some favorable changes in smoking habits. Nevertheless, the increases in the actual numbers of people smoking cigarettes is puzzling, considering both the general level of "risk consciousness" and the quantity and quality of information on the adverse effects of cigarette smoking. It is not just another hazard—cigarette smoking is the single biggest proven hazard in today's life.

Perhaps people's understanding of this issue has been blunted by the long controversy about the reality of the risk of cigarette smoking. A recurring theme in this overlong controversy has been that the risks are not real, and that the association between smoking and disease or death is "only statistical." In 1980, however, there appeared a new kind of information about the death-risk of cigarette smoking: the actuarial experience from the first life insurance company to offer a nonsmoker's life insurance policy, begun shortly after the first Surgeon General's Report in 1964. The information was contained in a paper given to the Society of Actuaries in 1979 by Cowell and Hirst,[11] two actuaries with the State Mutual Life Assurance Company, the firm which pioneered special insurance rates for nonsmokers.

The report by Cowell and Hirst summarized the company's claims experience during the years 1973–78. In this period, the firm had $2.7 billion of insurance in force for smokers and $5.6 billion in force for nonsmokers—figures which indicate that the concept of special insurance for nonsmokers had been a success in the marketplace. The company had paid 718 death claims during 1973–78, amounting to $13 million for dead smokers, and $11 million for dead nonsmokers. The claims paid for smokers were a third higher than the original projection; those paid for nonsmokers were about half that of the original projection, both projections having been based on the data presented in the 1964 Surgeon General's report. Overall, insured smokers died at 2.2 times the rate of nonsmokers. Table 2 lists the relative risks of death by various causes for smokers and nonsmokers among State Mutual's policyholders.

This new evidence puts the whole matter of the death-risk of

TABLE 2

STATE MUTUAL'S EXPERIENCE BASED ON 718 DEATHS
AMONG INSURED SMOKERS AND NONSMOKERS, 1973–1978

% deaths in categories	cause of death	ratio of death-risk smokers/nonsmokers
100.0	all causes	2.2
6.0	respiratory cancers	15.0
30.1	arteriosclerotic heart disease	2.7
2.5	hypertension and hypertensive heart disease	8.1
19.1	cancer (excluding respiratory cancers)	1.2
4.9	motor vehicle accidents	2.6
4.9	suicide	9.0
32.5	all other	1.9

Source: Cowell and Hirst, *Transactions of the Society of Actuaries*, 32 (1980): 1–29

Note: The percentage of deaths due to the various listed causes differs from that for the U.S. population as a whole. This difference relates to several factors: insurance purchasers represent a particular age group, are preponderantly male, and have to pass a physical examination before being issued a policy. The physical examination serves to exclude diabetics and those with hypertension-related diseases. Also, since the nonsmoker's policy went into effect only in 1964, the ages of policyholders who died during the years 1973–1978 were largely late thirties and early forties. Thus, the causes of death and their respective percentage contribution to total deaths are characteristic of that age range, not of the population as a whole.

cigarette smoking on a very practical, realistic basis. While one may have been skeptical about the data in the two Surgeon General's reports or suspicious of the biases of fanatical antismokers, one thing is certain: major life insurance companies act without illusions on the basis of economically motivated self-interest. More recently, the other insurance companies have reacted to this new information, and there are now over 100 companies, numbering among them the industry's largest, offering special premiums for nonsmokers. Moreover, the biggest industry critic of State Mutual's original policy back in 1964 has recently introduced its own policy for nonsmokers.[12]

There are certainly a number of logistical problems in the non-smoker's policy: (1) how to confirm that the insured is indeed a nonsmoker; (2) what to do when an insured smoker claims to have quit smoking; (3) what to do with policies already in force which do not distinguish between smokers and nonsmokers; (4) what to do with heavy versus light smokers. The difficulty of finding satisfactory answers to these and other questions is one of the reasons that there are still many more insurance companies that do not offer a non-smoker's policy than do.[12] But, the net effect of State Mutual's actuarial experience and the movement of the major insurers into singling out smoking as a premium-influencing factor is this: the conclusions of the two Surgeon General's reports are now backed by gold.

In the United States, the number of premature deaths caused by or accelerated by cigarette smoking is about 540,000 per year. It is the equivalent of three fully loaded 747 jumbo jets crashing every day. One might think that this fact is worth at least a medium-sized headline, since it amounts to about 1475 people dying every day. Of course, it happens every day and so ceases to attract attention. One wonders, if three jumbo jets did crash every day, how long would it be before they became back-page news? Certainly many much smaller catastrophes dominate the news, though never for long. Yet people's memories are long: one commentator remarked that many people still recall the TV news item about the deaths of cattle in the area around Three Mile Island when that event dominated the news —though few noted the correction made some time later that the cattle had died of ordinary causes in an ordinary way.

It should be noted that the principal impact of smoking on premature death comes about not from lung cancer, but from what Table 2 lists as "arteriosclerotic heart disease," the disease entity which we have referred to as coronary heart disease (CHD). The effect of smoking is "only" to double the risk of death due to CHD, whereas it multiplies the risk of respiratory cancers by 10–15 fold; but since CHD is the leading cause of death, its multiplication by a factor of two has a very big effect, one which is larger than that due to lung cancer.

It is odd, in a way, that no one has, to our knowledge, ever demonstrated outside a cigarette factory, or laid down in front of a cigarette delivery truck. However, what is probably a more constructive phenomenon is occurring: the growing exclusion of smokers from common facilities by the nonsmoking majority. Increasing attention to the risks of "second-hand smoke," in addition to its obvious unpleasantness, has given impetus to this change in many people's attitudes about shared smoke.

Alcoholic Beverages

The consumption of alcohol is so extensive that it is sensible to consider it not only from the behavioral and health points of view, but from the caloric and nutritional one as well. Setting aside their effects on mood and behavior, alcoholic beverages certainly represent a significant source of calories. A normal bottle of beer contains 14–18 grams of alcohol, corresponding to 100-130 calories. The alcohol content of a half liter of wine corresponds to about 375 calories. Since the average daily intake of calories is 2500–3000, the caloric content of the alcohol in alcoholic beverages can account for a fair fraction of caloric intake.

Certainly, the caloric content of alcohol is its most prosaic aspect, because alcohol's effects on mood and behavior make it both a valued and feared part of human life. Alcohol plays a role, in one form or other, in practically every human society; it appears in the oldest human writings, and Hippocrates prescribed it against depression— not an especially apt choice, since alcohol is itself something of a depressant. In its rich and changing history, alcohol has always been both a curse and a blessing.

Alcoholic beverages are hazardous because they are so strongly connected with two of the ten leading causes of death: accidents and cirrhosis of the liver. The role of alcohol in coronary heart disease is still equivocal, with some authorities under the impression that, taken in moderation, alcohol confers some modest benefit. We have already commented on the hypothesis put forward by St. Leger, Cochrane, and Moore on a possible protective effect of wine. From derelicts to university professors, however, there is no one without an opinion on alcohol. Yet there is an impressive amount of evidence that excessive alcohol intake has adverse effects on many body systems: the liver, heart, pancreas, gastrointestinal tract, brain, blood-forming organs, muscles, and sexual functions. Curiously, though, while much money is now spent on the surveillance of adverse reactions to prescription drugs, very little is spent on studying the effects of the chronic use of alcohol, which is by far the most commonly used drug.

The role of alcohol in death by accident is impressive, and confirms the old saying that many alcoholics kill themselves before the alcohol does.[13] In recent years, it has become increasingly common to measure blood alcohol levels in people involved in fatal traffic accidents, and, as noted earlier, these data show that at least one driver in half the fatal accidents is legally drunk. Less well-known are data indicating that about one-third of pedestrians killed each year were themselves legally drunk at the time of the accident.[14] It is common knowledge that alcohol plays a role in other kinds of accidents, too, but formal documentation is sparse.

Not every case of cirrhosis is alcohol-based, for the disease has other causes than excessive alcohol consumption. Also, many people drink a great deal over many years and do not develop cirrhosis. Nevertheless, there is a very clear connection between alcohol consumption and the development of cirrhosis.[15] In the United States, the death rate from cirrhosis was reduced during the years of Prohibition. In Britain, the number of deaths from cirrhosis decreased by a factor of seven during World War II—a time when high taxes and limited pub hours made the consumption of alcohol more difficult. France, as is generally known, has the highest per capita consumption of alcohol and also the highest rate of deaths due to cirrhosis. An important French study[16] has shown that there is no measurable risk of cirrhosis in men if consumption of alcohol is below 80 grams per day. Some risk is apparent when consumption is between 80 and 160 grams per day and is further increased when consumption exceeds 160 grams per day. The data for women are much less clear, but they suggest that women are more likely to develop cirrhosis at the 80 grams per day intake level than males, and that some women develop cirrhosis from as little as 20 grams per day.

One bottle of wine contains about 80 grams of alcohol, and a pint of whiskey has 200-250 grams, depending on proof. Thus, one has to be a steady, heavy drinker in order to develop cirrhosis, unless there is underlying liver disease to complicate matters, and you probably have to "drink your meals" from time to time.

It is useful to look at the insurance perspective on alcohol. A number of insurance studies have shown that people classed as "alcoholics" have a mortality rate which is 2.5–3 times the standard for age and sex, with the increased mortality arising mainly from accidents (especially car accidents) and suicides, as well as from diseases of the gastrointestinal tract and cirrhosis. These studies did not take into account differences between regular and spree drinking, although U.S. insurance data show that spree drinkers are at higher risk than steady drinkers, mainly through car accidents and suicide.

What does all of this mean for a person who believes that his or her drinking behavior falls into the category which one would generally recognize as being "social" and "socially acceptable"? Table 3 gives the insurance actuary's answer, which is probably the most nearly dispassionate view attainable of an area of human life about which there are many more opinions than facts: it is the actuary's job to put only an economic value on risk—high enough to give his company a fair return, but not so high as to price the insurance product out of the market.

TABLE 3

ADJUSTMENTS IN LIFE INSURANCE PREMIUMS IN MALES FOR VARIOUS DEGREES OF ALCOHOL CONSUMPTION

	Extent of Alcohol's Effect		
frequency of occurrence	jovial	boisterous	uncontrolled
6 times/year	standard	standard	+50%
monthly	standard	+50%	+100%
weekly	+25%	+75%	+150%
daily	+100%	+150%	decline

Source: Brackenridge, R.D.C., *Medical Selection of Life Risks,* p. 734

Note: +25% means that the premium is 125% of standard for age; +100% means that the premium is 200% of standard for age.

A pithy characterization of alcohol's risk has recently been given by Dr. Alex Comfort, noted for his widely read book *The Joy of Sex.* Prompted by his observation that 40–50% of the medical caseload at Los Angeles County Hospital is directly alcohol-related, he wrote as follows in the leading English medical journal: "Our attitude toward alcohol is basically not evidential but sentimental, rather as we are slow to admit that a family member is delinquent or insane. If cocaine is an Edwardian roué, marijuana a grubby counterculturist, and LSD a crazy with a knife, alcohol is a beloved if disreputable old uncle whose peccadilloes are excused because he is friendly and keeps a good cellar. So much so that even substance abuse experts bridle at the idea that he is a child molester who should be incarcerated. We obviously need to moderate his excesses, but suggesting that he be banished is like attacking Santa Claus. . . . Faced with the epidemiological facts—that alcohol is the main single preventable cause of trauma, impulsive crime, child and spouse abuse, birth defect, and sociosexual difficulty—we wriggle. . . and join the body of counselling, common now in America, that teaches 'sensible drinking' and how to avoid detection while driving under the influence. . . . The public awareness that 'doctors do not smoke cigarettes' (at least in public) has been salutary. A similar awareness that 'doctors do not drink alcohol,' remote as it is from our convivial reputation, might do likewise."[17]

Oral Contraceptives

Documenting the effectiveness of oral contraceptives is relatively straightforward because women of reproductive age seeking to become pregnant have on average 4 chances in 5 of doing so within a year's time.

Users of the oral contraceptive pill have—if they take the pill faithfully—a risk of pregnancy of about 1 in 1000 per year: their safety-degree status with respect to conception is 3.0 SDU. If they don't take the pills faithfully, however, the risk of pregnancy concentrates to around 1 in 20 per year, and their safety-degree status with respect to conception declines to 1.3 SDU.[18] This number is rather unsatisfactory, and so those who have difficulty taking the pill regularly and reliably should consider other means of contraception whose efficacy does not depend so much on regular self-medication.

When the first oral contraceptives were introduced in the early 1960's, attention focussed on their striking effectiveness in preventing pregnancy. Clinical studies had documented not only the 1 in

1000 per year risk of pregnancy in women using the pill, but also that those who decided to seek pregnancy could stop the pill and switch with little or no delay over to the normal 4 chances in 5 of becoming pregnant within the year.

This unprecedented degree of highly effective, convenient, and reversible contraception gradually attracted many women, so that, by the end of the decade, about one-third of the women in the reproductive age range in North America and Western Europe were using "the pill," as its wide usage led it to be called. This meant that by 1970 something like 20 million or more women were using the pill in countries where health care, medical records, and vital statistics are rather carefully looked after. As the cohort of pill-users grew into the millions, it became inevitable that any very infrequently occurring adverse events of pill use would begin to appear.

In the original trials, there had been only a few thousand women under study, and so the occurrence of one or two of a particular adverse event might or might not mean anything in relation to the oral contraceptive they were taking. After all, if you observe a few thousand people carefully for a year's time and do nothing at all to them, some will die from various causes, some will become ill with various diseases, and so forth. Against this continual background of life's adversities, one has to judge whether the drug is doing something unusual. Consequently, in the clinical trials, it was only possible to measure the medical safety-degree of pill use to the 1–2.5 SDU range (1 in 10 to 1 in 300), because it usually takes five or more adverse reactions to arouse suspicion that something unusual is happening in a big clinical trial. By 1970, the stage was set for the arrival of information about what adverse reactions there were with the oral contraceptives to the safety-degree range of about 5.0 SDU (1 adverse reaction in 100,000 pill users per year).

It had begun to become apparent in the late 1960's that, when the very unusual event of a heart attack or stroke occurred in women of reproductive age, it usually turned out that they had been using an oral contraceptive. Neither heart attacks nor strokes are unusual adverse events in the population at large, but they are exceptionally rare occurrences in women who have not yet undergone menopause. When this association became apparent, the plight of the victims created a huge sensation in the news media. U.S. Senator Gaylord Nelson held public hearings at which testimony was heard from victims who had been taking oral contraceptives and from their families.

It has been said that many women who saw TV reports of these hearings threw away their oral contraceptives, turned to older, "safer" methods of contraception—and became pregnant.

Whether that is true or not, the hitherto "clean" reputation of the pill was lost, and it was not until almost a decade later that the actual levels of risk could be measured from good information that was simultaneously gathered on both victims *and* nonvictims using oral contraceptives, plus information on women of the same age and situation in life who used other methods of contraception, or none at all. The best such information came from a big study carried out in England by the Royal College of General Practitioners (RCGP).[19] The RCGP study was begun in 1968 and is still continuing, although it has reported out data at intervals since the latter 1970's.

The RCGP study revealed that most of the risk of pill use was concentrated in two special groups: (1) women over age 35, and (2) women who smoked. Hence, the original cohorts of pill-users and nonusers each had to be divided into four smaller cohorts: (1) women under 35 who don't smoke; (2) women under 35 who do smoke; (3) and (4) women 35 and older who don't and do smoke. The RCGP study is based on 23,000 women who entered the study during 1968–69 and were using the oral contraceptive at that time; at the same time, another 23,000 women who were not using the oral contraceptive were also entered and followed with the same questions and tests as those who were pill-users. Over the years, reports have been gathered on a six-monthly basis from their family doctors. These reports keep track of changes in contraceptive method, along with various medical events in the women's lives, including death and its cause.

The current results from this very large and long study are that, with respect to deaths due to circulatory diseases, the safety-degree of pill use is 4.9 SDU (1 death per year in 80,000) in nonsmokers under 35; this very low level of risk may be unrelated to pill use, for the different number of deaths between nonsmoking pill-users and nonusers in the RCGP study was simply too small indicate a clear relation to pill use. For women under 35 who smoke, the safety-degree status declines 4.0 SDU (1 death per year in 10,000). With increasing age, the safety-degree status declines further to 3.7 SDU

(1 death per year in 5000) for nonsmokers between 35 and 44; for smokers between 35 and 44, it is 3.2 SDU (1 death per year in 1600). For women 45 and older, the safety-degree status of pill use declines still further: for nonsmokers it is 3.3 SDU (1 death per year in 2000), and for smokers it is 2.7 SDU (1 death per year in 500).

These figures all refer to risk just of circulatory diseases related to the pill, over and above the risk of deaths due to circulatory diseases in women using other methods of contraception. Table 4 compares in total 16 groups of women who have never used the pill with those who have ever used the pill. If you study the table, you will note that women who currently use the pill or who have ever used the pill (even though not currently using it) are combined in one group. The reason for this is that women who have once used the pill but stopped seem to be subject to the same risk as women who continue to use it—a rather surprising result that has not had much public comment.

The most noticeable thing about the figures in Table 4 is that either smoking or pill use decreases safety-degree status by 0.3–0.6 SDU, but when the two are combined safety-degree status declines by 0.8–1.1 SDU. In other words, either smoking or pill use concentrates risk by 2–4-fold, but the two together concentrate risk by 6–14-fold.

TABLE 4

PER-YEAR RISK OF DEATH FROM CIRCULATORY DISEASES RELATED TO ORAL CONTRACEPTIVE USE, AGE, AND SMOKING

age	Women who are pill-users now or in the past		Women who have never used the pill	
	nonsmokers	smokers	nonsmokers	smokers
Under 25	less than 1 in 100,000	1 in 9600	less than 1 in 100,000	less than 1 in 100,000
25–34	1 in 23,000	1 in 7000	1 in 37,000	1 in 22,000
35–44	1 in 4700	1 in 1600	1 in 16,000	1 in 6600
45 and over	1 in 1900	1 in 500	1 in 8800	1 in 3600

Source: Note 19

Individuals should look at these risk estimates and make their own judgments as to contraceptive method and smoking.

Those judgments should be made recognizing that, even though the data came from a very large study that has gone on for over a decade, there are still many uncertainties. For one thing, there were only one or two deaths from circulatory diseases in some of the cohorts. Such small numbers put considerable uncertainty in the estimate of the unicohort size, because the chance occurrence of one more or one less victim would have a big effect on the estimate of unicohort size. Nevertheless, the RCGP study has the largest number of participants and thus gives the clearest definition of the smallest measurable risks associated with the use of oral contraceptives.

Another point about the RCGP study is that inevitably there are certain things that, if one had it to do over, one would do differently from the beginning of the study in light of what was subsequently learned. The most important of these relates to how smoking was measured. It turns out that women were asked about their smoking habits at the time they joined the study in 1968-69, but not afterwards. When the study was designed, smoking was not recognized to be such a large hazard. Because of this omission, there are probably a fair number of ex-smokers being counted as smokers. There may also be some women who originally were nonsmokers but subsequently started smoking. There are, however, probably far fewer of these than of smokers who subsequently quit; surveys of smoking habits show that there are many more smoking adults who have quit smoking than there are nonsmoking adults who have started smoking. Most people, if they are going to start smoking, do so in their adolescent or very early adult years. If all that is applicable to the RCGP study, there were probably a fair number of ex-smokers erroneously counted in the various cohorts of smokers. If so, then the true risks for smokers may be greater than Table 4 indicates.

A final point to make is that the process of understanding oral contraception is not finished. Clearly we know much more now than we did a decade ago, and especially so compared to the moments of high drama when the first revelations of pill-related risk made people wonder if we would soon be tripping over women dead in the streets. Now, however, what we need to learn is how to define the important pill-related risk factors more clearly. Take, for example, smoking pill-users over age 45, whose per-year risk of death from circulatory disease is 1 in 500: in five years time, we would expect 5 in 500, or 1 in 100, to die. Yet there are 99 who do not. Constant comparison of victims and nonvictims and research on the mechanism of disease increase the ability to discern factors that separate potential victim from nonvictim. It is a slow and usually undramatic process.

Concluding Thoughts

In 1970, a burst of victim-oriented reporting created concerns about the risks associated with use of the oral contraceptives. Those concerns persist today, almost 15 years later, and it took almost a decade to understand the apparent way in which pill use, age, and cigarette smoking interact to concentrate risk. For women under the age of 35, however, regardless of whether they smoke or not, use of the oral contraceptive is a smaller risk than is use of a car. Given the available information, it is penny-wise and pound-foolish for a woman under the age of 35 to worry about the pill, or forego its use because of risk concerns, without worrying more about her car and at least giving serious thought to abandoning its use because of its risk. Worry if you will, but worry about the bigger risks rather than the smaller ones.

The history of the dramatic revelations about the risks of using oral contraceptives, followed by a decade of undramatic work to measure and understand how big those risks really are, is a good introduction to the problems of understanding risks with prescription drugs in general—the subject of a later chapter. For the present, we can note that if alcohol were a prescription drug, it would have been long ago driven from the market in a hailstorm of victim-oriented publicity. The worst disaster on record involving a prescription drug probably cost about 3000 lives;[20] in contrast, alcohol's yearly toll in the U.S. alone is at least 20 times higher than that, including alcohol-related road accidents accounting for about 25,000 victims, a fair share of other fatal accidents, homicides, and suicides, plus half or more of the 30,000 deaths from cirrhosis. Maybe alcohol will prove to be offsetting all this mayhem through a protective effect against coronary heart disease, but that is only a hypothesis at present. But what ultimately offsets the adverse effects of alcohol consumption is the fact that most people like alcoholic beverages and are willing to pay very stiff taxes and even engage in illegal activities (as was evident during the Prohibition era in the United States) to have alcoholic beverages available.

Practically everyone likes the unequalled convenience of the automobile, which is clearly an accepted trade-off against the overall per-year risk of 1 in 4000 of being killed in one. Separating drinking and driving has until recently proved to require more political will and collective self-discipline than we could muster. But the adverse consequences of drinking and driving have recently gotten much attention in the news media, and that seems to have mobilized unprecedented political pressure for improvement. Only time will tell how much improvement is possible.

The life insurance companies have recognized cigarette smoking as a "life-style" choice that is a big enough risk factor to influence the setting of life insurance premiums. The insurance firms, however, have set these premiums in a way that effectively has the nonsmoker subsidizing the smoker. The smoker pays the standard rates for age and sex, with the standard rates having been set on actuarial experience with an approximately 50–50 mix of smokers and nonsmokers. Thus, the standard rates underprice the smoker's risk and overprice the nonsmoker's. The nonsmoker gets about a 20% discount off the standard rate—varying a bit from firm to firm. Yet the risk differential between smokers and nonsmokers is a factor of about two, i.e. 0.3 SDU. If the full value of the risk differential was translated into premium differences (and not held back for overhead, profit, and reserves), one might expect to see nonsmokers paying half the premiums of smokers, i.e. nonsmokers would pay about one-third less than the standard rate for age and sex, and smokers would pay about one-third over standard. The insurance marketplace is probably not yet prepared to force smokers to pay higher than standard premiums, but this too may come, as nonsmokers seem recently to have gotten the upper hand on smokers in many aspects of life.

The faddish way the news media focus publicity on risk-related stories is illustrated by contrasting the attention paid to victims of cigarette smoking and victims of AIDS. Throughout 1982 and 1983, AIDS was a major subject of news media attention, with ample space and airtime given to each new finding, plus many human interest stories focussed on the plight of individual victims. The total number of reported AIDS victims stood at 3572 at the end of February 1984, with 1536 known deaths.[21] Some cases of AIDS are not reported to public health officials, so perhaps the total number of deaths might—at the outside—be as many as 10,000 since the disease was first recognized in 1981. Even that almost certainly overestimated figure is equivalent only to one week's premature deaths in the United States from smoking—a disproportion that certainly suggests faddish reporting on AIDS.

Certainly the news media are not wholly silent on smoking-related risk, but the coverage comes nowhere near what AIDS has gotten. It is true, of course, that AIDS tends to strike at fairly young people —the median age of AIDS victims is 36[21]—but the lethal effect of cigarette smoking already shows up among people in their thirties and forties. It was from that age group, for example, that most of the claims came that were paid by State Mutual in its pioneering program with separate life insurance for smokers and nonsmokers. The only evident conclusion is that AIDS is a media fad and gets a lot of attention, but the awesome toll related to cigarette smoking is not a media fad and gets relatively little attention. There are some cigarette advertising revenues for the print media that may have a bit of influence, too.

NOTES TO CHAPTER 5

1. Brody, J. "Personal Health: Seatbelts can lessen injuries in a crash, but their use is declining." *New York Times,* December 19, 1981; Waymark, P. "Motoring. Keeping death much more off our roads." *The Times* (London), June 8, 1978; "Motoring. Seat belt law gain would be enormous." Ibid. April 19, 1981.

2. "Death on the road." *Wall St. J.,* April 14, 1982; Dicke, W. "States heeding pleas to strengthen laws on drunk driving." *New York Times,* April 16, 1982.

3. Kivinen, O. "Legislation curbs Finland's reckless drivers." *The Times* (London), February 20, 1981.

4. *Transport Statistics, Great Britain, 1969–1979.* London: HMSO, 1980, Table 2.61.

5. U.S. Bureau of the Census. *Statistical Abstract of the United States, 1980.* Washington, D.C., Table 1111.

6. Ibid. Table 1110.

7. Ibid. Tables 1113, 1114.

8. National Loss Data Institute. "Claim frequency results by size of claim, 1978–1980 models." Research report HLDI I 80–81, September 1981.

9. U.S. Public Health Service. *Smoking and Health.* PHS Pub. No. 1103, 1964.

10. U.S. Department of Health, Education, and Welfare. *Smoking and Health.* DHEW Pub. No. (PHS)79-50066, 1979.

11. Cowell, M.J., and B.C. Hirst. "Mortality differences between smokers and nonsmokers." *Trans. Soc. Actuaries* 32 (1980):1–29.

12. Hayes, T.C. "Insurance gain for the nonsmoker." *New York Times,* April 11, 1981.

13. Brackenridge, R.D.C. *Medical Selection of Life Risks.* London: Undershaft Press, 1977.

14. U.S. Department of Transportation, National Highway Traffic

Safety Administration. *Fatal Accident Reporting System, 1980.* DOT HS 805 953, October 1981.

15. Sherlock, S., ed. *Alcohol and Disease. Brit. Med. Bull.* 38 (1982).

16. Lelbach, W.K. In Gibbon, R.T. et al., eds. *Research Advances in Alcohol and Drug Problems.* New York: Wiley, 1974, pp. 93–198.

17. Comfort, A. "Alcohol as a social drug and health hazard." *Lancet* 1 (1984): 443–44.

18. Ryder, N.B. "Contraceptive failure in the United States." *Family Planning Perspectives* 5 (1973): 133–42.

19. Royal College of General Practitioners, Oral Contraceptive Study. "Mortality among oral contraceptive users." *Lancet* 2 (1977): 727–31; "Further analysis of mortality in oral contraceptive users." *Lancet* 1 (1981): 541–46.

20. Inman, W.H.W., and A.M. Adelstein. "Rise and fall in asthma mortality in England and Wales in relation to use of pressurized aerosols." *Lancet* 2 (1969): 279–84.

21. Curran, J. "The epidemiology of AIDS." Paper presented at meeting of Federation of American Societies for Experimental Biology, St. Louis, April 2, 1984. (Dr. Curran directs the AIDS task force of the U.S. Center for Disease Control.)

6

Medical and Surgical Risks

The title of this chapter could serve for a 1500-page textbook of medicine and surgery, but our aim here is more modest. It is to illustrate some of the important ways in which treatment-associated risk is identified and measured in contemporary medicine. Coronary heart disease and hypertension are two major diseases considered in some detail. Coronary bypass surgery is prominent in the treatment of CHD, and the problems of its evaluation compared to drug treatment illustrate a whole class of treatment-related risk-assessment problems. The treatment of hypertension, on the other hand, is an area where the insurance perspective is uniquely strong, allowing a striking comparison between the risks of treating and not treating. Then we examine the process by which prescription drugs are tested. Drugs are the mainstay of modern medicine, and so the limits on risk detection in drug testing have wide impact on treatment-related risks. Here the comparative risks of treating versus not treating reveal some curious quirks in how small risks can become the basis of big controversies, while big risks go unnoticed. To begin, however, it is useful to understand the limits on the individual physician's ability to detect treatment-related risk.

Risk as Perceived by the Individual Physician

There are natural limits on the individual physician's ability to perceive treatment-related risk. These limits have to do with the size of any one physician's practice.

To understand the origin of those limits, consider how a busy practice operates. If the physician works six 10-hour days a week and spends two hours per day in activities not involving direct contact with patients—reading, administration, filling out forms, and so forth—there will be approximately 50 hours a week for seeing patients. If, on the average, the physician sees three patients per hour, then in a week's time he or she sees 150 patients, and in a year's time about 7500. These numbers will vary among physicians, but they can be taken to indicate that an individual physician could see between 5000 and 15,000 patients per year, depending on how much time each patient gets and on how heavy a workload the physician can assume. To make the numbers easy to follow, and without doing great violence to reason, let us use 10,000 patients per year per physician.

Let us, for the moment, make some preposterously oversimplified assumptions about the variety of patients a physician sees. Let us suppose an ultimate super-specialist who sees only patients with one disease, that the disease only involves one sex, and that all the patients are of similar age and socio-economic status. With all these idealized conditions, this one super-specialist can visualize a year's events within a homogeneous group of 10,000. Now we have to ask the question: how many adverse events have to occur before some kind of association with treatment is suggested? One event is not enough: it is merely something that happens, and things happen to people all the time for all kinds of reasons. There are no hard and fast rules, but generally it takes four, five, or six similar events to trigger the suspicion of association. Let us use five, to make the calculations easy. If the physician's memory and associative abilities can span across a full year, and across 10,000 patients, then there is a chance that the physician working in this hypothetically homogeneous practice could detect adverse reactions at the level of 1 in 2000 patients per year. This limits the one physician's ability to define the safety-degree status of a treatment to 3.3 SDU. With an elephantine memory spanning 20,000 patients in two years, risks of maybe 1 in 4000 could be perceived, extending the definition of safety-degree status to 3.6 SDU.

Of course, not even the most super-specialized physician sees patients of such uniformity. Instead of seeing 10,000 lookalikes, physicians see real patients who divide into reasonably homogeneous cohorts of the same disease, same severity of disease, same treatment program, same sex, similar age, similar build, same grouping of other diseases, similar alcohol consumption, same medications for conditions other than the one of current interest, similar smoking habits, and so forth. These factors divide the 10,000 patients into groups of, at most, a few hundred, and more typically a few dozen. Thus, the heterogeneity of people, their diseases, and their treatments markedly constrict the individual physician's perception of treatment-related risk. The individual physician is, in a functional sense, "blind" to treatment-related risks more dilute than 1 in about 200, with the definition of safety-degree status restricted to 2.3 SDU, if that.

Yet adverse reactions to drugs in the range of 1 in 1,000 to 1 in 30,000 have triggered drug withdrawals or drastic curtailment in drug usage, with much attendant publicity and concern. These risk levels signify that the public wants a drug's safety-degree status to be at least 3.0 SDU, and perhaps as high as 4.0 or more. When a serious adverse drug reaction is first identified, the majority of individual physicians are usually in the position of having prescribed the suspect drug without having observed anything untoward, and of learning about newly identified risk associated with the drug through professional channels within hours before or after it is revealed publicly and becomes a topic for the news media. A relatively few physicians will have seen an individual case or two of the suspect adverse reaction, and it is usually only by a process of central assembly and monitoring of such information that adverse reactions can be identified. How that assembly and monitoring is done, and by whom, has been a subject of unresolved debate and much misunderstanding on the part of both the public and the medical profession since the thalidomide disaster in 1962. We shall return to this subject later.

Many forces acting on medicine since World War II have increasingly brought physicians together in various kinds of groups and away from the "solo" practice that formerly dominated medicine. As a consequence, group practices, health maintenance organizations, and urban medical centers can provide a much-expanded number of patients within one organizational framework, beyond the 10,000 or so that an individual physician might be able to see yearly. To the extent that physicians working in groups can pool their experience, there is some opportunity for recognizing more dilute risks than the individual physician is able to. However, merely getting 20 physicians together in a meeting does not guarantee that they will be able to recognize a 20-fold more dilute risk than any one of them could, acting alone. To recognize these more dilute risks requires formally organized research.

Sometimes adverse reactions may cluster in a particular locale for reasons that may or may not ever become clear. Obviously, that makes it easier to make the association between adverse event and treatment. Another factor that makes association easier is when the adverse reaction is something medically unusual. For example, it was the rarity of heart attacks or strokes in young women that led to recognition of one of the risks of oral contraceptive use.

On the other hand, it may be difficult to recognize the occurrence of a treatment-related increase in commonly occurring adverse events. This problem is illustrated by the difficulty of recognizing the two-fold increase in CHD among male cigarette smokers. Cigarette smoking is of course not a treatment, but the example can serve to illustrate the point. The effect of smoking on the risk of CHD was not recognized until the data were analyzed in formal studies designed to test the theory that cigarette smoking caused lung cancer. Smoking was causing hundreds of thousands more heart attacks than lung cancers, but both smoking and heart attacks were so common already among middle-aged men that the association was, so to speak, camouflaged, and was revealed only by careful data analysis, not by sudden recognition at the bedside.

Thus, there are different patterns of recognition of treatment-related risks as they variously reveal themselves in shifting patterns of disease. Computers and research programs notwithstanding, much of the recognizing is done by individual physicians, whose powers of observation and association make the critical connections. Once the suggestion is made and communicated among doctors of an apparent association between a treatment and an adverse reaction or disease, there is often an echoing "me-too" response from many physicians who had previously observed the same thing but had not previously been motivated to communicate it. Sometimes that "me-too" phenomenon brings a sudden flurry of reports which creates a distorted impression that there is a sudden epidemic of the newly recognized problem.

Research Methods of Studying Treatment-related Risk in Medicine

Because of the natural limits on the ability of individual physicians to perceive treatment-related risks, formal research programs in this field have been organized in a number of medical centers.

A basic method of studying treatment-related risk factors is the "case-control" method, which is appropriate for analyzing to see if relatively frequently-occurring adverse reactions are treatment related. Here, one starts with records of patients who experienced the particular adverse reaction—the "cases." One then identifies the "controls," a group of patients who are matched as well as possible to the "cases" with respect to age, sex, socio-economic status, and so forth, but who have appeared in some other medical context at about the same time as the "cases." One then analyzes the records of the patients from both groups for differences with respect to the presence or absence of particular factors between the two groups. If there is a preponderance of a particular factor among the "case" group, there is a basis for postulating its being a risk factor.

The case-control method has provided evidence for the theory that postmenopausal estrogen therapy is a risk factor for development of cancer of the endometrium, the lining of the uterus. Case-control studies have generally shown that estrogen therapy has been used by a larger percentage of patients with cancer of the endometrium than of control patients with other conditions. There has been a great deal of controversy about the design of such studies, especially about whether the "cases" and the "control" patients are strictly comparable, and whether peculiar biases creep into the conclusions as a consequence.

Another simple but tedious way to identify risk factors and quantify the risk they pose is to do a retrospective assessment of patient records. It is not a very powerful method, because information later deemed pertinent is sometimes not written in a patient's record.

Both the retrospective record review and the case-control methods are useful in generating hypotheses, but this kind of evidence has to be supplemented with data from other kinds of studies in order to make a convincing distinction between risk factor and coincidence.

A third method for identifying and measuring treatment-related risk is the "prescription-event monitoring" (PEM) study. This is a new method, recently developed in the United Kingdom by Dr. William Inman of the Drug Surveillance Unit of the University of Southampton. To use the PEM method requires one of the special features of the National Health Service, the governmental agency that pays almost all of the medical and drug bills for the entire population of the United Kingdom. After a patient has a prescription filled by a pharmacist, the pharmacist routinely sends the prescription to the Health Service for payment; from that central point, the PEM study group gets a copy of all prescriptions for whatever drug is currently being studied. Each prescription shows the patient's and the physician's name and address, and the dates of writing and filling. The PEM study group then sends a questionnaire to the doctor, identifying the patient, the drug, and the date of prescription, and asking the doctor to list the events that the doctor's record shows occurring in the patient's life within a specified time interval after the prescription was filled. Naturally, all this information is held in confidence by the PEM study group.

Between 10,000 and 20,000 PEM questionnaires are sent out and about 75% are completed and returned. Analysis of the questionnaires reveals whether particular events happened with unexpectedly high or low frequency. When there is a particular event of special interest, a second questionnaire is sent to obtain more detailed information about that one aspect of the patient's record. The PEM method appears to be capable of identifying treatment-related adverse reactions down to a risk dilution of 1 in as much as 3000, or to a safety-degree index of 3.5 SDU.

These research methods have become steadily more important in the detection of treatment-related risk and figure in the subsequent discussion of how prescription drugs are tested before and after market introduction. Now we turn to evaluating treatment-related risk in two major diseases: CHD and hypertension.

Comparative Risk-assessment in the Treatment of Coronary Heart Disease

An important area of progress in the treatment of coronary heart disease has been the reorganization of in-hospital care facilities for heart attack patients.[1] The so-called coronary care unit (CCU) is a special ward staffed by people skilled in the various aspects of caring for acutely ill, life-threatened cardiac patients. It has been an espe-cially important development, because there is a 1 in about 4 risk of death due to myocardial infarction during the first fortnight after one occurs; this corresponds to a quite low safety-degree status of 0.6 SDU. Many patients who fully recover have harrowing episodes of irregular heart rhythm during the first few days after their infarction; these rhythm disturbances can be fatal, but careful monitoring and prompt treatment prevents many deaths.

There has been some criticism of CCU's as being too expensive, too technological and impersonal, and of unproven effectiveness. The physicians and nurses involved in acute care of heart attack victims and post-operative cardiac surgical patients give these criticisms no credence. They see too many instances of deaths prevented by emer-gency measures in now-simple and expeditious ways that would be impossible to deploy effectively if patients with acute cardiac condi-tions were scattered around a general hospital. Some critics question whether preventing these deaths costs too much; this raises a pro-found ethical issue that is beyond the scope of this book.

One of the most spectacular developments of the 1970's has been coronary bypass surgery. About 100,000 of these procedures are now performed annually in the United States, and the numbers continue to grow. This is a formidably complex procedure which would have been unthinkable only 25 years ago. During most of the procedure, the body's needs for oxygen have to be met by an external mechanical blood pump, which also provides the same air exchange functions as does the lung for oxygen and carbon dioxide. Obstructed coronary arteries are bypassed by connecting short pieces of vein to either side of the obstructed region, providing an alternate channel around the area of obstruction in much the same way as freeways pass around an urban area of congested traffic. The veins are taken from the patient's own legs. Coronary bypass surgery is complex and costly—in excess of $20,000 for the diagnostic tests, the procedure, and the postsurgical care.

The 100,000 bypass operations done each year in the United States may be compared to 1.25 million coronary occlusions and 800,000 deaths due to CHD. From these numbers, it is apparent that there is a good deal of coronary artery disease which is not currently being treated surgically. There are several reasons for the discrepancy in numbers. One is that many people who have an acute coronary occlusion and myocardial infarction did not have enough pre-existing coronary artery obstruction to warrant surgery. But another, equally fundamental reason for the discrepancy is that it has not been clear until very recently that coronary bypass surgery was preferable to more conservative, medical management in terms of both quality of life and life expectancy. Now, however, there has been a major report from a large, multicenter study in Europe which clearly validates the claims that coronary bypass surgery both improves and extends life in patients with CHD that is of sufficient degree to cause angina.[2]

The specific details of the trial are important, however, because there are multiple patterns of coronary artery obstruction, and the comparative results of surgical versus nonsurgical treatment differ among the various patterns of obstruction within the three major coronary arteries and their larger branches. Those details go beyond the scope of our interest here. There is not an overall risk figure for bypass surgery that we could cite that has any meaning, because there are so many different patterns of CHD, each with its own set of risks.

Organizing the clinical trials to compare bypass surgery with various nonsurgical alternates has proven to be quite complex. One of the big concerns about such trials was that they should begin only after there was a broad consensus on the techniques for bypass surgery and on the criteria for selecting the appropriate technique of bypass for patients with the various patterns of obstruction in the three coronary arteries. If major trials had gotten started while there were still unresolved differences of opinion about patient selection and technical aspects of the surgery, then there was concern that the value of bypass surgery might be improperly judged. From the early years of bypass surgery to the present, the mortality during the procedure has declined from as high as 1 in 20 to less than 1 in 100—an increase of 0.7 SDU. Part of the reduction in operative mortality lies in improved techniques, but part also lies in knowing which patients have disease too advanced for surgery. The real aim of the clinical trials, however, was to follow surgical and nonsurgical patients with initially comparable disease for at least two years, and preferably longer, to see the comparative survival of the two groups and the comparative extent of CHD in the survivors.

Consequently, over a decade of bypass surgery was done before formal, comparative trial results became known. In the interim, the preponderance of cardiological and surgical opinion grew to support bypass surgery, but by no means unanimously. That necessarily left individual patients in a quandary and often meant that whether or not a particular patient with CHD got bypass surgery depended upon whether the consulting cardiologist was for or against bypass surgery. It has certainly been clear from the earliest days of bypass surgery that it made great improvements in the quality of most patients' lives in the weeks and months after surgery; indeed, that was one of the main reasons for its rapid growth. At the same time, it was clear that many patients never returned to work afterwards, and that some went on to develop obstructions in the bypass channels, with angina, heart attacks, heart failure, and so on. Hence, there was uncertainty until formal comparative trials could be done as to whether bypass surgery had any impact on life expectancy compared to nonsurgical treatment.

From an epidemiological perspective, there has, in effect, been a big "experiment of nature." In the United States, the training of bypass-oriented cardiologists and cardiac surgeons grew throughout the decade, so that every major city had at least one or more bypass teams doing as many as two dozen bypass procedures per week. In the United Kingdom, on the other hand, only a few bypass teams have been allowed to operate within the National Health Service, and so patients simply have had to wait in line, unless they could afford private care outside the NHS. Understandably, controversy has surrounded both the unrestrained growth in the United States and the restricted availability in the United Kingdom.

The decision to perform coronary bypass surgery is dependent upon the outcome of an X-ray study of the coronary arteries called coronary angiography. A fine catheter is inserted into an artery in the leg and threaded toward the heart and into one of the coronary arteries. A "contrast" solution which shows up on X-ray is injected through the catheter and into the coronary artery. The flow of contrast solution along the artery reveals points of narrowing in the artery and its downstream branches. This procedure is repeated in each of the three main coronary arteries. The results provide the basis for deciding which vessels need to be bypassed and which not.

The concept of passing fine catheters from a distant blood vessel up to the heart had its origins with the work of a German physician,

Werner Forssmann, in 1929. He recognized the diagnostic importance of being able to draw samples of blood from the various chambers of the heart, especially in patients with various congenital heart
defects. He demonstrated cardiac catheterization by performing it on
himself, and his 1929 paper in a German medical journal shows an
X-ray picture of Forssmann's chest with a catheter seen passing from
his right arm into one of his heart's chambers. Together with a
number of other important advances in the late 1940's and early
1950's, Forssmann's technique played a decisive role in the development of surgery for various congenital heart defects, and later on his
technique was adapted to pass catheters into the coronary arteries.
Forssmann shared the Nobel Prize for his work in 1949. His bold
self-experimentation is a good example of what one might call "pro-
ductive" risk. It is a reminder, in an era when the ethics of medical
experimentation are much debated, that self-experimentation is
sometimes the best resolution to real ethical dilemmas which can
arise in the design of the best-intentioned clinical trials. Self-experimentation has a long tradition in research medicine.

It would be simple if the story ended here, with the value of bypass
surgery now reasonably well established by well-controlled clinical
trials. Just as the controlled trials were getting under way, however,
a new procedure called coronary angioplasty was being tried out for
treating obstructed coronary arteries. This procedure involves passing a special, narrow-gauge angioplasty catheter upstream from an
artery in a leg or arm and into a partially obstructed coronary
artery—just as is done in coronary angiography, as described above,
but with a difference. The angioplasty catheter has a tiny, inflatable
balloon near its tip; the balloon can be inflated by injecting fluid into
a special port at the opposite end of the catheter, through whose wall
there passes a narrow channel leading to the balloon. By means of
a special guide-wire, the tip of the angioplasty catheter is threaded
past the point of partial obstruction or narrowing, and the catheter
positioned so that the balloon's inflation will dilate the artery at the
point of narrowing. Only certain patterns of narrowing are amenable
to angioplasty, but those that are can evidently be treated much more
simply and less expensively than with bypass surgery.

Angioplasty seems to be an important advance, but it has only
been since about 1981 that very many patients were being treated
with this new procedure. This development once again poses all the

same questions about patient selection criteria and standardization of technique that bypass surgery did in its early years. Thus, it will be some years before the comparative value of angioplasty versus other modes of treatment will be firmly established by controlled trials in the various patterns of CHD. In the interim, there will undoubtedly be a good deal of controversy about the procedure and its risks relative to those of bypass surgery or of drug treatment alone.

Risks Associated with Hypertension

The life insurance companies understood the risk of premature death due to hypertension sooner than did the medical community. The landmark study in this area was published in 1959 under the prosaic title of "Build and Blood Pressure Study, 1959."[3] It drew on life insurance data in the United States from 1935 through 1954, and thus dwarfs the scope of any medical experiment ever done. As late as 1959, many physicians believed that the insurance practice of charging extra premiums for high blood pressure was unjustified, if not downright fraudulent: the publication of "Build and Blood Pressure Study, 1959" dispelled such ideas by demonstrating the sound actuarial basis of stepping up premiums with increasing blood pressure. The life insurance risk tables did not arise out of abstract theory nor out of medical research, but are simply based on past experience, in which findings on insurance examinations are correlated with claims. The most recent insurance data from the "Build and Blood Pressure Study, 1979"[4] now show that therapy which succeeds in normalizing the blood pressure can normalize the characteristic death risk for the patient's age and sex.

The currently accepted medical definition of hypertension for the purposes of starting treatment is 160/95 millimeters of mercury. In contrast, the actuarial tables used for determining life insurance premiums call for the first jump above the normal premium for people in their forties if the blood pressure exceeds 136/88 millimeters of mercury, and for stepwise increases in premium with each 4 millimeter increase in systolic pressure, or each 2 millimeter increase in diastolic pressure. The tables show that the risk of premature death associated with a blood pressure of 160/95 is twice that in a person of the same age and sex who has normal pressure.

This difference between current medical and actuarial views reveals a peculiar quirk in the perception of risk. To illustrate, let us take the hypothetical example of a 45-year-old male patient whose blood pressure measurements average out at 152/88 millimeters of mercury. His physician elects not to treat, in keeping with current medical practice, and instead recommends weight loss, exercise, and no smoking. In keeping with current patient practice, the patient makes some efforts in this direction, takes off several pounds, but does not make any permanent changes; his blood pressure remains at the 152/88 level. The actuarial tables show that, if this patient were applying for life insurance, he would have to pay a premium that is 50% higher than that for a 45-year-old male of normal blood pressure and build. In effect, the medical judgment not to treat leaves the patient permanently in a risk category that is 50% higher than the normal value for his age. The normal 45-year-old male's per year risk of dying from any and all causes is 1 in 225 (a safety-degree status of 2.4 SDU), but that of our patient is 1.5 in 225, or 1 in 150 (2.2 SDU). Thus, the high blood pressure reduces his safety-degree index by 0.2 SDU.

The medical judgment on whether to start drug treatment to normalize blood pressure revolves around the impact of drug treatment on the quality of the patient's life. None of the currently available drugs for treating hypertension is completely devoid of side-effects, such as drowsiness, impotence, loss of appetite, nausea, dryness of the mouth, weakness, and so forth. In a direct sense, none of these side-effects is life-threatening, but their occurrence can disrupt people's lives in various, sometimes important ways. Judging this impact in relation to a risk-diluting reduction of blood pressure is part of the art of medicine. That judgment underlies the current view that treatment to normalize pressure be limited to pressures over 160/95.

There is a peculiar asymmetry in this logic, however, as the following bit of fancy will illustrate. Instead of saying that the physician decides not to treat our 45-year-old patient, let us say that the physician decides to treat him with a hypothetical drug called ONU-RONE (pronounced "on your own") which, though believed effective, is not. Nor does it do anything. Then another male patient comes along, also age 45 and with the same build and history as our first patient, but he has a little higher pressure of 160/95, so he gets treated with a low dose of one of the thiazide drugs, which restores his pressure to normal. Untreated, his per-year risk of death was double the normal risk for his age: 2 in 225, or 1 in 112. The thiazide treatment normalizes both blood pressure, and the risk reduction that accompanies the normalization of blood pressure far exceeds the risk of using the drug. The net effect is to dilute the patient's per-year risk of premature death to the normal figure of 1 in 225. The patient on the thiazide would appear to be in a risk category that is preferable to that of the patient taking ONURONE.

Suppose now we treat a lot of 45-year-old males with mild hypertension, and all the ones with pressures of 160/95 or a bit more get the thiazide, and all those with somewhat lower pressures get ONURONE. We follow the two groups for several years, and lo and behold—the mortality in the ONURONE group is 50% higher than that in the thiazide group, and calculation shows that being on ONURONE adds a per-year death risk of 1 in 450. By current standards of acceptable drug-related risks, then, ONURONE should be banned. As we shall see below, there have recently been several major drugs withdrawn from the market because of the risks they posed, with the most hazardous having an apparent death-risk of 1 in about 500.

The point of this little vignette is that it is sometimes instructive to convert a no-treatment decision into a decision to use ONURONE, and to hold ONURONE against the same standards of acceptable risk as we hold active treatments. This is uniquely possible with hypertension because of the singularly intensive scrutiny it has had from the actuarial perspective, based on pressure measurements and subsequent events in hundreds of thousands of lives.

The insurance studies are not experimental, for they simply correlate what was written down during an insurance applicant's insurance examination with what was written down later on the death certificate. If there is any experimentation involved in actuarial studies, it is that the insured themselves "experiment" with different styles of life, habits, and so forth. There are certainly many limitations—some obvious, some not—in actuarial studies. One limitation is the fiction that two numbers measured with a blood pressure cuff on several occasions serve to define "the" blood pressure for months or years. Nevertheless, the very large numbers of people included in actuarial studies go a long way toward cancelling out some of these vagaries. It is useful to note that the validity of actuarial risk assessment is one of the cornerstones of the life insurance industry's continuing profitability, about which there is little question. It will be important to learn how the actuaries rate the risk-reducing potentials of the newest antihypertensive treatments, and whether partially controlled high blood pressure reduces risk to a degree wholly accounted for by the reduction in blood pressure. Answers to those questions will be some years in coming, for the actuarial method requires years for adequate numbers of people to complete the cycle from insurance application to death certificate.

Many potential improvements in the treatment of hypertension are currently under evaluation. It is an area where the big investments in medical research over the last three decades by both governments and pharmaceutical companies have produced important dividends that translate directly into dilution of the risk of premature death, and of the risk of occurrence of major disease conditions, such as stroke, that have a very adverse effect on the quality of life. Some older drugs are also now being tested with new methods of administration, e.g. transdermal systems ("skin patches"), which seem to have advantages over the tablet form of the drug.

Probably the most important research issue in hypertension just now lies outside the rubric of laboratory science: to find the best ways to reach the entire population of hypertensives with the treatments already in hand. As noted in Chapter 4, only about one-quarter of the patients with hypertension are adequately treated. Another important research issue in hypertension is to develop a broad base of actuarial data on hypertensive patients treated with various antihypertensive drugs. Such data would resolve much of the current uncertainty about how high the blood pressure should be allowed to go before treatment is begun.

A final point about hypertension is that premature death is not its only adverse outcome. Strokes and kidney failure are also consequences of hypertension. Strokes are responsible for paralysis, speech defects, and all sorts of behavioral disorders, and so exact a heavy toll that is not reflected in mortality data.

Risks Related to Drugs and Drug Regulation

Twentieth century technology has transformed two old institutions, the doctor and the drug, from relatively harmless comforters and anodynes into powerful forces capable of strong actions, good and bad. Drug regulation in the United States appeared in three successive steps: (1) in the first years of this century, following a number of deaths due to a contaminated vaccine; (2) during the 1930's, following a number of deaths due to a sulfa drug product that was formulated with a toxic solvent; (3) in 1962, following the recognition that thalidomide was responsible for children being born with deformed limbs. All three steps focussed on tightening standards of manufacturing, testing, and labeling to minimize the risk of adverse reactions; the most recent big changes added for the first time the requirement that drugs be proven effective for uses claimed for them by their manufacturer.[5]

Each country has its own special approach to drug regulation, but the economic and technological power of the United States is such that the activities of the Food and Drug Administration (FDA) are closely watched internationally, and frequently imitated by other countries, though each country brings a special character to their drug regulatory system: the Japanese are extremely rigid; the Americans demand complete documentation of every aspect of the drug's testing program, irrespective of the mountain of paper—and cost—entailed; the British are sensible and flexible; the French have a system which is a unique amalgam of the bureaucratic and the personal; the Germans and the Canadians lean heavily on the FDA's policies.

The bias in all drug regulatory systems is toward preventing unexpectedly hazardous drugs from reaching the market. That bias is understandable from the history of how drug regulation came into being, through public reactions to a series of disastrous incidents involving relatively small numbers of victims compared to other hazards in our lives. This bias poses a curious paradox, as illustrated by the following rather simple-minded parallel. We disrupt traffic and incur rather special risks to rush injured or seriously ill people to the hospital by ambulance so that they can come as quickly as humanly possible to the best available treatment, and sometimes we bend heaven and earth to rush a special medicine to a few people who need it. Yet somehow none of this sense of urgency carries over to the regulatory review of new drugs.

An example of the cost in human lives of the slow pace of the drug regulatory system is the seven years it took for FDA approval from the time of the first publications showing that administration of beta blocker drugs reduced mortality in the first few years after heart attack. The results of the first clinical trials were reported in 1974, and in 1976 the Swedish regulatory authorities approved this use for one of the beta blocker drugs—alprenolol—then already available in the Swedish market. The first FDA approval of this usage for a beta blocker came in November 1981. In 1975, Professor William Wardell of the University of Rochester had called this beneficial action of the beta blocker drugs to the attention of the then-commissioner of the FDA, Alexander Schmidt, together with calculations indicating that each year's delay in approving this use would cost about 20,000 lives.[6] Six years after Wardell's letter, when the first approval finally came, FDA Commissioner Arthur Hayes announced that, indeed, the newly approved product would save 17,000 lives per year. Nobody thought to haul him up to the Capitol, sit him down in front of the TV cameras and a Congressional investigating committee, and ask him what about the 100,000 people who died in the time between the first publications and the approval, without which few physicians will use a drug. In effect, Americans had to use ONURONE for a half dozen years even though something demonstrably effective was already available.

Yet, when it recently developed that there had been five deaths from allergic reactions associated with the widely used analgesic drug ZOMAX, there was a strong reaction in Congress and the launch of an investigation to learn how this terrible thing had been allowed to happen to the American people.

Critics of drug regulation point out that the only time that Congress, the President, and the American people were of one mind in praising the FDA was when Dr. Frances Kelsey delayed the approval of thalidomide in the United States. President John F. Kennedy transformed her into a heroine by presenting her with a special medal in the White House Rose Garden. The message was not lost on her colleagues at the FDA or in other regulatory agencies around the world: there is no credit to be gained for lives saved due to speedy regulatory action, but a very small number of fatalities or other severe adverse reactions to a drug will lead to public humiliation and scorn for any regulatory official who may have acted other than very cautiously and conservatively in reviewing the drug.

If one were to judge the overall value of drug regulation strictly on a body-count basis of lives lost due to regulatory delays as against lives saved due to keeping unduly dangerous drugs from the market, one would have to question seriously whether drug regulation is a very good bargain. With little or no regulatory involvement, many other industries design, test, manufacture, and market complex products on which many lives depend, and it would appear that both competitive forces and the pressure of product liability lawsuits are effective checks on the sale of unduly risky products. At the very least, we ought to be a sophisticated enough society to be able to see and understand the risks that are prolonged, as well as the risks that are minimized, by regulatory review. A simple-minded stranger looking in might wonder: if we have ambulance crews on duty around the clock and allow them to run red lights when called, should we not have our drug regulatory agencies working a three-shift, seven-day week to minimize the fatal consequences of delaying the introduction of improved drugs?

The FDA and other drug regulatory agencies around the world get most of the criticism whenever the subject of long delays in bringing new drugs to market arises. However, there are two other often overlooked factors that contribute to these delays. One of these is that only large pharmaceutical firms can mobilize the resources to develop and test a new drug, but one of the inevitable consequences of large size in any organization is that it necessarily becomes slow and bureaucratic in its operation. The second delaying factor is a technological one. As pharmacologists and physicians have become increasingly cognizant of the power of modern drugs, the processes for testing new drugs have become increasingly elaborate and searching. There has been a steady expansion in the kind and number of animal toxicologic tests run on new drug candidates, and the whole field of designing clinical trials has been fundamentally transformed during the last two decades. Thus, the whole process of new drug development is vastly more complex and time-consuming since the days when insulin was rushed from the laboratory to the bedside. It is probably amenable to some considerable pruning, but there is little incentive in the current regulatory environment for that to happen.

In clinical trials of various treatments, one seeks to standardize diagnostic criteria and methods, to standardize the severity of disease in the patients admitted to the trial, and to standardize the various treatment regimens which the trial is designed to compare. Standardizing the cooperation of the patients with the prescribed regimens, however, is easier said than done—even when everyone acts in the best of faith and solemnly swears to do just what the doctor asks.

Clinical trials have come to play an increasingly important role in modern medicine, putting different treatment methods to the test of quantitative comparison in as controlled a fashion as ethical medical practice allows. When a new treatment modality appears for a previously untreatable disease, the controlled clinical trial will naturally include a no-treatment group, though often disguised from patients, nurses, and doctors by use of a placebo, i.e. an ONURONE treatment. Contemporary standards of ethics mandate that participants in the trial know they are in a trial and be informed about the various treatments that they may (or may not) actually receive. The designs of such studies are a not-always judicious blend of scientific experiment and everyday medical practice.

There are many vexing problems in the design and execution of clinical trials, but they are one of the very important advances which have come into clinical medicine in the last quarter-century. Their routine use in the evaluation of virtually all new methods of treatment—plus their use in the retrospective assessment of many time-honored methods of treatment—is gradually transforming medicine from an almost wholly empirical art to an amalgam of quantitatively validated technology and art. Clinical trials are gradually providing the main outlines of how the best practice should be carried out, but clinical judgement and the art of medicine continue to guide most diagnosis and treatment. Thus, the physician's judgment will continue to be an important element in the risk of disease, however much it may seem that technology may have displaced the art of medicine and the essential human contact between patient and physician or nurse. In medicine, the patient is an object of a discipline which, in using technological-scientific procedures, puts on a scientific face but is both more and less than a science in the extent to which it draws on the art of human judgment tempered by experience.

The growth of medical knowledge based on well-designed clinical trials is a slow process. Clinical trials take a great deal of time to plan, to be reviewed by the necessary disinterested individuals for ethical concerns, to find the appropriate patients to enter into the trial, to carry out the sequence of treatments called for, to analyze the data, and finally to communicate the data to other physicians and health care personnel. There are pitfalls in the process, many of which come down to bending the need for scientific rigor to the exigencies of caring for patients. The trial has to have enough rigor to give a definite answer to the question of which treatment modality is best, or the better of two; at the same time it has to be a close enough approximation of routine clinical practice so that treatment efficacy shown in the trial will also be found in practice. Some big clinical trials take three to five years to complete, especially if they involve questions about diseases that progress slowly.

Yet there is a huge numerical gap between even the largest of clinical trials and the potential patient population that would use a new drug. Some of the biggest trials are those in which contraceptives were evaluated: these have had between 10,000 and 25,000 participants. Most new drugs, however, are tested in 1000–2000 people. In the case of the oral contraceptives, there are about 12 million women in the United States using these products and probably upwards of 50 million worldwide. In the case of drugs for hypertension, there are about 40 million hypertensives in the United States. Certainly not all will ever take any one drug, but, if a drug appears to be especially efficacious and well tolerated, and poses little risk, it may be used in half or more of the patient population. Consequently, the clinical trial population and the population who may use the product in the market will differ in size by hundreds of thousands to millions. That number gap has the important consequence of making the first few years' use of the drug after market introduction into a big but poorly controlled experiment.

The initial years of market experience are necessary to close the number gap between the population size in the clinical trial and the population size needed to define safety-degree to the 4–5 SDU range (i.e. risks of 1 adverse reaction in 10,000 to 100,000 patients). This point has already been mentioned in the discussion on oral contraceptives in Chapter 5, but it is a very important fact of life about which our society manages to delude itself. To illustrate why the number gap exists, suppose the clinical trials have involved 5000 patients, which is an unusually large number; if 50 patients have similar adverse reactions, it is reasonably certain that the risk of that adverse reaction can be defined as 1 in 100 during the time period involved. Suppose, however, that only one patient develops a particular kind of adverse reaction. It is difficult to know what to conclude about a single event—it may or may not be related to the drug, and so the matter has to be held in abeyance until more experience is gained with the drug. Thus, having 5000 people in the clinical trial does not allow definition of a risk level of 1 in 5000, but something rather more like 1 in 1000.

Suppose five patients developed similar adverse reactions in a group of 5000 patients: one has an approximate idea that the risk is 1 in 1000. This figure is only an approximation, however, for it may be that there was a chance clustering of a few "extra" adverse reactions within the study group and that the true risk is less. On the other hand, the events in the study group may somehow have minimized the occurrence of the adverse reaction, such that in subsequent market experience with the drug, the adverse reaction turns out to occur at a 2–5 times greater incidence than in the trial. As a practical matter, the biggest unicohort size one can define with reasonable accuracy in a clinical trial is about one-fifth the size of the trial's population. If, however, the patients in the trial have to be considered as being divided into subgroups—by age, sex, other disease conditions, etc.—then the biggest unicohort definable will be about one-fifth of the biggest subgroup.

The initial use of the drug in the first year or two after its market introduction builds up large numbers of users—assuming the product is widely prescribed—and will necessarily begin to reveal adverse reactions which occur at the 1 in 10,000 to the 1 in 100,000 level of incidence. As in the clinical trial phase of experience with the drug, it is not possible to draw any conclusions from a single adverse reaction. Therefore, it usually takes 4–6 occurrences before an association with the drug is suggested. However, one of the things lacking in the United States is a means of insuring that adverse reactions to drugs are reported; as a result, more than nine-tenths go unreported. Thus, it may take over 2 million people's use of a drug before the full extent of its risk is reasonably well defined to the 1 in 50,000 level— per use if it is an acute-use drug, per year if it is a chronic-use drug. If we had a mechanism in place that insured efficient and timely reporting of adverse drug reactions in the first years after a new product entered the market, we could reduce both the number gap and the time required to identify drug-related risk. Even with an efficient system of reporting adverse drug reactions, however, there will still be a large number gap between the biggest clinical trials and the smallest numbers needed to reveal all the risk information we crave to know about any widely used drug.

Therein lies one of the reasons for saying that life is an experiment: there is no earthly means to finance or manage a clinical trial that could define the degree of drug safety to more than 3 SDU (1 adverse reaction per treatment period in 1000 patients). Yet our social and political behavior indicates that we reserve the right to react with shock, horror, and witch-hunting when drug-related risk shows up at the 3–4.5 SDU level (1 in 1000 to 1 in 30,000).

The number gap is a fact of life, but it is not generally understood. When a newly introduced drug is associated with adverse reactions, there is usually a big uproar and witch-hunt—talk of prosecuting people in the company which developed the drug, suspicious congressional cross-examination of FDA people who reviewed and approved the product, and a usually brief but intense coverage of the subject by the news media. By the time media attention shifts to a fresh subject, the drug in question usually has acquired such a widespread reputation as a poison that it is practically useless thereafter. Many months or years later, when the nature of the association has been worked out and reported within professional circles, the news media give little attention to the resolution of the story, which sometimes exonerates the drug.

The automobile manufacturers seem to be able to recall their products without such catastrophic losses in credibility, but drugs are much more politicized, despite the fact that automobiles kill many more people than drugs do.

For example, McNeil Pharmaceutical recently recalled, on its own initiative, its pain-relieving non-narcotic drug, ZOMAX, for reevaluation in light of a small but growing number of reports of serious and very rarely fatal allergic reactions to the drug. There were five known fatalities possibly attributable to use of the drug, which had been widely prescribed and so had a very large cohort of past and present users. Prior to McNeil's voluntary recall of ZOMAX, the recall of a drug because of possible adverse reactions had meant the drug's end as a product. McNeil's stated intention, however, was to clarify the risk situation and then decide whether to reintroduce the product, and if so to make changes in instructions to physicians and patients which would act to minimize risk. This "recall for re-evaluation" was a bold and innovative step, signifying a new degree of realism in evaluating the risks of adverse reaction to a widely used drug.

However, a congressman promptly demanded an investigation of what the FDA had done wrong, what the company had done wrong, and so forth, effectively taking the matter out of McNeil's hands and turning it into a media happening. The concept of a "recall for re-evaluation" is ethical, scientifically sound, and beneficial to the public health, but no pharmaceutical company is likely to repeat McNeil's experiment for a long time to come. Instead, recalls will continue to be postponed until adverse reactions are clearly occurring at a risk level which is high enough to force everyone involved to jettison the product permanently. This policy means that: (1) we shall continue to lose opportunities to preserve useful drugs by making risk-reducing changes in their instructions for use; (2) more people will have to suffer adverse reactions to trigger a permanent recall than a recall for re-evaluation.

An intriguing and not yet fully understood footnote to the ZOMAX episode was revealed about eight months after McNeil's voluntary withdrawal. A prescription-event monitoring study of ZOMAX in England showed that patients taking the drug appeared to have about half as many heart attacks and strokes during their time on the drug as would have been expected for their age group. After the drug was withdrawn and the patients all had to turn to other drugs for pain relief, the rate of heart attacks and strokes resumed at the usual rate.[7] If this unexpected finding is in fact related to the use of ZOMAX, it would certainly suggest that many more premature deaths were prevented by the use of the drug than it may have caused, if even the worst assumptions about its risk were true. The basic fact is that drug use, both in clinical trials and in everyday medicine, is a risk discovery process. Clinical trials can only screen for relatively high-risk problems at the 1–3 SDU level; the discovery of the more dilute risks—at the 3–5 SDU level—has to occur in the course of the drug's use in everyday medicine.

Useful new drugs do not grow on trees, but now cost an average of $70 million and take seven to ten years each to develop. Every new stricture in the heavily politicized arena of drug regulation adds new layers of cost and time. Each new layer of cost effectively raises the minimum patient population size for which drug development is economically justifiable. The term "orphan drugs" has recently appeared. These are drugs for diseases that affect too few people to allow a return on the expense to develop, test, and register the drug product. The orphan drug phenomenon has been created by successively more complex and costly regulations governing new drug development.

Pharmaceutical innovation is a goose that has laid many golden eggs in the past half century. One cannot but wonder how hard the process can be squeezed before investment simply moves into other areas,[8] leaving it to governments to develop the new drugs. Reviewing the meagre pharmaceutical innovations which have come out of the state-run industries of Eastern Europe does not inspire one to believe that this would be a very effective way to meet present and future disease challenges.

Not all the news is bad, however, as a drug gains use-experience in the market, for sometimes unsuspected new therapeutic uses are identified for older drugs—the above-mentioned apparently favorable action of ZOMAX, for example. Once the initial several million patients have used the drug and its overall risk picture is reasonably well-defined, these new uses are indeed bonuses. They do cost money to document in clinical trials and to gain approval from regulatory authorities for inclusion in the indicated uses for the product. These costs pose a major problem when the discovery of a new use comes at or after the end of the drug's patent life, for thereafter the drug is public property, and a new claim registered by any manufacturer is more or less automatically available to all. That quirk in the regulatory and patent laws deprives all manufacturers of the economic incentive to innovate with older drugs, which is one reason why most manufacturers will opt to bring forward a new, "me-too" drug of the same class as the older one, around which to develop new uses. That has two disadvantages: (1) it keeps the regulatory system clogged reviewing "me-too" drugs; (2) each new drug raises a whole new set of risk questions, which can only find minimal answers in clinical trials. Because of the number gap, about 2 million patients have to undergo the involuntary experiment of testing for adverse reactions that occur at the 3–4.5 SDU level (1 adverse reaction per treatment cycle in 1000 to 50,000 patients).

One area of recent pharmaceutical innovation which partly side-steps this problem is the development of new drug delivery systems, or therapeutic systems. These are special dosage forms which meter the drug into the body at low, usually steady rates for extended periods of time. They have their own patent protection and thus can be used in conjunction with some older drugs to develop better tolerated, less frequently dosed forms while still relying on the existing risk definition of the drug that came from its initial years in the market. Controlling the rate of entry of drug into the bloodstream can have an important influence on balance between therapeutic actions and side-effects of many drugs. These new drug delivery systems make it both scientifically and economically possible to extend or improve the uses of some older drugs. Examples of such products are the "skin patches" which administer nitroglycerin for angina, scopolamine for motion sickness or vertigo, clonidine for hypertension, and estrogen for the menopausal syndrome and to prevent postmenopausal mineral loss from bones. These technological advances are gradually turning the major pharmaceutical companies away from their long-standing, single-minded focus on new chemicals as the sole means of pharmaceutical innovation.

Everyone should understand that there is no such thing as a risk-free drug, just as there is quite obviously no such thing as risk-free surgery. It is unfortunate that the term "drug safety" is used so widely in so many contexts, both lay and professional, for it is fundamentally misleading and contributes to the confused politicization of pharmaceuticals. U.S. drug regulations require that the "safety and efficacy" of each new pharmaceutical product be proved, thereby implying promise of the unattainable goal of absolute safety. German regulations avoid the confused semantics of the term "safety," and ask instead that the product should be "free of concern," which is also unrealistic, for how can any intelligent person be "free of concern" in the face of a defined risk of death or serious injury? The choice of words in these two sets of drug regulations symbolize the lack of realism and confusion with which we, as technologically advanced societies, confront risk. Often while we dither, patients are left with ONURONE.

Part of clinical judgment is to balance risk and benefit in the use of a drug. With great insight, Plato used the term *pharmacon* to mean both "medicament" and "poison," leaving it to the context to indicate which meaning was appropriate. It is not always easy to make such judgments in clinical practice, nor can these judgments be made "free of concern." The use of an effective anticancer agent may necessitate—and warrant—the acceptance of a 1 in 10 risk of fatal bone marrow suppression, but when the antibiotic chloramphenicol turned out to have a 1 in 30,000 risk of fatal bone marrow suppression, its previously general anti-infective use was promptly restricted just to the treatment of typhoid fever, for which it was uniquely effective and still offered an overwhelming advantage compared to other treatments.[9] A diuretic drug called tienilic acid had to be withdrawn several years ago when it turned out, after its first half-year in the U.S. market, that its use carried a 1 in 500 risk that the patient would develop a sometimes fatal liver disorder;[10] curiously, the same drug had already been in the market in France for several years without this problem having become evident, nor was there any evidence that it was occurring in France when very careful studies were done there after the problems became known in the United States. That discrepancy remains a mystery. Aspirin is probably the most widely used drug of any—a recent British survey showed that 4.5 million out of the 57 million total population took it at least once a week, and half a million people took five or more a day.[11] Aspirin has its recognized risks—among them are gastrointestinal bleeding and ulceration, plus precipitation of asthma attacks in people with a certain kind of allergy problem—but the risks of these occurrences are very dilute. However, the exceptional person who has encountered an adverse reaction to aspirin is well-advised to use another agent in the future.

The most troublesome kind of adverse effect of a drug is the one which takes many years to appear. Two examples will illustrate. The first is an antidiarrheal drug, clioquinol, which had been widely used in many countries for many years throughout the world before its use in Japan was associated with several hundred cases of serious neurological damage, blindness, and a number of deaths.[11] Protracted investigation has failed to give a satisfactory explanation for how this catastrophe occurred when and where it did, but an extensive litigation process put the blame on the drug and held the pharmaceutical companies involved liable. The second example is a true "time bomb"—diethylstilbestrol (DES). This artificial estrogen compound had been developed in the 1930's; among its clinical uses during the 1940's and 1950's was the treatment of impending miscarriage. In the late 1960's a small number of young women in Boston were found to have a previously extremely rare form of vaginal tumor; case-control analysis showed that during the fetal lives of these young women their mothers had received DES treatment for impending miscarriage. In earlier years, this choice of treatment had been especially strongly advocated within Boston medical circles, which probably accounts for why the problem was first recognized in Boston, instead of elsewhere. Other—seemingly minor—abnormalities in the genital tract are also observed in about 1 in 3 of either males or females exposed to DES in fetal life; fortunately, the lifetime risk of developing the vaginal tumor in the exposed females appears to have been about 1 in 7000 (3.8 SDU).[12] The whole story will not be known, however, until the people exposed during fetal life have lived their entire lives.

There is no conceivable clinical trial or drug regulatory mechanism which could have prevented either catastrophe. Both could, of course, have been prevented if, back about 1900, all countries had legislated against administering synthetic chemical substances to humans, just as we can readily prevent jet plane crashes by banning jet planes. The cost in human suffering and in premature death of restricting our pharmacopoeia to the ONURONEs of the 19th century would create such a preposterous imbalance of risk and benefit that there can be no alternative to accepting occasional disasters as part of the price of improved lives and health for the vast majority. Nor should we delude ourselves that drugs extracted from natural sources—plants or animals—offer any inherently greater insulation from risk, for every natural substance has its undesirable, frankly toxic, and sometimes lethal actions.

The only hope for minimizing the risk of such events in the future is the added understanding that we gain with each passing year from the big investment being made in biomedical research. It may eventually enable us better to foresee certain kinds of problems and avoid having always to deal with them in retrospect.

We have been lucky to have gained so much and lost so little as modern technology has moved so rapidly into medicine. Infrequent disasters involving small numbers of people have brought governments into the process in the name of protecting the public health. We should pay much more attention than we now do to the health consequences of the slow pace of pharmaceutical innovation and regulation, for the resulting forced dosing with ONURONE can be responsible for many thousands of premature deaths. The whole area of medicine and drugs is so thoroughly politicized that the foreseeable changes will probably bring both a slower pace and more governmental involvement, not less. An important area for improvement is the monitoring of unexpected drug actions—both adverse and beneficial—during the drug's use in the first few million patients. Improved monitoring would reduce the number gap standing between risks definable in clinical trials and risks acceptable to society.

NOTES TO CHAPTER 6

1. Levy, R.I., and J. Moskowitz. "Cardiovascular research: decades of progress, a decade of promise." *Science* 217 (1982): 121–29.

2. European Coronary Surgery Study Group. "Long-term results of prospective randomized study of coronary artery bypass surgery in stable angina pectoris." *Lancet* 2 (1982): 1173–80.

3. Society of Actuaries, *Build and Blood Pressure, 1959.* Chicago, 1959.

4. Society of Actuaries, *Build and Blood Pressure, 1979.* Chicago, 1979.

5. Young, J.H. "Public policy and drug innovation." *Amer. Inst. History of Pharmacy* 24 (1982): 1–56.

6. Wardell, W. Personal communication.

7. Inman, W.H.W. Personal communication.

8. Smith, T. "The drug industry. The goose that lays the golden eggs." *Brit. Med. J.* 281 (1980): 1255–57.

9. *Physicians' Desk Reference,* 38th ed. Oradell, N.J.: Medical Economics, 1984, p. 1454.

10. "FDA's SELACRYN AR file lists 1083 reports," *SCRIP* (London), nos. 584 and 585, April 22 and 27, 1981.

11. Laurence, D.R., and J.W. Black. *The Medicine You Take: Benefits and Risks of Modern Drugs.* London: Croom Helm, 1978.

12. Herbst, A.L., H. Ulfelder, and D.C. Poskanzer. "Adenocarcinoma of the vagina." *New England J. Med.* 284 (1971): 878–81; Herbst, A.L., D.C. Poskanzer, S.J. Robboy, C. Friedlander, and R.E. Scully. "Prenatal exposure to stilbestrol: a prospective comparison of exposed female offspring with unexposed controls." Ibid. 292 (1975): 334–39.

7

Food and Risk

This is a difficult topic, and one which cannot be approached from the same quantitative point of view that we have applied in previous chapters to other areas of risk in human life. This is so because there are simply too many unknowns, too many fertile imaginations offering unproven or unprovable ideas, and too few opportunities to define quantitative relations in the area of diet and risk. Accordingly, in this chapter we review this field qualitatively in the context of material already covered about the major causes of death and their trends. Three big issues discussed are: (1) the role of dietary fat in development of coronary heart disease; (2) dietary factors and the development of cancer; and (3) possible risks associated with food additives. As in other fields, it is useful to begin with a bit of history.

All the major vitamins were discovered during the first half of this century. These were landmark scientific discoveries, and in some instances the stories of their discoveries read like detective stories.[1] These discoveries have rid us of beri-beri, pellagra, scurvy, and rickets—the most vividly remembered of the vitamin deficiency diseases. Conquering them was not at all straightforward, for they had many confusing earmarks of infectious diseases. During the decades of the vitamin discoveries, the major concerns about diet and risk focussed much more on deficiencies in one's diet than on what was included but shouldn't be. Today, most of the concern focusses on the latter.

Much less dramatic than the discovery of the vitamins but nevertheless also important was the work done during the same decades to provide the basic information on caloric, vitamin, mineral, protein, fat, and carbohydrate contents of all the major foodstuffs. This included much experimental fieldwork in animal nutrition, which has improved the productivity of the cattle, hog, chicken, lamb, dairy, and egg industries. All this information laid the groundwork for understanding daily calorie requirements in human nutrition, plus the evident requirements for protein and the various vitamins and minerals. The relations were drawn between nutrients, as chemically defined, and the various foods from which one prepares meals. All this work transformed understanding of the empirical, regional culinary know-how and food preferences of human experience by providing quantitative relations between food choices and the body's evident requirements for calories and the essential chemical constituents of food.

The story is not yet finished, for even in the past few years there have been striking advances in the application of new principles of nutrition to the medical care of both acutely injured and chronically ill patients, through the use of intravenous solutions of amino acids and concentrated sugars—called intravenous hyperalimentation. The full impact of these advances has not yet been seen, but the area is one of intense investigation and rapid change in medical and surgical practice, with sometimes dramatic improvements in critically ill patients related to the application of these new nutritional principles.

Diet and Heart Disease

By 1940, coronary heart disease (CHD) had emerged as the leading cause of death, as mortality due to infectious diseases dropped among infants, children, and young adults, and more people lived beyond age 50. There was also evidence that CHD was growing in its own right, and not just being revealed in bigger numbers because people were living longer. After World War II, the understanding of this disease became a leading priority in medical research.

In addition to the well-established and already-discussed adverse influence of cigarette smoking on CHD, a very large body of circumstantial evidence now links dietary fat consumption with CHD. An important part of the evidence came out of an unusual study by the U.S. Public Health Service of the inhabitants of Framingham, Massachusetts during a period of almost 25 years.[2] It was an observational study, not an experimental one, and of all the findings from those many years of observation, one of the most important was the identification of the factors that increase one's risk of CHD: hypertension, cigarette smoking, heart enlargement, and elevated levels of cholesterol in the blood. These risk factors were identified by collecting observations on people over the years, and then looking to see what factors correlated most closely with the development of CHD. In this sense, the Framingham study was not unlike the various studies by the insurance industry, except that there were periodic medical exams in the Framingham study which allowed the documentation of disease appearance or progress; the insurance studies usually only correlate what is found at the initial medical examination with what ends up later being written on the death certificate.

The Framingham study was not the first to suggest that cholesterol levels in the blood were an important risk factor for CHD, but it showed how much more likely the people with high cholesterol levels were to develop CHD than were those with low cholesterol levels. Previous studies had been retrospective and had shown that people who already had CHD tended also to have high cholesterol levels.

It is known that the cholesterol level in the blood is increased by a high dietary intake of fat, especially of the saturated fats such as butter, lard and other animal meat fats, and hydrogenated vegetable cooking fats which are solid at room temperature. Thus, because a high cholesterol level in blood is a risk factor for CHD, it is a reasonable inference that diets high in saturated fats predispose to CHD.

Yet the link between dietary fat intake and CHD is a loose one: some who eat very Spartan diets get CHD, and others who eat all the "wrong" things do not. It would be very helpful to have a study in which two carefully matched groups of people ate different diets, but it would take many years, be very costly, and would be exceptionally difficult to monitor to insure compliance. It would have to be started at a rather young age, for some people in their twenties already have some narrowing of their coronary arteries. Conceptually, such a life-long study is highly desirable and has been considered, but its immense practical problems have precluded it.

Long-term feeding studies in animals have lent support to the dietary fat-CHD link. Yet it is also clear from studies in humans who have already developed CHD that switching to a low-fat diet does not appear to reverse the disease or to lessen its severity. This observation does not disprove the theory, but if CHD had proved diet-reversible it would certainly have strengthened the theory. Some may challenge the assertion that CHD is not reversible by diet, for combined programs of diet, weight loss, and exercise can lead to considerable clinical improvement in some patients with CHD. But there is no convincing evidence that dietary change alone can "melt" the cholesterol-rich obstructions in the coronary arteries, even when the cholesterol level in the blood drops.

So there is strong suspicion, but not proof, that CHD could be prevented or minimized by changing the diet toward a lower content of fats in general, and saturated fats in particular, and by reducing the dietary intakes of cholesterol and sodium. The American Heart Association (AHA) recommended just that change to the American public in early 1982, but not without a great deal of internal debate beforehand, and not without a great deal of skepticism publicly expressed by many experts in nutrition. All the pro and con evidence is summarized in a publication* by the AHA, describing what has led it to take the unprecedented step of recommending a reduction of dietary fat intake to 30% of total calories (from the current average value of 40%) with less than 10% of calories being saturated fat, plus the other changes noted above.

The meat, dairy, and egg industries have a large interest in this matter, for if there were a large shift in dietary preferences in the directions recommended by the AHA, it would considerably reduce the consumption of meat, milk, and egg products. Egg yolks are one of the richest sources of dietary cholesterol, and beef and pork have relatively high saturated fat contents; also, many prepared meat products, such as sausages, cold meats, hot dogs, and so forth, are

---

* The publication can be found in the April 1982 issue of the Association's journal, *Circulation,* starting on page 839A. A copy of this publication can be ordered from the American Heart Association by writing to them at 7320 Greenville Ave., Dallas, Texas, 75321, and asking for publication No. 72-202-A.

well over 50% fat. As a consequence, the meat, dairy, and egg industries orchestrate a vigorous, contrary response whenever there is any suggestion that meat, milk, and egg products are anything less than wonderfully nutritious parts of a well-balanced diet. It is a personal judgment whether this is greedy self-interest operating in a public-be-damned manner, or the quite proper defense of good products against unwarranted, scientifically unproven assertions.

The evidence about the role of dietary fat intake in CHD remains circumstantial, and thus has many elements of ambiguity. No one likes ambiguity, and so people seek ways to resolve it. One of the political mechanisms for resolving ambiguity is the appointment of an expert committee charged with preparation of an authoritative report. Besides the above-mentioned report by the AHA, four groups of experts have issued authoritative reports within the past half-dozen years, not only in the area of diet and CHD, but in the more confusing area of diet and cancer.

This has all had the effect of drawing the field of nutrition away from its century-long tradition of solid, scientific strength and into an arena of wishful thinking and clashing political, social, and economic interests. Available scientific information cannot provide immediate answers to the kinds of questions now being asked, and the pace at which new scientific information becomes available is too slow to satisfy the public's current demand for instant resolution of the uncertainties about diet and health—hence the expert committees. It should be noted that no one needs an expert committee when the scientific evidence is clear; also noteworthy is the fact that it is very hard to find people who qualify as real experts in nutrition who have not had extensive involvement with the food industry. That industry, like most other modern industries, is technologically advanced, information-intensive, and dependent upon close contacts with the best expertise in the scientific fields that are basic to its products. From the point of view of contemporary politics, however, it means that anyone has license to disregard the views of any professor who has ever consulted with any food manufacturer or industry group. You can read what follows in light of the fact that neither author of this book has ever had any involvement with the food industry—beyond the eating of its products; neither are we experts in nutrition. We bring only general medical and scientific training and experience to the reading of what the experts have written.

The first expert report on rebalancing our diets came from a committee of the U.S. Senate which had been chaired by then-Senator George McGovern. The 1977 report, "Dietary Goals for the United States," was drawn from recommendations made by many experts who had testified before the committee, and it prescribed what people should eat if they were to avoid what the report called "the epidemic of killer diseases" which was stalking the nation.[3] (It is useful to remember that since everybody eventually dies of something, there is destined always to be an "epidemic of killer diseases.") The main recommendation of "Dietary Goals" was that Americans should eat less meat. It was widely hailed by people who see great value in the so-called "health" foods, and was roundly criticized by the food industry. Some of the language from "Dietary Goals" was written into the 1977 agricultural appropriations bill, which led to the establishment of a research center for human nutrition within the U.S. Department of Agriculture.

In 1980 this center issued, in collaboration with the U.S. Department of Health and Human Services, a booklet called "Dietary Guidelines." It recommended that Americans ". . . eat a variety of foods, maintain ideal weight; avoid too much fat, saturated fat, and cholesterol; eat food with adequate starch and fiber; avoid too much sugar; avoid too much sodium; and if you drink alcohol, do so in moderation." While these guidelines sound remarkably like what most mothers tell their children, "Dietary Guidelines" was vigorously attacked by the U.S. meat industry. When the Reagan administration came into being, it was only a few months before both "Dietary Guidelines" and the Human Nutrition Center at the USDA ceased to exist. The beef industry has been well represented in the Reagan administration: the then-new Deputy Secretary of Agriculture had been Executive Director of the American Meat Institute, and one of the Assistant Secretaries of Agriculture had been a lobbyist for the American National Cattlemen's Association.[3]

The next expert report to appear came in 1980 from the Food and Nutrition Board of the U.S. National Academy of Sciences—*Toward Healthful Diets.*[4] The Food and Nutrition Board (FNB) is the group which, since 1941, has recommended the daily allowances of essential nutrients in the U.S. diet. These are called "Recommended Daily Allowances" (RDA's) and are now part of the labelling of many food products. The FNB was mostly made up of biochemists, and they cast a rather dim eye on epidemiological data, writing that "epidemiology establishes coincidence, but not cause and effect," though it can "lay groundwork for further studies."

With that perspective, the FNB said: "there is no basis for recommendations to modify the proportions in the American diet at this time." They added a noteworthy point: "Any public official considering a new public health program for disease prevention must evaluate the potential effectiveness of the proposed action before recommending its adoption. If there is uncertainty about its effectiveness, there must be clear evidence that the proposed intervention will not be harmful or detrimental in other ways. In the case of diseases with multiple and poorly understood etiology, such as cancer and cardiovascular disease, the assumption that dietary change will be effective as a preventive measure is controversial. These diseases are not primarily nutritional, although they have nutritional determinants that vary in importance from individual to individual. Authorities who resist recommendations for diet modification express a legitimate concern about promising tangible benefits from controversial recommendations that alter people's lives and habits. . . . Those experts who advocate a more aggressive approach and seek to change the national diet in the hope of preventing these degenerative diseases assume that the risk of change is minimal and rely heavily on epidemiologic evidence for support of their belief in the probability of benefit. Neither the degree of risk nor the extent of benefit can be assumed in the absence of suitable evidence."

The FNB's statement epitomizes the controversy: most people and many scientists are not convinced by epidemiological data—that is to say inferences as to cause and effect which are drawn from observations on experiments of nature, as opposed to controlled experiments in the laboratory; they are not willing to undertake the mammoth task of getting hundreds of millions of people to change their diets on the basis of inferences about risk factors, which they see as a weak form of scientific evidence about cause and effect. Most scientists and physicians recognize hard scientific evidence to be the basis for humankind's progress from short, disease-ridden lives to the long, healthy lives that the vast majority of people in the Western world enjoy today. They fear that the pressure to "do something," despite all the uncertainty about diet, will take us away from what has served us so well in the recent past.

Criticism of "Toward Healthful Diets" focussed on the scope and range of the ties of some individual committee members to various parts of the food industry. The report had little impact in the face of a great and widely felt urgency to change people's diets.[5]

The next report to appear was the aforementioned set of recommendations by the American Heart Association in 1982. It is a well-balanced report, which covers both the pro and the con evidence.

The most recent report to issue came also in 1982. It concerned dietary factors in the development of cancer and grew out of a request in 1980 from the National Cancer Institute to the National Research Council to study this subject. The 1982 report is called *Diet, Nutrition, and Cancer.*[6] One of its recommendations is similar to that of the AHA: reduce dietary fat intake from its current level of about 40% to 30% of caloric intake. This change was recommended because the committee concluded there was sufficient evidence to view high fat consumption as a significant risk factor for breast and colon cancers.

The balance of saturated and unsaturated fats was also dealt with, because polyunsaturated fats appear to act to promote tumor formation in certain animal studies—yet they also have an ostensibly beneficial effect of reducing the blood cholesterol level. The AHA had taken cognizance of this problem and had recommended that polyunsaturated fats be not more than 10% of caloric intake—but by no means is it clear where the greater risk lies.

The report on "Diet, Nutrition, and Cancer" makes an astounding claim: "It is highly likely that the United States will eventually have the option of adopting a diet that reduces its incidence of cancer by approximately one-third." Commenting on this assertion at the time the report was issued, the committee's chairman, Prof. Clifford Grobstein, said: "The evidence is increasingly impressive that what we eat does affect our chances of getting cancer. This is . . . good news because it means that by controlling what we eat we may prevent such diet-sensitive cancers."[7] Then he added the bad news that the committee "does not yet think it possible to say . . . how much the incidence of particular cancers might be reduced by dietary alteration. Certainly we have no ideal cancer-preventing diet to announce." The changes they did recommend should, he said, "reduce anxiety" about cancer. These included: reducing fat intake to 30%

of total calories; minimizing consumption of salt-cured, pickled, or smoked foods; increasing consumption of fruits, vegetables, and whole-grain cereals; minimizing carcinogenic additives to food; and moderation in the consumption of alcohol. They also called for more research on substances called mutagens, which are present in some foods, and which may increase the risk of the development of various cancers.

The postulated link between diet and cancer rests on two lines of evidence. The first is that the incidence of most types of cancer in the United States has not increased during this century, with the notable exception of the cancers of the respiratory tree, including the lungs. These respiratory cancers are related to cigarette smoking through evidence which, in relation to what we are considering in the dietary field, is stunningly clear-cut. At the same time, there has been a big drop in gastrointestinal cancers, perhaps related to the trend away from smoked, salted, and nitrated meats and fish—and perhaps not, as we noted in Chapter 3 in discussing the big decline in stomach cancer that has occurred since about 1920. In other respects, cancer incidence has remained more or less constant throughout the period of great expansion in the chemically based industries, and without the environmental controls and workplace safety regulations that have only come into being within the past few years—too recently to have had any impact on cancer statistics.

The second major line of evidence for the diet-cancer link is that cancers of the liver, stomach, esophagus, and mouth have a much *higher* incidence in nonindustrialized than in industrialized countries. When people migrate from nonindustrialized to industrialized countries, the incidence of these various kinds of cancer shifts to the rate characteristic of the new home.

Based on these two lines of evidence, the committee concluded that the most common cancers "are related, for the most part, not to industrialization, but to various other long-standing features of our life-style, especially diet."[8] Curiously little attention has been paid to the committee's exoneration of industrialization, whose pollution of earth, air, and water has been such a widely discussed topic in recent years.

The current U.S. Secretary of Agriculture has been quoted as saying, "I'm not so sure government should get into telling people what they should or shouldn't eat." One can have a certain sympathy with that straightforward, simple view, given all the controversy.

A considerable dampening of the zeal to urge fundamental changes in diet has come from the results of a major study on risk factors in heart disease, published after all the expert committees had had their say, and just a few months after the American Heart Association published its dietary recommendations. This big risk-factors study carried the formal title of "Multiple Risk Factor Intervention Trial" (MRFIT).[9] It was begun in 1973 with the purpose of measuring the benefits of reducing major risk factors for CHD in patients who were, according to the risk factors defined in the Framingham study, in the top 10% risk group for premature death due to CHD. The three major thrusts of the study were to reduce cholesterol levels by changing diet, to reduce or stop smoking, and to treat whatever hypertension might exist.

To this end, 12,866 men age 35–57 who precisely met the selection criteria for the MRFIT study were chosen from a much larger group and enrolled. They were divided randomly into two groups. The intervention group received special programs of dietary advice, counseling on smoking, and hypertension treatment. Members of the other (control) group were merely referred to their physicians with the information that they were in a high-risk group for CHD. Both groups were followed equally closely over the succeeding years, and the results were published in September 1982. Overall mortality was the same in both groups, as was mortality from both CHD and all other causes. The control group turned out to have about half the mortality that had been predicted from the Framingham data and also a lower mortality than expected from the modest downward trend in overall CHD mortality in the population. Both groups showed reductions in cholesterol level and in cigarette smoking, though the reductions in both were smaller in the control group than in the intervention group. Intervention resulted in a larger than expected reduction in smoking but a smaller than expected reduction in cholesterol levels. Those who quit smoking in both groups experienced less mortality from both CHD and all other causes than those who continued smoking, as did those who were nonsmokers all the while.

The results of the MRFIT study were a big disappointment to many who had concluded that incontrovertible evidence supported the role of diet in development of CHD. Indeed, some people have argued that the whole theory should be abandoned as being of no practical value, given the effort put into effecting dietary changes and the lack of beneficial results in the MRFIT study. That is probably too extreme a view, given the balance of evidence, plus the recently published results of a multiyear trial in Oslo, Norway, showing beneficial results with a cholesterol-lowering diet combined with efforts to reduce smoking.[10,11]

Meanwhile, what is a prudent person to do?

A reasonable thing to do is to read the AHA recommendations, MRFIT notwithstanding: these recommendations are thoughtful and balanced, as well as being quite readable. They focus on the biggest single cause of death but are not oblivious to the possible tumor-promoting effects of the polyunsaturated fats. "Diet, Nutrition, and Cancer," on the other hand, is difficult to read for someone not accustomed to biomedical scientific literature; moreover, irrespective of the importance of its subject, the report does not come to a conclusion which can be readily translated into food choices, other than what the generalities mentioned above suggest.

Beyond that, everyone has to make up his or her own mind, based on dietary preferences and individual assessment of the strength of the evidence for dietary changes. If you smoke cigarettes, you should certainly invest both your concern and your will-power in the effort to quit smoking: the evidence for the adverse effects of cigarette smoking on both CHD and various cancers is black and white, compared to all the dull shades of gray in the area of diet and CHD or cancer. It may be prudent to try the AHA recommendations for a few weeks, so as to assess in your own view the degree of hardship they pose. If you find them acceptable, it may be reasonable to choose them as a well-reasoned set of dietary recommendations. If following them only creates another source of turmoil or guilt in your life, focus your will-power on something else. In either event, it is a good practice to maintain variety in your diet, to minimize continuity of exposure to such mutagens or carcinogens as may be present in one or another kind of food.

FOOD ADDITIVES AND RESIDUES

Large-scale food processing and distribution is about a century old, having come into being as mechanization of the farms displaced a large fraction of the populace from rural to urban life; the simultaneous advent of the railroads made it possible to ship the harvest to the food manufacturer and packaged food products to the urban consumer. By 1900 there were a number of abuses in the food industry sufficiently flagrant to bring political action. The best publicized involved filthy conditions in meat packing plants, the use of acutely toxic substances such as formaldehyde and borax as food additives, and willful misbranding.

The recent terrible catastrophe in Spain from industrial rapeseed oil sold fraudulently as olive oil is a page out of the food industry's history in the first years of this century.[12] By 1914, most Western countries, responding to public outcry, had legislated a governmental role in regulating food processing and manufacturing. It is well to recall that knowledge about bacteria and their role in the then-commonest fatal diseases was only several decades old, so the growing public awareness of potentially lethal microbes in foods created an extra impetus for reform.

All the while, the majority of food manufacturers were undoubtedly making quality products, according to the standards of the time, while the flamboyant abuses of a few undercut the credibility of the whole industry and prompted bursts of political action and regulation. In between these catastrophe-inspired lurches into regulation, the food industry provided a major stimulus to the development of sterilization techniques and other aspects of applied microbiology, to insure that canned products would consistently be free of bacterial contamination. As recently as 1971, the canning industry was forcibly reminded that there is zero tolerance for error in this area, for a major U.S. producer was forced into bankruptcy after shipping canned vichyssoise soup contaminated with botulinus toxin. A number of people became ill, and some died. So did the soup company.

In 1900, it might not have been possible to detect such an event, but today outbreaks of food poisoning are very conspicuous. There is a whole surveillance mechanism for sudden outbreaks of disease—the Epidemic Intelligence Service of the Center for Disease Control in Atlanta—which continually monitors for such events. All technologically advanced countries have similar agencies. When a problem is identified, the food regulatory agencies have legal powers to remove unsafe food products from the market. Their practical ability to do so is facilitated by modern manufacturing practice that identifies each lot or batch of product by number, with records to allow rapid tracing of shipped goods in the supply chain.

Food processing and packaging is a technology-based industry and has provided the impetus for many advances in microbiology, chemistry, materials, and engineering. Some changes have been mandated by governments, but most of the improvements have come from competitive pressure to adopt new technology. The awesome array of products on the shelves of a modern supermarket is the result. Aside from the food industry's ability to please almost every palate and to provide a very broad range of products with long shelf-lives, it provides a strong defense against famine, one of humanity's three ancient scourges, beside plagues and war.

As sanitary problems have faded from public view—even if, through occasional lapses, they will probably never disappear completely—public concerns shifted in the early 1970's to a new focus: insidious threats to life and health from advertent and inadvertent additives to food, which currently number in excess of 6000 different substances. The perception of problems posed by these additives and residues has been enhanced by the tremendous advances in the ability to measure complex chemicals in ever-tinier amounts.

In the "good old days" impurities were expressed in percentage terms. Procter & Gamble, for example, used to claim that its Ivory brand of soap was "ninety-nine and forty-four one-hundredths percent pure." That claim may have sounded impressive years ago, but in today's language it translates to impurities at the level of 5600 parts per million—which lacks both the meter of the original phrase and its implication of penultimate purity.

The ability to measure substances at a level of one part per million (1 ppm) started during the 1960's; today it is an exceptional substance which cannot be measured at the 1 ppm level, and some can now be measured at the level of a few parts per billion (ppb). These are measurements capable of detecting, for example, a few grains of salt added to an Olympic-sized swimming pool.

There is a large psychological impact in the difference between "zero" and 0.0000001%, which is the percentage equivalent of 1 ppb.

For this reason, the phenomenal growth of capability in analytical chemistry has had the sobering consequence of making us aware that many substances, long thought not to be present at all, are in fact there at the ppm or ppb level. Analytical chemistry continues to gain capability, so that we can expect to see some measurements being reported at the parts per trillion level. This forces those involved in the growth, processing, and consumption of food—i.e. literally everyone—to ask, and answer: what effect does the presence of the substance at the reported level have on humans?

The advertent additives we know are already there, so one might suppose that there might not be any unpleasant surprises to pop up out of the new-found ability to find chemical needles in haystacks. Even that turns out not to be so, because every chemical product has some level of impurities in it—like Ivory Soap. Suppose, for example, a chemical food additive contains an impurity at the 1 ppm level—in other words, the additive is 99.9999% pure. By anyone's standards, this is an exceptionally high degree of purity. Now, suppose the additive is used in food processing at the 0.1% (one part per thousand) level—typical additive uses being as coloring agents, antioxidants and other preservatives, blending/mixing aids, and emulsifiers. The contaminant in the additive is now present in the processed food at the 1 ppb level. The problem becomes more complex in storage and at the time when the product is cooked, prior to consumption. Both storage and heat are capable of changing the chemical nature of both the original additive and its contaminant, and one could well expect to find a number of contaminant-generated substances at the parts per trillion level at the time of consumption.

Another aspect of the additives problem are those which end up inadvertently in food. These are environmental contaminants—drugs used to treat food-producing animals, feed additives, pesticides used to treat animals or plants, industrial chemicals, and so forth. In addition, there are substances which may leach from packaging materials into packaged food—an example from long ago having been lead extracting from the solder used to seal tin cans. Also, there are various substances from the environment which happen—during growth, harvesting or slaughtering, shipping, processing, or in the package—to find their way into food destined for human consumption.

Should we give up food?

No one can know what adverse effects may be caused by this myriad of additives and residues. What we do know, however, is that mortality has been declining steadily throughout this century, except for its one year upturn during the 1918–19 flu epidemic. Mortality from coronary artery diseases and strokes has been steadily declining for over a decade. Overall cancer mortality has remained about constant (when the aging of the population is taken into account), and the only group of cancers increasing are those clearly linked to cigarette smoking. It is possible that the substitution of modern techniques of food preservation for traditional methods of salting, curing, and smoking has played a role in the big decline in cancers of the upper gastrointestinal tract. There are no evident big increases in nonfatal diseases relatable to diet or specific foods. There are certain people with food allergy problems, irritable bowel syndrome, and Crohn's disease. In fact, there is some suspicion that the numbers of people developing Crohn's disease may be increasing, so it should be carefully watched, but it remains a very infrequently occurring condition.

If we are poisoning ourselves in some way or other through modern techniques of food production, processing, and packaging, then the risk they pose is sufficiently dilute not to have offset the steady improvements in health and life expectancy that have come about from other aspects of modern technology. It is, however, possible that there is some kind of delayed-action "time bomb" ticking somewhere in the food chain, but it has yet to manifest itself.

Yet this whole area of modern life is a source of chronic unease, punctuated by occasional episodes of acute public reaction, the most striking of which concerned artificial sweeteners. It is useful to understand what happened in that episode, for it brings us to the most recent developments in this troubled area.

Since 1958, advertent food additives in the United States have been subject to the Delaney Amendment, which prohibits use of any substance as a food additive when that substance has been found "by appropriate toxicological tests" to induce cancer in animals or man. This requirement was added to a piece of 1958 legislation that gave the FDA power to require food manufacturers to prove the "safety" of new additives before they could be used in food products. Previously, FDA action had to be taken against an already-marketed product, after animal tests or other evidence had shown it to be hazardous. There was wide support to make this change in the FDA's powers, but Congressman James Delaney took the occasion to add his amendment to the legislation. Although it was clear at the time that the Delaney Amendment was going to pose difficult problems in the future because of its absolute language, it was also clear that the FDA could not get the new power it sought without the Delaney Amendment, and so it became law.

The moment of truth for the Delaney Amendment came during the cyclamate/saccharin controversy, which established that people would choose to keep available a desirable one-of-a-kind food product in the face of evidence which would require the total banning of the substance from the market. It was a watershed event in public attitudes about risk and about the scientific status of the testing of food additives.

Cyclamate had been introduced as a low-calorie sweetener during the 1960's and had rapidly achieved wide usage because of its superiority to the older, slightly bitter-tasting saccharin. In 1970, animal studies were completed which showed that cyclamate produced bladder cancers when fed in very large quantities to rats. This finding triggered the ban of cyclamate, as the Delaney Amendment required.

The ban came just as the California fruit harvest was ready to be canned. Part of it was to be canned with cyclamate for use by diabetics and others seeking low-sugar, low-calorie foods. The ban resulted in the bankruptcy of a major canning cooperative, because it was left with a whole year's supply of unsalable product, despite assurances from the FDA at harvest time that it would be possible later to find a legal basis for selling the products. Most other countries judged cyclamate to be satisfactory for human use, so it remained in many markets. That was no help to the California cooperative, for it is illegal to export food or drug products which are not qualified for sale in the United States. The ban on cyclamate left saccharin as the only low-calorie sweetener in the U.S. market.

A short while later, other animal tests showed that saccharin, like cyclamate, is a weak carcinogen in rats. This result necessitated that saccharin, too, be banned totally. That would have occurred, but for a large public outcry to the contrary. Congress began to hear from their constituents in large numbers that they were not going to be done out of low-calorie sweets just because some rats got cancers at unimaginably high doses of sweetener. Much was made of the fact that the cancer-producing dose in rats was equivalent to a human's drinking of 800 cans per day of artificially sweetened soft drinks.

There then ensued a brisk and emotional debate on the risks and benefits of low-calorie sweeteners, with testimonials to their essential role in the management of diabetes and in America's unrelenting war on obesity. Congress responded by exempting saccharin from the Delaney Amendment, allowing it to remain in use, provided that all saccharin-containing products be labelled with a prominent statement that they contain saccharin, which has been shown to cause cancer in tests on laboratory animals. That shifted responsibility to the consumer for decision in the face of ambiguity, while giving the consumer the essential facts. The closest thing to a practical concern about saccharin (or cyclamate) had been the possibility of small children consuming many cans of artificially sweetened soft drinks; it seemed reasonable to assume that the label provided sufficient warning to any responsible parent.

Many people were concerned by the social and intellectual implications of the cyclamate/saccharin episode. The regulators had their hands tied by the Delaney Amendment. It is an ill-considered but politically unchangeable law—who would vote to legalize the addition of cancer-causing substances to people's food? The public got ambiguous and otherwise confusing signals from the scientific experts involved, and heaped considerable scorn on the basic concepts of toxicity-testing procedures on laboratory animals—the basic means by which Western humankind is going to figure out what can stay and what must go among the 6000+ chemicals that end up as additives or residues in food. At the same time, the food industry was left uncertain as to how it was going to go about its business in the future.

The U.S. food industry reacted to this situation in an innovative, politically adroit, and socially constructive way. In 1976, the major U.S. food companies formed and funded a group called the Food Safety Council for the purpose of bringing together people from academia, consumer groups, government, and the food industry to establish a coherent policy on testing procedures for food additives and residues. It took about four years for the scientific aspects of the group's work to be completed and published, and another two years for comments to come in from various interested people and groups, plus final review and publication, which occurred in mid-1982.

The final report is entitled "A Proposed Food Safety Evaluation Process."* It is a model of carefully reasoned presentation of the problems, the available methods for solving them, the logic which underlies the methods, their recognized limitations, and the time required to generate the information needed to make rational decisions. The report also includes recommendations on the regulatory process, which is in the continually difficult position of (1) needing to generate decisions—and sometimes rules—on the basis of incomplete information; (2) having its past actions often made to look unscientific as new information becomes available; and (3) often being the sole focus of criticism when something previously thought safe turns out to be the cause of disease or death in humans.

The full impact of the Food Safety Council's final report is yet to be felt. Because the scientific portion of the report had such broad participation in its preparation, however, it seems reasonable to expect that it will be the guide to handling food hazard issues for some years to come. One can assume that the report is part of the food industry's lobbying effort with Congress. The issues are hard ones, without easy answers: the available methods for answering questions are time-consuming and sometimes provide data which are difficult to interpret and sometimes downright misleading. The questions are too important to leave entirely to the political arena, but they are also too important to leave entirely to the scientists without broad public understanding and support.

Of the "expert" reports which have been generated in recent years, those of the AHA and the Food Safety Council deserve wide public attention. No person seriously interested in issues of food hazards can credibly sound off in public on the subject without being fully cognizant of the Food Safety Council's report. The conclusions of the report are not going to make the concerns and problems in this difficult area go away overnight, but they set forth a process for resolving problems, with a clear indication of the time required to get the answers.

We are the first generation to have to confront the chemical con-

---

* Copies may be obtained by sending $5 to: The Nutrition Foundation, Inc., 888 17th Street, Suite 300, Washington, DC, 20006.

tamination of food and the intimidating problems that poses. In this situation, we find it useful to recall that humankind is only four generations into the era of understanding the world of bacteria which exist all around us, and within us. It had a tremendous impact on our great-grandparents to realize that the causes of the then-leading killing diseases were invisibly small microbes crawling all over everything around them, even—and sometimes most of all—themselves and their loved ones. Modern principles of sanitation entered their lives in the context of that profoundly disturbing revelation, and the change was not without some rather striking distortions in human behavior, as some people concocted odd ways of trying to sanitize everything around them.

We have gradually come to terms with the germs all around us, . even though people still contract bacterial infections, some of them fatal. Taking bacterial cultures in food preparation areas—even the finest restaurants—reminds any who care to inquire that a kitchen is not an operating room, for proper food handling and sterility are two quite different things. We have learned to co-exist with both the bacteria and the knowledge of their omnipresence and potential for mischief. We could, of course, require all food preparation to be done in aseptic, low-particle count, clean-room facilities, as are used in the manufacturing of certain kinds of sterile drug products. Instead, we compromise by using a set of principles and procedures of sanitation which are not perfect, for we still have the occasional outbreak of food-borne bacterial or viral gastroenteritis, diarrhea, or hepatitis. Nevertheless, the methods we have ended up with are a reasonable compromise. Microbes ceased being a major focus of people's phobias at about the half-century point in the microbiologic era.

We are still at an early point in the chemical contaminants era. They are a source of great anxiety, much public commentary, and governmental action. The latter naturally follows when the public becomes "upset," as an older generation used to say before the advent of television converted the occasional public "upset" into a state of permanent inversion. We are the first-generation immigrants into a new world of omnipresent, strange chemicals, revealed in increasing numbers by new analytical methods with an ever-increasing ability to detect ever-tinier amounts. We have not yet come to terms with this chemical "world," which is in some respects newly created by the presence of novel synthetic substances. In other respects, however, this chemical "world" is very old, but information about its existence is new, because we have only recently learned the chemical correlates of old practices. We are just now struggling to assimilate this new information—a process analogous to the sanitation and hygiene which our great-grandparents had to learn. We can be pardoned for being a little crazy in the process, but perhaps we can benefit from their experience. We have something they did not: a long and healthy life for a large majority.

NOTES TO CHAPTER 7

1. Schultz, M.G. "Joseph Goldberger and pellagra." *Amer. J. Trop. Med. Hygiene* 26 (1977): 1088–92.

2. Kannel, W.B., and T. Gordon, eds. *The Framingham Study: An Epidemiological Investigation of Cardiovascular Disease.* Washington, D.C.: U.S. Government Printing Office, 1976.

3. Broad, W.J. "Nutrition research: end of an empire." *Science* 213 (1981): 518–20.

4. Food and Nutrition Board, National Research Council. *Toward Healthful Diets.* Washington, D.C.: National Academy of Sciences, 1980.

5. Broad, W.J. "Academy says curb on cholesterol not needed." *Science* 208 (1980): 1354–55.

6. Committee on Diet, Nutrition, and Cancer, National Research Council. *Diet, Nutrition, and Cancer.* Washington, D.C.: National Academy Press, 1982.

7. Maugh, T.H. "Research news. Cancer is not inevitable." *Science* 217 (1982): 36–37.

8. Note 6: Chapter 2, p. 5.

9. Multiple Risk Factors Intervention Trial Research Group. "Multiple risk factor intervention trial." *J. Amer. Med. Assoc.* 248 (1982): 1465–77.

10. Hjermann, I., et al. "Effect of diet and smoking intervention on the incidence of coronary heart disease: report from the Oslo Study Group of a randomized trial in healthy men." *Lancet* 2 (1981): 1303–10.

11. Oslo Study Research Group. "Commentary. MRFIT and the Oslo study." *J. Amer. Med. Assoc.* 249 (1983): 893–94.

12. Gillman, P., and I. Hilton. "Revealed: a family quest for cheap oil that ended in jail." *The Sunday Times* (London), February 14, 1982.

8

Risk-Related Codewords

This chapter covers a diversity of topics with the single aim of achieving a realistically balanced understanding of the meanings of the four leading risk-related codewords in current usage. The first of these codewords is "natural," which is widely used as a codeword in consumer product promotion to conjure up confidence and the illusion of safety. The other codewords are "chemical," "technological," and "nuclear." These will be explored through the analysis of some of the specific problems that have helped to burden these terms with special adverse meanings in the public mind. The problems we discuss are dioxin, DDT, asbestos, formaldehyde, and the generation of electric power by controlled nuclear fission.

Some believe that the world has been destroyed by chemistry and other technology, and yearn to start anew in a pre-technological, still "natural" world. Others shun contemporary developments and seek alternative life-styles. It is understandable that many people fear "chemicals," and uncritically admire that which is "natural"—a theme that has been picked up in the promotion of many foods. It is understandable that people confront the increasing technological transformation of society with worry and fear. Many events *are* worrisome—the seeming pervasiveness of chemical contamination of water and earth, appalling mistakes in nuclear power plant construction and operation, adverse drug reactions, food additives with uncertain effects, and on. . .and on. It is possible to recognize terrible dangers in practically everything that goes on today. But at the same time it is paradoxical and frustrating to observe how we, as a society, give the greatest attention to events of least significance. It is of course the purpose of this book to give a basis for focussing on the big problems rather than being distracted by the small ones, however newsworthy they may be in the first moments of revelation.

Many people recognize in every food product they buy in the supermarket the fingerprint of the chemical industry, and turn towards "natural" or "organic" products, produced as in the "good old days." It is widely understood that "natural" or "organic" equates with "good." There is a certain anonymity in the big supermarket, filled with products which for the most part have been processed and packaged by large companies. By contrast, there is a certain sense in a farmers' market or a fruit and vegetable stand of knowing the path from the farm to the plate—a reminder of how it used to be before machines intervened to harvest, transport, process, package, and widely distribute food. Yet, all things "natural" are also "chemical," and so cannot be taken to be innocuous or, ipso facto, good. A few facts about food chemistry illustrate this point.

Let us imagine a meal composed of natural products as nature has given them to us: carrots and radishes, onions and broccoli, eggs, cheese, an apple, and, for drinking, pure water. Our knowledge of the chemical components of these foods will probably never be absolutely complete, because they contain dozens of different chemicals. Yet knowledge of food chemistry is fairly well-developed, and sufficient to indicate the major chemical constituents in these familiar foods.

Everyone knows that carrots are good, especially for the eyes and for night vision. Also, there has been recent evidence gathered that the beta-carotene provided by carrots is a good scavenger for some of the naturally occurring mutagenic substances in other foods. Less well-known is the fact that carrots contain carotatoxin, a rather strong neurotoxin, whose chemical structure would alarm any toxicologist asked to consider it as a food additive. There are no long-term toxicological studies on carrots, but the acute toxicity and chemical structure of carotatoxin alone are so fearsome that this biochemical would not be at all acceptable as a food additive. Furthermore, carrots also contain myristicin, which can cause hallucinations. There are some incompletely identified substances of the isoflavone group in carrots; these have an estrogenic action, which means that they may mimic the major female sex hormone. One might wish, on all this evidence, to give up carrots.[1]

Radishes present another problem. They contain two substances which can cause goiter: about 2 ounces of radishes are sufficient to have a clinically demonstrable effect on iodine metabolism. Thus, no radishes.

Onions contain some fascinating substances, including the one which brings tears during peeling, but those we might really cry about reside in a complex, ill-smelling mixture of di- and tri-sulfides, which also have a goiter-inducing action. That they also cause bad breath is a problem for others.

Broccoli contains five goiter-inducing substances, two in large amounts. These various chemicals, as well as some goiter-inducing chemicals which the body synthesizes from certain other substances contained in broccoli, interfere with iodine metabolism at five differ- ent points in the biochemical pathway by which iodine is incorporat- ed into the thyroid hormones. So, we should forswear broccoli.

In eggs, let us simply ignore the question of the high cholesterol content of the yolk, and turn instead to the content of Vitamins A and D. Vitamin A presents a dilemma which is as significant as it is peculiar: in experimental animals, either a deficit or an excess of Vitamin A causes fetal deformities. The safety factor for Vitamin A is small, and warrants attention during pregnancy. Excessive con- sumption of Vitamin D can lead to calcification of certain tissues.

Cheese contains a large amount of blood pressure-increasing amines, notably tyramine. For most of us the intake of these amines does not pose a problem, for there is an enzyme system called mono- amine oxidase which attacks these amines, converting them into inactive chemicals which are harmlessly excreted. But certain blood pressure-reducing drugs block the action of monoamine oxidase, which makes the ordinarily harmless consumption of cheese into an occasion of hypertensive crisis.

While an apple a day may keep the doctor away, an interesting chemical in apples is phlorizin, which blocks various enzymes and can interfere with the kidney's reabsorption of glucose, causing sugar in the urine.

Setting aside any question of contaminants or pollutants in water, the toxicity of chemically pure water is clearly established, for excessive water intake is demonstrably fatal.[1]

These examples, while true, are also absurd. It is not our purpose to say that the normal foods which we buy and eat are dangerous— not those mentioned here, and not others. They are nutritious and without evident harm, when they are components of a balanced, varied diet. Some of the properties mentioned above, however, can become the source of health problems if one's diet becomes permanently based on one or two foods.

In the area of pharmaceuticals, the last half-century has seen a move almost altogether away from nature-derived products based on plant and animal extracts. Human-directed synthesis of chemicals has been the basis for most of the major new pharmaceuticals of the past few decades, with the major exception that many of the important antibiotics have been produced by cultures of microorganisms especially selected because of their genetic ability to synthesize the antibiotic. With the most recent developments in the biotechnology of recombinant DNA, it is now possible to modify the genetically directed chemical synthetic machinery of bacteria to synthesize even the most highly complex drug and hormone molecules—ones which have hitherto been technically impossible or uneconomical to make by human-directed synthesis.

Human insulin is the first pharmaceutical synthesized by recombinant DNA technology to have gone through clinical testing and to have entered the market for general medical use. This important advance promises to end the exclusive dependence of the world's insulin supply on the availability of pancreases from slaughtered swine and cattle. It also allows humans to use an insulin preparation which is identical in chemical structure to that secreted by the human pancreas, whereas pork and beef insulins differ enough in chemical structure to create immune reactions in some diabetics. One rather loses track of what is "natural" or "unnatural" in this story.

A major reason for chemical synthesis of pharmaceuticals is to make products which have the best possible definition of purity. The synthetic approach begins with starting materials of defined purity and composition, and proceeds step by step to an end result that can be expected to give a consistently reproducible product—if the starting materials and the steps of the reaction are controlled. Having a chemically reproducible product, batch after batch, is fundamentally important for the biological testing process, in animals and humans. Documentation of the biological and clinical effects of the product can then rest on a secure basis that what is being administered is, within very narrow limits, always the same thing.

Sometimes, the starting material is part of a plant or an animal tissue. Then it is necessary to extract and purify to come to a chemically defined substance of reproducible purity. That substance may be either the drug itself or a chemical intermediate which can be converted by human-directed synthesis into the drug.

In the past, much use was made of medicinals that were made as simple extracts of plants or even as pills compressed from leaves, flowers, roots, or fruit. Such pharmaceuticals are not chemically defined, because they are a happenstance mixture of a usually very complex array of chemicals present in plants that grew in a particular locale in a particular season. A reminder of the variability inherent in such products is the ritual of smelling and tasting a freshly opened bottle of wine, to determine if the wine is acceptable: irrespective of the source and year of its grapes and the reputation of the winemaker, there are times when the wine is "bad."

Besides the difficulties in standardization, there is another problem with chemically undefined medicinals. Modern pharmacological thinking has focussed very strongly on documenting the biological and clinical effects of single chemical compounds. It is a big, expensive, multiyear task to develop the full range of documentation for the use of a single chemical substance as a drug; typically it comprises a hundred or more volumes of information. Documenting the biological and clinical effects of two substances in combination involves not only the separate documentation of each substance, but a third mountain of paper concerning how each influences the actions of the other. Going beyond two substances multiplies the problems so frightfully that only a uniquely valuable therapeutic action is now regarded as justification for registering a new, multi-agent pharmaceutical. A simple plant extract may have a useful therapeutic activity, but it also will typically contain dozens of chemicals.

The branch of pharmacology which studies plant extracts offers some examples of a useful therapeutic action of a crude extract which could never be accounted for in terms of the actions of the major chemical constituents of the plant. It apparently needed a particular combination of substances from among the many present to produce the therapeutic action of the crude extract. Lest this be misinterpreted as some kind of innate natural "goodness" which transcends chemistry, it should be noted that most of the therapeutically important actions found originally in plants and plant extracts have been reduced to a chemical basis. The problems of standardizing a chemically undefined plant extract from batch to batch are formidable, for they have to rely on biological tests, which are inherently quite variable, and so give a rather uncertain measure of product uniformity from batch to batch.

Human-directed synthesis is not without its problems, too, for sometimes residual impurities cannot be avoided, and sometimes these pose toxicity problems, not only in pharmaceuticals but in other man-made chemicals as well. Indeed, it has been an unavoidable contaminant in the process of synthesizing a once widely used herbicide, 2,4,5-T, that has given us much of the dioxin contamination we face today. (The proper chemical name of dioxin is 2,3,7,8-tetrachlorodibenzo-*p*-dioxin, but this substance has become so widely known as dioxin that we shall call it that, even though there is another compound which is, in fact, properly called dioxin.) The story of dioxin is both illustrative and symbolic of the underside of the once-proud slogan of one of the major chemical firms: "better things for better living through chemistry."

Much of the story of dioxin[2] is the story of the herbicide 2,4,5-T, since dioxin was always an unavoidable contaminant, although this fact was not recognized until a decade after 2,4,5-T was introduced in 1948. The unprecedentedly high toxicity of dioxin in certain animal tests was not discovered until 1970. Thus, many years passed before people understood the potential for problems that were lurking in the more or less carefree use of 2,4,5-T. It was used extensively, beginning in 1948, as a weedkiller on rangeland, pastures, rice fields, and in nurseries. Its rapid biodegradability was seen as one of its advantages. During the Vietnam War, it was used until 1970 to defoliate groundcover in various preparations that were sprayed aerially, the best-known being Agent Orange, a 50–50 mixture of 2,4,5-T with another herbicide. The spraying program was terminated due to ecological concerns just as the extreme toxicity of dioxin came to be recognized.

There had been a series of human health problems associated with the production of 2,4,5-T almost from the beginning. In 1949, 1953, and 1956, industrial accidents occurred at plants making the herbicide (along with its yet-unrecognized contaminant, dioxin), and these accidents produced, between them, several hundred cases of a skin condition known as chloracne. The connection of chloracne to dioxin was not made until 1957, by a physician involved in treating workers at a German chemical firm; also in 1957, dioxin was first identified as an unavoidable contaminant in the process of synthesizing 2,4,5-T. It was not until 1970 that animal toxicity tests on dioxin revealed that minute quantities could cause fetal deformities and fetal death; the same year the U.S. Department of Agriculture suspended uses of the 2,4,5-T that would lead to the greatest human exposure. In 1971, the recently founded Environmental Protection Agency (EPA) banned the use of 2,4,5-T on most food crops.

By 1971, however, the production of 2,4,5-T was no longer the only source of dioxin. It was in 1971 that a man with a truck in Missouri began hauling away dioxin-contaminated industrial waste materials, which he sometimes used as a ground-spray for dust control and otherwise disposed of in an undocumented, helter-skelter fashion—an act of human folly that was not to come to light for a decade.

In 1976, a chemical plant in Seveso, near Milan, Italy, exploded, releasing several pounds of dioxin into a densely populated area. There were 134 cases of chloracne among about 500 people treated for possible toxic symptoms. A total of 37,000 people were exposed to dioxin in some amount in this catastrophe, making dioxin a major news item.

In 1978, the EPA began the process of totally banning 2,4,5-T, based on additional toxicity test results showing the ability of dioxin to cause cancers, birth defects, and fetal deaths. The following year the ban went into effect. Also in 1979, a series of legal actions were begun by veterans of the Vietnam War, related to claimed toxic effects consequent to exposure to Agent Orange and other dioxin-contaminated defoliants used during the Vietnam War.

Dioxin-related events have occurred at a brisk pace since 1980. The EPA has moved to require advance notification of disposal of dioxin-contaminated wastes. The FDA has advised people not to eat fish containing 50 parts per trillion dioxin—thereby putting the idea of parts per trillion into the public vocabulary. The haphazard disposal of dioxin-contaminated wastes in Missouri came to light, and with it, the shocking dioxin contamination of the whole town of Times Beach, Missouri, was discovered, leading the EPA to try to purchase the entire town because it was judged uninhabitable.

Meanwhile, dioxin contamination of fish in the area around Midland, Michigan, home of Dow Chemical Company, became an issue. Studies of this problem led to several surprising findings which indicated that the synthetic processes involved in 2,4,5-T production were not the only source of dioxin. Dioxin is a product of various kinds of relatively low-temperature combustion processes, including the usual municipal trash incinerators and, to some small extent, the burning of wood in an ordinary fireplace. In contrast, high-temperature combustion processes, such as industrial incineration processes operating in excess of 1000°C, tend to destroy dioxin already present in waste, and to prevent formation that would occur at lower combustion temperatures. Fish can be another source of dioxin, which may come via fly ash from certain combustion processes. The fly ash apparently gets into streams and thus comes in contact with fish. Fly ash binds dioxin very tightly, and, through an as yet unknown mechanism, some freshwater fish can concentrate dioxin by several thousand-fold from their environment.

Dioxin is one of the most potent man-made toxic substances. In guinea pigs, which is the species most sensitive to dioxin's toxic effects, only three natural substances—diphtheria toxin, tetanus toxin, and botulinus toxin—are more potent killers. The lethal doses of dioxin in other species, however, vary quite widely, with the lethal dose in the hamster being 5000 times more than in the guinea pig. Regardless of these wide differences, however, dioxin is undeniably one of the most toxic substances known, man-made or natural. Studies on rats show that dioxin is about three times more potent as a cancer-causing substance than the fungus-produced natural toxin aflatoxin B_1, which is one of the most potent cancer-causing substances known and probably an occasional natural contaminant of certain foods.

The toxicity of dioxin for man is less clear. Its link to chloracne is established, and about 600 cases are known from the nine industrial accidents that have occurred since 1949, including the one in Seveso. Those who developed chloracne, which occurs promptly after heavy exposure, would appear to be the most heavily exposed of all who have come in contact with dioxin; presumably they are all being closely followed medically. Chloracne is disfiguring, but in most of the cases it has disappeared after a few months, though some severe cases have continued for as long as 15 years. Liver damage has been reported in two of the ongoing studies of exposed people, but people appear to recover normal liver function after several years. There is also evidence for some neurological changes, noted especially among a group of 78 workers at a Czechoslovakian 2,4,5-T plant where continuing leaks during a five-year period in the late 1960's exposed the workers sufficiently to produce chloracne.

As yet, there is no evidence for either unusual types or numbers of cancers in the people who had been exposed to enough dioxin to have developed chloracne. However, a Swedish study has shown a five- to six-fold increase in soft tissue tumors (sarcomas) in people who had used dioxin-contaminated herbicides, compared to people with no such exposure. Dioxin exposure among people using the herbicides would be expected to be of a much smaller degree than in most of the various industrial accidents—unless there was some kind of gross misusage of the herbicides by the people involved in the Swedish study. There are no known instances of chloracne resulting from exposure during herbicide use. Sarcomas are relatively infrequently occurring tumors, a fact which complicates their study. (In fact, a fortunate aspect of their infrequent occurrence is that even a five- to six-fold increase would not suffice to bring them into the top ten causes of death, which, as we have previously discussed, account for about four-fifths of all deaths.) Clearly, further study is needed to clarify the apparent contradictions between this Swedish study and the results to date in the people heavily exposed in industrial accidents, who have not yet shown any unusual numbers or types of tumors, including sarcomas.

There is a big and growing program of surveillance of the people known to have been exposed to dioxin, including the Vietnam War veterans who were exposed during the aerial defoliation program. Here again we meet the unpleasant but inescapable fact of the "experiment of nature." One must decry the fact that people were unwittingly exposed to dioxin, that there have been nine big industrial accidents in the 35-year history of producing dioxin-contaminated chemicals, and that knowledge of its poisonous qualities came after, rather than before, wide use of dioxin-contaminated products. But these are facts, and the tasks now are two: (1) to learn from this series of fiascos how better to anticipate and control the manufacture, use, and disposal of toxic substances; (2) to learn as much as is humanly and ethically possible about the consequences of human exposure.

There are many studies under way, and results will become available during years to come. There will continue to be a great deal of controversy, for several reasons: (1) experiments of nature can never have the degree of control, definition of variables, and precision of information that one has in laboratory experiments; (2) there are many contending economic and political interests in the outcome of the studies. It is a foregone conclusion that some people will, according to their interests, exploit the studies' inevitable ambiguities.

An earlier surge of public concern about mercury contamination of fish faded when it was learned that this undeniably toxic substance had been in the food cycle for centuries. There is some indication that dioxin may have been part of the human environment since the discovery of fire. Yet there can be no doubt about the unprecedented magnitude of the recent, widespread contaminations with industrially produced dioxin. It will probably be another decade before the consequences of these mishaps are reasonably fully understood. Meanwhile, one has the choice of lapsing into "chemophobia" or of maintaining equanimity in the face of the uncertainties that can only be resolved in time—and even then some ambiguities may remain.

In favor of equanimity is the fact that the whole dioxin fiasco developed, not in a vacuum, but in an era of rapid development of knowledge and increasing sophistication in the uses and abuses of potent chemicals—of both natural and synthetic origin. One might characterize this development of understanding as a progressive shedding of naïveté about the hazardous side of chemicals with beneficial actions—in human and veterinary medicine, agriculture, industry, construction, food processing and packaging, and in the food we eat. We have learned a great deal during the past few decades, and, in relation to the benefits we have gained, it would appear that the "tuition" we have paid in terms of adverse consequences has so far been very small. But the information is often too complex to fit the journalistic format, which so dominates the way information is communicated today.

If "chemical" continues to be a codeword for "poison," and if "chemophobia" dominates the public discussion of these often difficult and complex problems, we gain nothing and lose much, because, in the final analysis, things chemical do not have an existence separate and apart from things "natural." The most potent toxic substances still come from the domain of the "natural"—botulinus toxin, diphtheria toxin, tetanus toxin, aflatoxin B_1, and a host of others. These could be grounds for a "naturephobia" for those who wish to indulge, but it is more useful, perhaps, to recall some of the germ phobias of our great-grandparents and grandparents. These phobias had their roots in realistic concerns, which persist today because germs and other micro-organisms still kill people and cause all kinds of diseases. We have, however, evolved a whole technology for contending with micro-organisms, and we have four generations of experience in living with them. Chemicals made by human-directed synthesis have figured large in human life for only about a generation and a half. As a society, we have not yet fully come to terms with that fact—perhaps a bit like the Turks with their automobiles, as we saw in Table 1 of Chapter 5.

The beginnings of adverse change in public perception of "chemistry" and "technology" occurred with the revelations in the early 1960's about the adverse ecological effects of widespread DDT use. Rachel Carson's widely read book, *Silent Spring,*[3] appeared in 1962 —the same year that the thalidomide disaster came to light—and brought the problems with DDT use to broad public attention. These two landmark events made 1962 a watershed year for public opinion about technology-related risk.

At the beginning of DDT's use, only its many advantages were seen, and they were responsible for a Nobel Prize in 1948 for its discoverer, the Swiss chemist Paul Muller. DDT introduced a new technology of insect control: the synthesis of a specific chemical which was capable of acting as a selective poison for insects, while being—it was believed—free of toxicity for man and other animals. In this sense, DDT was analogous to a drug, which is expected to act selectively on the disease process while not interfering with the normal functions of the body. DDT was the first of many insecticides created by human-directed chemical synthesis.

After World War II, DDT was rapidly put into effective use throughout the world, notably against the mosquitoes which spread malaria. On a worldwide basis, malaria was probably among the top five causes of human death prior to the advent of DDT—although the numbers are somewhat vague because the countries with the biggest malaria problems also provided the least reliable data on mortality and causes of death.

By 1960, however, it had become evident that DDT was remaining for long periods of time in water and in the ground, and that it was being concentrated in the tissues of a number of kinds of birds and fish, with toxic consequences and the death of many of these animals. Carson's book painted a heart-rending picture, and contributed directly to the complete ban of DDT in the United States after her book appeared.

Malaria had not been present in the United States since the first decades of this century, long before the advent of DDT. Malaria had been eradicated by the laborious processes of land drainage and other pre-insecticide means of mosquito control, as well as by case-finding and quarantine of malaria victims. Consequently, when DDT was banned, there was no resurgence of malaria in the United States. That was not the case in other countries—for example, Sri Lanka, where DDT had been responsible for mosquito control and a drastic reduction in both sickness and mortality from malaria. Unfortunately for the people of Sri Lanka, their government opted to follow the Americans in banning DDT, whereupon sickness and deaths from malaria promptly rose substantially.[4]

The history of DDT shows not only another example of belated recognition of adverse consequences of an agent with obvious benefits; it also shows how the balance of risks and benefits is not the same in one place as another. Just as there are sometimes dangerous and difficult-to-foresee consequences of introducing a new technology, there may sometimes be dangerous and difficult-to-foresee consequences of abandoning a technology that has already found a niche in the environment of a country or region.

Closer to home are two different, difficult, and currently controversial examples of the same problem of balancing benefit and risk. These are the two economically important substances, asbestos and formaldehyde.

Asbestos

Asbestos designates a group of materials which have a long history of use in the construction industries, including piping for water and sewer lines, and the fabrication of flooring, roofing, and insulation materials. Asbestos is also an important, essentially irreplaceable material in brake linings for cars and trucks.

The health problems caused by asbestos are related almost altogether to inhalation by workers in the asbestos industry of asbestos fibers suspended in air.[5] There are three major diseases related to asbestos: (1) fibrosis of the lung, called asbestosis; (2) cancer of the lung—the same type caused by cigarette smoking; and (3) an unusual, malignant tumor of the lining of the lung's surface, called mesothelioma. In each instance, however, many years have to pass before the disease becomes apparent; hence, a disease being identified today is the result of exposure to asbestos which was inhaled 20–40 years ago. Exposure does not have to be constant, for there are many documented instances of asbestos-related disease appearing 20 or more years later, without apparent exposure in the interim.

Hence the triad of asbestos-related diseases is another "time bomb," and the long delay between exposure and the appearance of disease poses two special problems: (1) the full magnitude of the epidemic is not known, for there may be many more cases "incubating" than one can now know; (2) today's and tomorrow's diseases relate to the industrial practices of many years ago—the type of asbestos used, the methods of working with the materials, and the standards and procedures in use to minimize inhalation of fibers. In the United States, industrial use of asbestos accelerated markedly during World War II, but mainly with a type of asbestos which is little used today. It appears that much of the asbestos-related disease appearing today is related to manufacturing practices of the 1940's that are no longer in use today. That is one peculiarity of today's asbestos problem.

A second peculiarity is that one of the three asbestos-related diseases, bronchogenic carcinoma of the lung, is almost entirely limited to cigarette smokers. This cancer is the same "lung cancer" whose risk of occurrence is multiplied about 15 times among cigarette smokers, unrelated to asbestos exposure. In asbestos workers who smoke, the risk of developing bronchogenic carcinoma of the lung is 80–90 times greater than among people who neither smoke nor work in the asbestos industry. The added risk for nonsmoking asbestos workers to acquire this cancer is only 2–3 times greater than the low risk prevailing among people who neither smoke nor have ever worked with asbestos. It appears that inhaled asbestos fibers strongly synergize with inhaled cigarette smoke in causing lung cancer.

In asbestos workers who also smoke cigarettes, lung cancer incidence is increased to the point of causing 35–40% of all deaths, so that it rivals heart disease for being the leading cause of death. Asbestos workers who smoke appear to have an overall mortality which is three times higher than that among nonsmoking asbestos workers—a risk concentration of 0.5 SDU; smokers who never worked in the asbestos industries have an overall mortality which is 1.5–2 times higher than that among asbestos workers who never smoked—a risk concentration of 0.2 or 0.3 SDU. Thus, cigarette smoking is a risk-amplifier for asbestos, and vice versa. Among nonsmokers, asbestos-induced disease appears to concentrate the risk of premature death by 10% (0.04 SDU).

The other type of lung tumor caused by asbestos, mesothelioma, appears to be unrelated to smoking. This is a tumor that very rarely occurs other than in former asbestos workers. Indeed, it was the appearance of this tumor in substantial numbers which aroused suspicions and led to the systematic studies that showed the association between previous asbestos work and subsequent development of both mesothelioma and bronchogenic carcinoma of the lung. Mesothelioma is much the less frequently occurring of the two cancers: it appears that 2–3% of those who had worked with asbestos during the 1940's and 1950's are destined to develop a mesothelioma, and possibly as many as 10%. It is a malignant tumor with little prospect of cure.

A big unknown is whether today's practices in the asbestos industry are still liable to produce mesotheliomas 20–30 years hence in today's workers. No one knows, but two changes have occurred in recent years: (1) the industry has shifted almost entirely from the type of asbestos fiber then in use—the shift having been dictated by market forces, not by health considerations; (2) the establishment of much stricter particle inhalation standards and the mandatory use of inhalation masks may have reduced or altogether avoided the problem. No one can know for another two or three decades.

Optimism was high in the 1930's that the particle-inhalation standards put in place then would prevent future problems. Indeed, these standards did have a major impact on pulmonary fibrosis (asbestosis). This condition is not a tumor but a nevertheless ultimately fatal condition in which there is a gradual impairment of lung function, with progressively more severe shortness of breath and limitation of oxygen supply to the body. Yet while those first standards for inhaled particles largely did away with asbestosis, they failed to prevent subsequent development of mesotheliomas and bronchogenic carcinomas. Today's standards are ten-fold more stringent than those of the 1930's, but it is not known whether they will suffice to prevent the cancers.

Experimental studies in animals have been carried out, but are felt by many experts not to be very informative, because of basic differences in the way inhaled fibers are transported to the furthest and finest branches of the bronchial tubes. That transport process depends on factors in humans which are not readily mimicked in experimental animals.

Is there enough evidence to warrant a wholesale ban on asbestos products? If there were economically available alternatives, the answer might be yes. However, there are none.

To conclude this brief summary of a very complex field, it appears that, without stringent safeguards to minimize the inhalation of asbestos fibers during mining and manufacturing, the various forms of asbestos are major health hazards. The combination of a shift to the least dangerous form of asbestos, plus the imposition of strict controls on worker exposure to inhaled asbestos particles, may or may not have dealt satisfactorily with the problems. Smoking amplifies the risk of asbestos exposure very considerably. The asbestos industry is beset with lawsuits and uncertainty, all of which creates increasing opportunity for other materials which might substitute for asbestos, though one should recognize that merely being "not asbestos" will not absolve new materials from being possible hazards in their own right.

It is estimated that about 8500 people in the United States will die of asbestos-related disease between now and the end of this century,[6] assuming that currently available methods of treating mesothelioma and bronchogenic carcinoma of the lung do not improve. These 8500 deaths are projected on the basis of what is known about the numbers of people already exposed and risks determined from already-developed disease. To put this number in perspective, it corresponds to about two months' traffic fatalities, four months' traffic fatalities due to drunk driving, and about one week's premature deaths caused by cigarette smoking. It is about one-third more deaths than can be expected between now and the end of the century due to crashes of commercial airliners.

These body count comparisons do not alter the facts about asbestos, the problems it has already caused, and those that may arise from even the latest developments in industrial practice. They may, however, help keep a sense of order in social priorities and concerns and in determining how they might best be translated into political action.

Asbestos represents an old technology. Some of its former uses have been abandoned or have found better substitutes. Perhaps less hazardous new materials will be found that can substitute in some or all of the remaining uses of asbestos. Perhaps the recent technological improvements in asbestos-related work have diluted the risk of working with asbestos to the level of other industrial jobs. These, of course, are technological solutions which "technophobia" would obstruct.

Formaldehyde

While the evidence about the risks of asbestos comes from observations on humans, the possibly adverse effects of formaldehyde are based on extrapolations from test data on laboratory animals. Annual tonnage production of formaldehyde is about ten times that of asbestos, and formaldehyde is the 26th largest volume chemical produced in the United States. Like asbestos, its economic importance is based on "invisible" uses in a wide variety of products: building materials, polymers, resins, leather, fabrics, preservatives, embalming fluid, drugs, and cosmetics. Its use is basic, for example, in the manufacture of "permanent press" fabrics. It is also a constituent of certain kinds of industrially polluted air, and some foam insulation materials used in home construction today have turned out to release formaldehyde slowly into the air within the home. Thus, formaldehyde's potential toxicity may not be limited to the workplace.

While formaldehyde has always been recognized as a poisonous substance of relatively low potency, the new concern arises from a recently concluded study on laboratory rats which had been exposed for 30 months to various concentrations of formaldehyde in the air they breathed for 6 hours a day, 5 days a week.[7] Some of the rats developed cancers in the nasal passages, the incidence being related to the concentration of formaldehyde in their air supply. Similarly exposed mice, on the other hand, did not develop the tumors. The study was published in 1980 and has caused a great deal of controversy about what, if anything, should be done to regulate the industrial uses of formaldehyde.[8] It is likely that the animal studies will be repeated and expanded in scope, and will stimulate renewed controversy as their results become available.

The long history of formaldehyde's industrial uses has not, however, produced reports of unusual tumors or other diseases among workers in the formaldehyde-based industries. Cancer of the nasal passages does occur in humans, but very rarely. It would be noticeable fairly promptly if it began to appear in unusual numbers in certain locales, for there is an ongoing surveillance of the incidence of all forms of malignant tumors. So at present, the available evidence for formaldehyde's carcinogenicity comes from one species of test animal, with negative results in the second animal species tested, and no supporting evidence as yet from humans.

The regulatory policies relating to the animal test data on formaldehyde are currently undergoing change. Since 1962, when major public attention began to be paid to environmental, workplace, and medical hazards, public policy has evolved toward the position that a substance would be officially regarded as carcinogenic in humans if it had been shown to cause cancer in experimental animals. Because of this policy, there was every expectation that the Occupational Safety and Health Administration (OSHA) would begin to take regulatory action to limit human exposure to formaldehyde in the workplace; moreover, it was also expected that regulatory action to limit formaldehyde levels in the air would be initiated by the EPA, which is charged with maintaining standards for environmental levels of toxic substances. A possible regulatory action, for example, might be to limit or ban altogether the use of formaldehyde-based insulation products; other actions could involve imposition of strict standards for the amounts and concentrations in air to which workers using formaldehyde were exposed. Such regulatory actions would have been consistent with the policies which developed from 1962 onwards. However, the Reagan administration has taken a new approach: neither OSHA nor EPA took regulatory action, on the grounds that there is no evidence that formaldehyde poses any threat to human health. This view appears to contradict an earlier OSHA view that results in animal studies would be used to establish the carcinogenic hazard to workers.

This new policy has prompted strong protests from individuals and groups which had played leading roles in forming the previous policy of minimizing potential human health risks as opposed to waiting until actual human health risks were evident. The new policy appears to be aimed at avoiding economic dislocations except when there is clear evidence of a human health hazard. One might characterize the two views as the "what if" versus the "what is" approach to health hazards.

For reasons we have already discussed, the "what is" method is really based on "what just was," for one has to count the toll of death and disease in order to develop clear evidence of a human health hazard.

Results from animal studies always require interpretation in order to place them in a context that makes them relevant to humans. In the case of the formaldehyde inhalation studies, the concentrations at which tumors developed in the rats were sufficiently high to be grossly repellent to anyone asked to breathe them. Also, until the studies are repeated, there remains the question of whether there was a concomitant viral infection of the nasal passages in the rats that might have played some synergistic role with formaldehyde in tumor induction.

Given the uncertainty of a potential toxicity problem in man, plus the lack of direct evidence for toxicity in workers from the formaldehyde-using industries, plus the economic dislocations of major regulatory actions, it appears to have been a proper decision to withhold action pending more compelling data.

Regulatory Dilemmas

The success or failure of the new policy will depend on the seriousness of purpose and care which is invested in identifying health hazards in advance of events which could be construed by the news media as catastrophes. The headlines are already written: BOSSES GET PROFITS; WORKERS GET CANCER!!! However, the economic consequences of costly regulations arc real, but never dramatic—price differences in pipe are not at all exciting and those losing jobs in the affected industry quietly join the ranks of the unemployed. To see the whole matter in the broadest perspective, one has to tally up the adverse health effects which follow from the frustration and stress of being unemployed. That problem is certainly far less dramatic than is a crusade against the exploitation of unwitting workers by greedy bosses, but recent work shows the relative increase in mortality due to cardiovascular diseases, suicide, and cirrhosis in the unemployed.[9] Thus, there may be both adverse health and economic consequences of regulations imposed in the name of reducing risks to human health. This subject is yet too new to have been widely analyzed and understood—as perusal of the various papers included in note 9 will indicate—but it can be expected to force people to look more broadly at the problems involved in regulating a hazardous industry, instead of concentrating only on the problems presented by the immediate victims.

To some, the prospect of basing corrective actions only on "body counts" is anathema. To others, the prospect of taking costly regulatory action on the basis of indirect and possibly misleading evidence amounts to squandering hard-won resources. In this clash of philosophies, it is useful to note that human progress has been built on adventurous, risk-taking behavior, with "what is" being in the ascendancy, not the "what if" of speculative, a priori analysis. Adventurous risk-taking has been the mainspring of the technological progress and economic strength that have brought the West to its current state of wealth, with unprecedentedly long and healthy lives for the vast majority of its people. At the same time, however, we have accumulated technologies of unprecedented power to do harm, so naive faith in progress and quick technological fixes is probably as harmful as "technophobia."

Nuclear "Technophobia"

Probably the supreme example of "technophobia" in contemporary life is the great controversy over the generation of electrical power by controlled nuclear fission. So many facets of this complex industry have been brought into public discussion that the subject requires a book in its own right, but a few aspects of the matter are worth examining from the perspectives we have tried to develop in this book.

The accumulated experience with commercial nuclear power dates back to 1957, when the first nuclear power plant went into service, although it is proper to include the technological experience with nuclear-powered naval vessels in any reckoning of the total human experience with power production by controlled nuclear fission. There are now several hundred nuclear-powered electric generating stations in service throughout the world, most of which started up during the 1970's. The industry's accident record is superior to that of the fossil-fueled power-generating industry, which is itself a low-risk industry.

Most of the fatalities associated with the fossil-fueled power industry come from accidents associated with coal mining—which is one of the highest-risk industries—and coal transport. It is well to recall that it takes about 100 rail cars of coal per day to fuel the largest of the fossil-fueled power plants. Indeed, coal-fired electric power plants account for 69% of U.S. coal production,[10] and 16% of U.S. rail freight-car loadings.[11] From these numbers, one could say that 69% of the 150 average annual number of deaths in coal mining accidents[12] are part of the cost of coal-fired power generation, i.e. slightly over 100 deaths per year. By the same kind of reckoning, 16% of the 1090 average number of accidental deaths at railroad grade crossings[13] are part of the cost of coal-fired power generation, i.e. about 175 deaths per year. Thus, there are over 300 deaths per year attributable to the use of coal in electric power generation. There are none in over 25 years attributable to the use of nuclear energy in electrical power generation.

About 12% of U.S. electric power generation is fueled by oil.[14] At even that low percentage, however, oil used in electric power generation is equivalent to one-fifth of the amount of oil the United States imports.[15] Thus, increasing the use of oil is unlikely for economic reasons. Nuclear power generation also currently accounts for about 12% of the total U.S. power generation.

The recent identification of coal-fired power generation as a major contributor to the increasingly severe acid rain problem is a new element in the risk-benefit calculation about fossil-fueled versus nuclear power. There is also an unresolved question about the extent to which the large volumes of carbon dioxide produced in the combustion of fossil fuels threatens to trap more heat in the earth's atmosphere, resulting in unforeseeable long-term climatic changes, the melting of some of the polar ice caps, and changes in ocean level.

On the other hand, there are certain troubling aspects about nuclear power, probably the most bothersome of which is whether it is truly possible to maintain absolute controls on the movement and fate of nuclear fuels, their byproducts, and their wastes. Many worry about the prospect of these materials being diverted into malevolent hands for the production of nuclear weapons, but the conversion of the fuels or their wastes to weapons-grade fissionable material requires the immense and special capabilities of a nation which is already in the nuclear weapons "club." Indeed, recurring confusion and misunderstanding about the vast differences between nuclear weapons and nuclear power generation underlie much of the public controversy about nuclear power. One has to understand this distinction in order to balance the foreseeable problems and costs of nuclear power against the increasingly less hidden consequences and costs of continuing to rely so heavily on fossil fuels for power generation. The modest conservation steps taken during the past few years have only slightly alleviated the problems, which pose a hard dilemma. However, the fatalities, acid rain, and carbon dioxide costs of coal are strong psychotherapy for nuclear technophobia. But no psychotherapy works if people cherish their phobias.

Looking Back

It is a puzzling paradox that, throughout the period of transition from short to long life expectancy, health-related issues were near the bottom of the social priority list. One sees in the industrial health controversies of most of the past 80 years a history of public and industry indifference, denial, and delay concerning the hazards of workplaces and products; people paid very close attention to what did and did not pay off in the economic sphere, but they largely ignored or denied the health consequences. However, just about the time that premature death had been substantially reduced and life became unprecedentedly less risky, there occurred a marked shift in public attitudes about workplace and product hazards; since 1962, governments have been impelled into increasing action to correct the historic imbalance between economic and health priorities. We seem now to be at a point of pause and assessment, after 20 years of rapid growth in regulation focussed on health priorities.

Intelligent regulation is itself a high-technology undertaking, for it depends upon the most advanced analytical techniques of chemistry and physics, diagnostic techniques of medicine, and computerized data processing and analysis. Probably the weakest link in the technological chain is our imperfect ability to do long-term epidemiological studies on various groups of people—an area which needs more research and better public understanding. But regulation is also a highly politicized undertaking that proceeds in periodic bursts of media-generated publicity, forcing complicated issues into the journalistic format of brief, victim-oriented reports. It takes a certain steeliness of mind in that environment not to lapse into chemo- or technophobia. Our hope is that the concept of comparing quantitatively defined risks of various contemporary hazards will improve the quality of public information and give a realistic balance to people's understanding of "natural," "chemical," "technological," and "nuclear."

NOTES TO CHAPTER 8

1. Hall, R.L. "Safe at the plate." *Nutrition Today* 12 (1977): 1–9.

2. "Dioxin." *Chemical & Engineering News; Special Issue.* June 6, 1983.

3. Carson, R. *Silent Spring.* Harmondsworth: Penguin Books, 1965.

4. Rothschild, Lord. "Risk. The Richard Dimbleby Lecture." *The Listener,* November 20, 1978.

5. Craighead, J.E., and B.T. Mossman. "The pathogenesis of asbestos-associated diseases." *New Eng. J. Med.* 306 (1982): 1446–55.

6. Editorial: "How to end the asbestos nightmare." *New York Times,* August 27, 1982.

7. Swenberg, J.A., et al. "Induction of squamous cell carcinomas of the rat nasal cavity by inhalation exposure to formaldehyde vapor." *Cancer Res.* 40 (1980): 3398–3402.

8. Smith, R.J. "OSHA shifts direction on health standards." *Science* 212 (1981): 1482–83; FDA Talk Paper, T 82-40. "Formaldehyde," June 17, 1982; Perera, F., and C. Petito. "Formaldehyde: a question of cancer policy." *Science* 216 (1982): 1285–91.

9. Draper, P., et al. "Micro-processors, macro-economic policy, and public health." *Lancet* 1 (1979): 373–75; Editorial. "Does unemployment kill?" *Lancet* 1 (1979): 708–9; Brenner, M.H. "Mortality and the national economy. A review, and the experience of England and Wales, 1936–76." *Lancet* 2 (1979): 568–73; Editorial. "Health consequences of redundancy." *Lancet* 1 (1981): 903; Gravelle, H.S.E., E. Hutchison, and J. Stern. "Mortality and unemployment: a critique of Brenner's time-series analysis." *Lancet* 2 (1981): 675–79; Brenner, M.H. "Unemployment and health." *Lancet* 2 (1981): 874–75; Rees, W.L. "Editorial. Medical aspects of unemployment." *Brit. Med. J.* 283 (1981): 1630–31; Frey, J.J. "Unemployment and health in the United States." *Brit. Med. J.* 284 (1982): 1112–13.

10. U.S. Bureau of the Census, *Statistical Abstract of the United States, 1981.* Tables 1011, 1332.

11. Ibid. Table 1117.

12. Ibid. Table 1310.

13. Ibid. Table 1112.

14. Ibid. Table 1011.

15. Ibid. Table 1005.

9

Life Is an Experiment

At the beginning of this book we posed five questions that the book would seek to answer: (1) how should risk be measured and expressed so as to permit distinction between big risks and small ones? (2) how can measured risk be related to a realistic conception of safety, quantitatively defined, and appropriate for balanced judgments of risk versus benefit in today's world? (3) what are the major risks of premature death in contemporary life? (4) how has the risk of premature death in the technologically developed countries changed within the past three generations, and how can these risks be projected to change in the future? (5) how does "victim-oriented" reporting by the news media distort the public perception of risk, and how could this be effectively changed?

The Safety-degree Scale answers the first two questions, as numerous examples have illustrated. The Scale runs from 0, when there is absolute certainty of death or other harm, to 8, when risk is so dilute as to be near, or just beyond, the limit of measurement by any of the available methods. Recall that 8 on the Safety-degree Scale means 1 adverse event occurring in 100,000,000 people—1 followed by 8 zeros—in a certain time period. That figure corresponds to half the population of the United States, so that the occurrence of one or two distinct adverse events could theoretically be detected at about the 8 SDU level through the U.S. data-collecting systems. If reliable data collection systems were put in place on an international basis, or in several of the largest countries whose populations together approach a billion, the Safety-degree Scale could go to 9—because 1 billion is 1 followed by 9 zeros. The essential point is that there is no upper limit on safety-degree, just as there is no such thing as absolute "safety." Instead, there are only progressively greater degrees of risk dilution, the measure of which involves the time-consuming and usually tedious process of counting not only the victims but also the nonvictims who appear to share the same exposure to risk as the victims.

Therein lies the answer to the fifth question, about "victim-oriented" reporting: understanding the magnitude of risk, or the degree of safety, of any human action does not come until there is reliable information about the numbers of both victims and nonvictims. Only then can the degree of safety be estimated. Just as an informed public demands to know the Richter number before reacting to the news of an earthquake, so an informed public should demand to have the best estimate available of both victims and nonvictims. Unfortunately, there is no special instrument, akin to the seismograph, to give an instant readout on safety-degree. There are, however, ways to make initial estimates of the numbers of nonvictims, using the tremendous wealth of data that come from the U.S. census and various other data collection systems such as the public health and traffic accident reporting networks—plus the rapid access to such data that computers provide. If and when an informed public demands such information, we shall see TV stations having epidemiologists as well as meteorologists on their staffs.

This is not to say that the local TV epidemiologist, sitting at the computer, can provide instantaneous, scientifically accurate answers to all risk questions in time for the 11 o'clock news. There is a process for answering risk questions, as we have illustrated in providing answers to the third and fourth questions we posed at the outset. The evolution of the top ten causes of death since 1900 occurred slowly enough, but in three generations it has resulted in a dramatic transformation of human life. The risk picture, once completely dominated by infectious diseases, is now dominated by risk factors relating to chronic diseases. These changes have brought the risk of premature death to an all-time low—a fact that is frequently obscured by a vocal minority who loudly proclaim the horrors and risks of modern technology and industrialization. But the facts are that we have traded in big risks for small ones over the past three generations, drastically reducing the risk of premature death but not altering the fact that everyone ultimately dies. For unclear reasons, many people's risk-consciousness has grown concomitantly during this period when the risk of premature death has fallen rapidly, with the paradoxical result that risk has declined greatly but fear has remained, or perhaps even increased from the times when a tenth of all babies died and most people died before age 50.

Medical progress has not changed the fact that just a few diseases account for a substantial majority of deaths. This fact can readily form the basis for the illusion that "killer diseases are stalking the land," as the McGovern Committee put it. Would it be any better if there were no leading causes of death, and each of the thousand recognized causes of death was responsible for precisely 0.1% of the deaths?

It seems that medical progress has succeeded in postponing premature death to a point that approaches the limits of human longevity. If that is so, then we may be nearing the time when future changes in the leading causes of death will have relatively little impact on longevity, and the critical questions will focus on the quality of the last years of life. There are valid grounds for real concern about the quality of one's last few years, and this is an area that can be expected to receive increasing attention from the public and medical researchers alike.

There is now a tremendous concentration of effort and recently gained know-how aimed at analyzing human life as an experiment, in order to attack the chronic diseases that dominate today's risks to life and health. More of that know-how now needs to "go public" in a systematic and effective way, to improve the reporting of risk-related events. Risk analysis can command public attention, just as technically complex weather reporting and forecasting have been transformed into public events by the satellite pictures, a vast information network, and rapid data processing. The Safety-degree Scale is put forward as a step in this direction, because it simplifies the comparison of risks and allows people to understand new events in the context of other risks in life. With the simple scheme of converting SDU into insurance premiums shown in Appendix A, you can translate risk into economic terms. You can then compare the cost of single-hazard insurance with the insurance cost created by all of the risks that go together to threaten your life at your present age. That comparison gives a useful perspective on how the risk posed by some new hazard relates to the risks that are already a part of your life. Making that comparison is a good antidote to anxiety and fear created by the latest scare stories.

The examples of well-analyzed risk in previous chapters give force to the idea that, indeed, life is a whole series of experiments in which the participants accept large or small risks, sometimes voluntarily but usually involuntarily and unwittingly. Almost all of these experiments go unnoticed and so are unrecorded. Their outcomes, however, sometimes do get recorded, provided the outcome is something that society has organized to record. Also, it is sometimes possible to piece together interpretable information about these experiments after the fact, especially when something really unusual turns up—for example, the very rare vaginal tumors in daughters of the women treated during pregnancy with DES, or the previously very rare mesotheliomas that have shown up in former asbestos workers. In both of these "time bomb" conditions, astute recognition of an apparent increase in a very unusual disease led to a systematic investigation that turned up a great deal more information and allowed interpretation of the "experiments" that had preceded these unfortunate outcomes. Clustering of hitherto exceptionally rare events is a fairly definite red flag that something new is happening, but it still requires unusually observant and thoughtful people to see beyond the individual patient to recognize an underlying trend.

However, while changes in these very rare conditions may be fairly readily recognized, they generally represent very dilute risks. Changes in common conditions—reflecting concentrated risks—are difficult for the individual physician to detect because the frequency of their everyday occurrence tends to camouflage change. Thus, detecting these big changes usually requires some kind of central data collection and analysis. Physicians, after all, treat patients one at a time: it is the extra dimension provided by epidemiology that leads a physician to consider patients in groups, to identify factors the victims share that set them apart from most nonvictims. It is an unusual physician who combines individual patient care with an epidemiologic perspective.

There is growing recognition that epidemiology—the science of recognizing and studying these "experiments of nature"—is one of the best ways we have to defend ourselves against hazards that have not been foreseen. Yet some of the examples we have discussed illustrate the fact that epidemiology is not held in very high esteem as a science, and that the kind of evidence it produces is often seen as weak and unconvincing. That was one of the main reasons for the many-year controversy about whether cause or coincidence linked lung cancer to cigarette smoking. The detailed mechanisms of the causal link are still not clearly defined, but that relative ignorance does not obviate the very concentrated risk of smoking nor the fairly rapid dilution of risk to the nonsmokers' level after cessation of smoking. The logic of the studies on smoking is the same as that used by John Snow to prove the water-borne transmission of cholera: retrospective studies prompted a theory, which was subject to a crucial test and confirmed in prospective studies on people who, for their own reasons, did or did not indulge in the activity thought—and then proved—to be causal.

Sometimes it is confusing, however, to try to reconcile the evidence from epidemiological studies with the fact that the majority of people exposed to the risk factor do not become victims, and that some victims appear never to have been exposed to the risk factor. This was evident in Snow's work on cholera: the vast majority who lived in houses served by Southwark & Vauxhall did not get cholera, for all kinds of reasons that undoubtedly would still defy precise explanation, for cholera behaves in some still-mysterious ways that all the accumulated knowledge in the intervening 130 years has not completely accounted for. Also, we have seen that some nonsmokers develop lung cancer, and that a narrow majority of smokers die of diseases unrelated to smoking. Even in the laboratory study of infectious diseases, where one sometimes seeks purposefully to establish a bacterial infection in experimental animals, it is usually necessary to go to extreme lengths to insure that a high percentage of inoculated animals develop the infection, and even so infection rates may not reach 100%. Even the worst epidemics invariably spare some people, for unknown reasons.

These facts serve as a reminder that disease transmission is complex. Nevertheless, it can usually be reasonably well understood in a very practical way from well-designed epidemiological studies, provided the right questions are asked. Good epidemiological studies can provide practical benefits even though there is an incomplete understanding of all the mechanisms involved—and sometimes no knowledge at all about specific bacterial, viral, chemical, or other causative agents. After all, it was deduced that sailors could prevent scurvy by eating citrus fruits long before vitamin C was discovered, and vaccination prevented smallpox long before the viruses of cow-pox and of smallpox were discovered. Sometimes laboratory science follows, and sometimes it leads, the discovery of practical steps which prevent disease and postpone death.

There is currently a considerable expansion in epidemiological studies. The biggest one of all time has just gotten under way, spon-sored by the American Cancer Society (ACS), as we noted in Chap-ter 3. The biggest concern about the ACS program is whether it asks the right questions. Recall the big multiyear British study by the Royal College of General Practitioners on oral contraceptives, in which each woman was asked about whether she smoked only at the beginning but never afterward. When that study was designed, smok-ing was not suspected to be a very important factor. Obviously, if there had been no questions asked at all about smoking, the study would have missed identifying the big contribution which smoking makes to the risk of oral contraceptive use. By asking about smoking only at the beginning of the study, it was not possible to identify those who started or stopped smoking thereafter, and so the RCGP study has probably underestimated the concentration of risk which smoking brings to oral contraceptive use. Of course, there are thou-sands of possible questions the RCGP study could have asked but didn't. Its main thrust was to measure the risk of oral contraceptive use and to ascertain if there were differences in risk associated with different pill strengths, which were in fact found and have led to a reduction in estrogen content. The identification of age- and smok-ing-related risks of pill use was an additional but unforeseen outcome of the study. One can only hope that the ACS study is designed well enough to reveal presently unsuspected causal relations.

Only time will tell whether the ACS questionnaire has been astute-ly designed, but it seems a useful and constructive step in basic fact-finding, which ought to give valuable new information. It may also serve to heighten public awareness of the "experiment of nature" aspect of life and to encourage a sense of social obligation about self-monitoring and recording information on the experiments of nature in which we all participate.

This social obligation falls on physicians as they witness big experiments of nature that occur each time a new drug is introduced into medical practice. Chapter 6 described the "number gap" between the number of patients in the largest practical clinical trials of new drugs and the much larger number of patients needed to reveal the full range and incidence of adverse reactions to a new drug. There is a very low efficiency in gathering information about newly introduced drugs, even during the first several years of use before the "number gap" closes.

The British have developed what is probably the best system yet for monitoring adverse reactions to drugs used in everyday medical practice: doctors are asked and periodically reminded to return such information on a simple form known as the "yellow card," a simple, postpaid form. Despite a substantial effort to make the yellow card system efficient, however, only about 5% of the adverse reactions to recently introduced drugs are reported by British physicians.[1] American physicians can report adverse reactions to the FDA, but the process is more complex than in Britain, and American doctors have not been so persistently reminded about doing so. Thus, efficiency in the reporting of adverse reactions in the United States is undoubtedly far lower than the disappointing 5% figure the British have achieved. Low efficiency in reporting adverse drug reactions effectively makes the "number gap" many times bigger than it needs to be to define the nature and risk of adverse drug reactions. Naturally, physicians have many more things to do—including many other forms to complete—besides filling out yellow cards or FDA forms, and in patients with multiple diseases, taking multiple drugs, it is often unclear which drug—if any—is responsible for what. Nevertheless, we should be able to have a more efficient monitoring of the first few years' use of new drugs.

The answer is not bigger clinical trials, for that would only further retard the flow of new drugs into general medical use. As we have seen, there is a curious type of blinkered vision in the politics of drug regulation that keeps all eyes focussed on relatively small numbers of adverse reactions to drugs, while ignoring the sometimes very large numbers of deaths and other human problems which are allowed to persist because of bureaucratic delays in bringing a new drug to the market—the ONURONE phenomenon. There once was a great sense of urgency to bring the first insulin and the first penicillin to the bedside, based on the recognition that every lost day meant needless suffering and death. That sense of urgency appears to have been regulated into oblivion as the whole process of drug research, testing, and regulatory reviewing has become bureaucratic, and dominated much more by concerns for the risks than desire for the benefits of new drugs.

We illustrated the cost of bureaucratic delay with an example of a new use for beta blocker drugs that the FDA estimated would save 17,000 lives per year by preventing heart attacks. FDA action did not come until seven years after the first published studies on this matter, and five years after the Swedish regulatory authority approved the new use. This single, five-year delay was responsible for more deaths —and probably for some comparably large number of people with cardiac disability—than all of the known drug-induced disasters of modern times. Thus, there are sins of omission as well as of commission in the drug regulatory process; the omissions appear to do much more harm than the commissions, but we totally ignore the bigger mischief and launch big witchhunts about the smaller one.

We silently pay a big price for always harping about making drug regulations ever tighter so as to give the greatest possible assurance that there will be the fewest possible unsuspected adverse reactions or deaths. Ever tighter regulations mean ever longer and more costly studies before a new drug can be made generally available. It would be better if we did three things: (1) improve the surveillance of drugs after they enter the market, where the numbers of people using the drug are large enough to define drug safety-degree to the dilute levels of risk that society likes to demand and that cannot be even remotely approached in clinical trials required before market entry; (2) loosen the requirements for testing before market entry; (3) analyze and publish the health and mortality consequences of nontreatment during the time that elapses between the first proof of effectiveness of a new drug and its market entry.

Yet, notwithstanding many problems, the overall consequence of all the technological progress of the past century has been to confine death very largely to the aged, whereas throughout all of human history death occurred more or less regularly among all ages of life. There is a further unprecedented aspect to death in today's world:

the increasing numbers of aged have clustered—or have been herded —into various communities, centers, and homes, so that most of the dying occurs within the communities of the aged, out of sight (and mind) of society as a whole. Thus, death has, so to speak, "disappeared" from the mainstream of life, where it was for all of previous human history. This "disappearance" of death must be having profound philosophical, religious, and social consequences, but, if so, they do not appear to be widely recognized in such terms. We wonder if one of the social consequences of death's "disappearance" is the emergence since about 1962 of exaggerated public fears about things which pose very dilute risks.

Of course, it is not only a question of big fears about dilute risks; there is also the paradox that exaggerated public fears about dilute risks coexist with bland public acceptance of some very concentrated risks. The major ideas behind this book came together as we tried to analyze that paradox in the context of people's reactions to news about unexpected, adverse drug effects.

The immediate stimulus to this book occurred when one of us (K.H.) was invited to participate in a public symposium in Germany in 1981 on the topic of "technophobia." As the two of us discussed the symposium and what the important underlying issues were, it was apparent that distorted public understanding of risk was an important element in "technophobia." Within the perspective of trying to correct that distorted understanding, we came to the central themes of this book.

With the aid of the Safety-degree Scale, we have reviewed some of the hazards in today's life—some of them well known, others not. There were a number of surprises for us as we assembled the information for the various hazards and expressed the risk of each with the Safety-degree Scale. (One of us [J.U.] who still smoked gave it up after seeing the full magnitude of the risk of cigarette smoking, and the wealth of evidence supporting it.) Both the Safety-degree Scale and the concept of unicohort size are new, but we believe that, in working through all the examples we have presented in the previous chapters, use of the Safety-degree Scale can bring a new element of public understanding of health-related risk, and the realistic view that safety is always a matter of degree, not an absolute.

The measurement of risk by after-the-fact body counting is a distinctly unpleasant fact of life. In principle, foresight should be much the better way: to use our ever-growing scientific, technical, and practical knowledge to anticipate hazards and prevent them, versus the alternative of shocking surprises, body counts, retrospective analyses of poorly defined "experiments of nature," and long waits for answers. Foresight would indeed be better if one could avoid its main pitfall: that it is usually possible to marshal convincing evidence to show why any proposed action cannot work or is too risky, or both. This essential difficulty with the "what-if?" mentality is implied by the subtitle of the German version of this book: "Risk—element of life and engine of progress."

Both foresight and body counts are useful tools in analyzing and minimizing risk, and they are not mutually exclusive. Reducing risk, however, is not an end in itself. There is no haven of absolute safety, so everyone has to tolerate a certain amount of risk. At the most basic level, there is an actuarially defined risk of death at each age of life. Understanding risk in the quantitative terms provided by the Safety-degree Scale (or by one of the alternate modes of quantitative expression described in Appendix A) is fundamental in balancing opportunity and risk.

A big and yet-undigested consequence of death's long postponement is to confront us with the problem of the quality of life in its eighth, ninth, and tenth decades. While we do a reasonably good job in collecting statistics about deaths and their causes, we have surprisingly little information on the prevalence of disabilities that can transform life from a joy to a torture. The start of understanding the full scope of this problem is to classify these disabilities, develop systematic ways to measure their severity, and to count them. We certainly recognize these disabilities at a clinical level, but we do not really count them. For example, there has been much attention paid recently to victims of Alzheimer's disease and the horrible impact of its virtual obliteration of memory; yet there is only a crude estimate of how many people have this disease.

In Chapter 3 we discussed how the collection of vital statistics, begun in the 1840's, played an important role in improving public health by distinguishing between the more and less important causes of death. The process of collecting such data is very dull, costs money, and takes a great deal of time before there are enough data on which to base conclusions—which may contradict impressions, received wisdom, and favorite but mistaken beliefs. Assessing vitality in the aged would give a whole new meaning to "vital statistics."

Collecting and analyzing such information is greatly facilitated by computers, but it also represents an unprecedented invasion of privacy. While it is trivial to confess to the American Cancer Society that you smoke cigarettes and eat broccoli twice a week, it is another matter to have to reveal on some government form that you are impotent, can't climb stairs, and have to have someone help you get on and off the toilet. It is a challenging task to preserve privacy and measure the scope and prevalence of disabilities. Moreover, the vast majority of people of every age of life have a direct, personal stake in understanding the problems and disabilities of the aged and in building knowledge of their antecedent risk factors.

Understanding risk is the key to striking the best balance between opportunity and fear. There is no opportunity without risk, but there can be risk without fear, especially so when you realize that something you now fear is less risky than the things you already accept without concern.

NOTES TO CHAPTER 9

1. Inman, W.H.W. *Monitoring for Drug Safety.* Philadelphia and Toronto: J.B. Lippincott, 1979.

Appendix A

A Survey of Scales for Measuring Risk and Further Information on the Safety-degree Scale

Among experts in public health, insurance, and other risk-related disciplines, there are several different ways of expressing risks in quantitative terms. The most commonly used scale is to express the number of events occurring per 100,000 persons per unit time. This index method has no special name, and because its unitage is a bit of a tongue-twister, it is convenient to give it some kind of name, so let us call it by an acronym for its unitage: epsykay-pee-put—*ep* = *events per*; *sykay* = CK, the Roman numerals for a hundred thousand; *pee* = *persons*; *put* = *per unit time*. The epsykay-pee-put scale has been the choice of people who work with population statistics, e.g. insurance actuaries, demographers, public health workers, and so forth. These are all people whose perspectives are not that of the individual threatened by a hazard, but are instead concerned at the professional level with events occurring in large groups or populations. The reference unit of 100,000 people—as opposed to 10,000 or a million—is an arbitrary choice but has a certain convenience gained from its familiarity among those who use it.

There is no difference, of course, between saying that there were 9.4 homicide deaths per 100,000 people last year, and that there were 94 homicide deaths per million people last year. However, if you are trying to make sense out of a large table of data on vital statistics, it obviously becomes very inconvenient to have more than one size of reference population, and experts are no less fond of convenience than anyone else. In our context of trying to define a scale for risk that can become a part of everyday language, however, the epsykay-pee-put scale is not one that is oriented to the individual, who naturally wants to know: what is my risk of coming to personal harm over this or that?

Another basis for indexing risks has recently been developed by people who analyze workplace hazards. This is called the FAFR scale—an acronym for "fatal accident frequency rate"—and has the units of the number of fatal accidents occurring in 1000 men in a lifetime of working at a particular job.[1] The FAFR scale allows a straightforward comparison of different jobs and thus gives a basis for ranking workplace hazards. The choice of 1000 men in a lifetime of working is arbitrary; it is approximately equivalent to 50,000 man-years or to 100 million man-hours. With a bit of arithmetic, you can show that 1.0 FAFR and 2.0 deaths per 100,000 per year are the same. On the FAFR scale, contemporary industrial safety is between 4 and 5 on a nationwide basis, based on data from recent years in Britain.[2] This means that, out of a thousand workers working together for 50 years, four or five will die in a job-related accident; it also means that, since everyone eventually dies of something, 995 or 996 out of the thousand die of something besides a job-related accident. The FAFR index is useful, but it is limited in its scope to its intended purpose.

Two researchers at the National Radiological Protection Board in the United Kingdom recently proposed to express risk as a shortened life expectancy.[3] To illustrate, one can show that a man of 20 who works for one year in deep-sea fishing loses 51 days of life expectancy. While this has some meaning if the person continues to work at that job, it loses meaning when he takes leave of the job. Thus, if he works in the industry for a while and dies in an accident, he is dead, and his life expectancy is zero; on the other hand, if he leaves his job to open a fishmarket, he immediately regains his lost life expectancy as if he had never been exposed to the hazards of deep-sea fishing in the first place. The average reduction of 51 days of life expectancy is one of those strange averages which are composed of two extremes: a few who die early, and many who die old. A good test for this method in a more familiar context is to consider what information you find in being told that an airplane trip will deprive you of some minutes of life expectancy, which you will regain at the end of the trip—if you don't crash: it is not wrong, it is just not very informative.

Safety-degree Scale

As described briefly in the latter part of Chapter 3, the Safety-degree Scale is based on the concept of unicohort size. A unicohort, to reiterate, is the average number of participants in a given activity (or members of a cohort) needed to produce one victim in a chosen time span. To convert, for example, a figure from the epsykay-pee-put scale to unicohort, simply divide 100,000 by the epsykay-pee-put rate: 20 deaths per 100,000 per year becomes a unicohort of $100,000/20 = 5,000$. To convert to safety-degree units (SDU), take the logarithm (base 10) of the unicohort size: the $\log_{10}$ of 5,000 is 3.7.

When the unicohort can be approximated as 1, 10, 100, 1000, 10,000, 100,000, and so forth up to 100 million, conversion to the logarithm is simply to count the number of zeros. Thus, a unicohort of 100,000 is an SDU value of 5.0. If the unicohort size is some intermediate figure, such as 219,000, then one of two methods may be used. The easiest is to have a calculator capable of converting numbers to their logarithms; enter the number, push the "log" button, and get 5.3, in the case of 219,000. (If your calculator expresses its results to, for example, four decimal places, you will get 5.3404; however, a single decimal place is sufficiently precise for human risk data, for reasons discussed below.)

If you do not have access to a calculator, you can use Table 1, which gives the conversions between SDU and unicohort size. To illustrate, we can use the unicohort of 814,000 for the per-trip risk of being killed in a commercial air crash. To convert this number into SDU, note first that 814,000 lies between 100,000 and 1 million, so that the SDU value will be between 5 and 6. . .and closer to 6 than to 5, because 814,000 is much closer to 1 million than it is to 100,000: the SDU value will be 5-point-something. To get the closest approximation, use Table 1: look in the horizontal row labelled "5" until you find the value closest to 814,000, which is 800,000 in the column headed "0.9"—giving the value 5.9 SDU for the per-trip degree of safety of commercial flying. To convert 5.9 SDU back to unicohort size, you look for the intersection of the row labelled "5" and the

TABLE 1

INTERPOLATION BETWEEN THE INTEGERS OF THE SAFETY-DEGREE SCALE TO CONVERT BETWEEN SDU AND UNICOHORT SIZE

SDU integers	SDU decimals										
	0	0.1	0.2	0.3	0.4	0.5	0.6	0.7	0.8	0.9	
0	1	1	2	2	3	3	4	5	6	8	single digits
1	10	12	16	20	25	30	40	50	60	80	tens
2	100	125	160	200	250	300	400	500	600	800	hundreds
3	1	1.25	1.6	2	2.5	3	4	5	6	8	} thousands
4	10	12.5	16	20	25	30	40	50	60	80	
5	100	125	160	200	250	300	400	500	600	800	
6	1	1.25	1.6	2	2.5	3	4	5	6	8	} millions
7	10	12.5	16	20	25	30	40	50	60	80	
8	100	125	160	200	250	300	400	500	600	800	

column labelled "0.9"; the intersection contains the figure 800 in the zone labelled on the right as "thousands"—thus, 800,000. There is a small error due to rounding off the 814,000 to 800,000, but it is only a few percent.

You will note that specifying SDU values only to a single decimal place imposes a certain degree of approximation on the data. For example, if the unicohort size were 700,000, it would be a toss-up whether to represent that figure as 5.8 or 5.9 SDU. In either case, it represents an error of less than 20%. That may appear to be somewhat cavalier in something which quantifies matters of life and death, but much of the basic data from which unicohort sizes can be determined turn out to have uncertainties of at least that size or greater. That is another of the "facts of life" about measuring risks: the data upon which risk measurements are based are sometimes of questionable reliability, usually because of uncertainties about whether all the right people were counted, or whether there was some peculiar kind of bias which resulted in only certain kinds of people being included in a count rather than all the people who should have been. This is an issue which comes up again and again in the discussion of specific hazards.

A further subdivision of the Safety-degree Scale into 0.01 increases or decreases is certainly possible, but is rarely warranted, because the available data lack the kind of precision implied when one tries to make distinctions between 5.90 and 5.91 SDU. That is about a 2% difference in unicohort size, and such fine distinctions rarely have practical value, even if the precision of the underlying data supported them. It is instructive to note that life insurance premiums are adjusted in light of various risk factors in a person's life in steps of 15–25%.[4] Each such step corresponds approximately to a decrease in safety-degree of 0.1 SDU, i.e. a risk concentration of 0.1 SDU.

As with the other scales we discussed for expressing risks quantitatively, the Safety-degree Scale has its strengths and weaknesses. One of its great strengths is compactness: from 1 in 1 to 1 in 100,000,000 is compressed into a scale which goes from 0 to 8; also, it translates readily into an expression of odds or risk which is easily grasped through the analogy to the class picture and its single victim. Another great strength of the Safety-degree Scale is that the expression of safety-degree is one and the same with risk dilution, and, as a consequence, the units of the Safety-degree Scale are units of risk dilution. An inevitable weak point of the Scale is its lack of familiarity, although this can change if the Safety-degree Scale is accepted and used, as occurred with the Richter Scale. Some people find it disconcerting that sometimes important risk comparisons are represented by only a few tenths of a safety-degree unit; this relates to the fact that a one-unit change on the Scale represents a ten-fold change in safety-degree or risk.

A fundamentally important feature of the Safety-degree Scale is that there is no number in the Scale for absolute safety, which does not exist, as reflected by the fact that there is no theoretical upper limit to the Scale. It has a practical upper limit, set by the limitations in population sizes from which risk data are gathered, but the Scale can expand if and when ways are found to widen the limits in data collection. "Zero" on the Safety-degree Scale is a unique point of absolute certainty that the adverse event in question will occur, signifying zero degree of safety.

The concept of measuring risk in units of safety-degree is novel, but simple. Increasing safety-degree means increasing dilution of risk. Decreasing safety-degree means that risk is increasing, or being concentrated. "Risk" and "safety-degree" are semantic inverses of one another. "Risk dilution" and "safety-degree" are synonymous, and, in fact, the German version of this book, published in 1983, used the term "risk dilution" exclusively and did not speak of "safety-degree." It was only in the months spent preparing the English version that we recognized the advantages in the concept of safety-degree, compared to risk dilution, as the basis for a quantitative scale for expressing risk.

An Economic Perspective on the Safety-degree Scale

In what follows, we relate the Safety-degree Scale to the principle of insurance, which allows SDU values to be interpreted in an economic context. The principle of insurance lies in giving risks an economic value, and converting those values into insurance premiums. The size of the premium depends on the size of the policy and the magnitude of the estimated risk. Life insurance will illustrate.

The principle of insurance is that all participants pay an affordable sum as premiums so that a few victims among them may receive a large sum. An example will illustrate: for a certain hazard, assume that one's risk of becoming a victim is 1 in 1000 per year, and that 1000 people are equally at risk of becoming a victim. If we want the victim to be compensated with $100,000, then we have to ask a premium of $100 per year from each of the thousand insured individuals. The total amount collected in premiums will be $100,000 —just enough to award the $100,000 payment to the anticipated single victim. Naturally, this example illustrates only the principle on which insurance is based, for it neglects the fact that insurance companies have to cover administrative and sales costs, maintain reserves in case the risk was underestimated, and obtain a profit. But the principle, simply expressed, is that one **thousand** people each pay one **hundred** dollars so that one victim can receive one **hundred thousand** dollars.

Insurance companies, as is well known, do not offer only life insurance but are also prepared to insure you against certain specifically defined hazards. What is required to write such insurance is data from recent past experience involving others who appear to have been sufficiently like you to warrant the assumption that their risk and yours are equal. (When you learn from the news media of some untoward event, you are moved to identify with the victims and to make that same assumption—"it could have happened to me.") The Safety-degree Scale can be used very simply to estimate how much you would have to pay in insurance premiums to insure yourself against the risk in question.

To illustrate how it works, let us assume that you want to insure yourself against the risk in question for $1 million—a tidy sum, the receipt of which might be expected to assuage a good deal of anguish over one's becoming a victim. We simply write the size of this policy in one row and place under the zeros the integers of the Safety-degree Scale in ascending order:

$ 1 0 0 0 0 0 0 . 0 0	policy size
0 1 2 3 4 5 6 7 8	integers of the Safety-degree Scale
$ _ _ _ _ _ _ _ . _ _	premium

Using this little device, we can calculate the premium needed for the example we considered previously, the risk of being killed in the crash of a commercial airliner. The per-trip risk was 5.9 SDU. To use this device, we have to round off to the nearest whole SDU value, namely 6 SDU. Simply write a 1 in the space in the bottom row under the 6 in the middle row, and fill in zeros in the spaces to the right. As you see, the premium is $1.00. If you take 100 trips in the course of a year, then the annual premium would be $100. This is illustrated as follows, for a single plane trip:

$ 1 0 0 0 0 0 0 . 0 0	policy size
0 1 2 3 4 5 6 7 8	integers of the Safety-degree Scale
$ _ _ _ _ _ _ 1 . 0 0	premium

For 100 trips per year, there is a per-year death risk of 3.9 SDU, which rounds off to 4 SDU, and so the premium would be:

$ 1 0 0 0 0 0 0 . 0 0	policy size
0 1 2 3 4 5 6 7 8	integers of the Safety-degree Scale
$ _ _ _ _ 1 0 0 . 0 0	premium

It is possible to calculate these hypothetical premiums more precisely, based on the SDU value carried to the first decimal place. But since they are only rough estimates and do not take into account realistic pricing of actual commercial insurance, it is not worthwhile to go further. This little device is useful, however, to give a quick estimate of the hypothetical cost of insuring yourself against various risks when they are expressed in SDU. To get a more precise cost, divide $1 million by the unicohort size.

Chronological Age and Risk-Age

If the previous section was written for those readers who want to see an economic value put on everything, this section is for those who dislike the idea of growing older. The notion we wish you to consider is that everyone has, in effect, two ages—a chronological one, based on your date of birth, and a risk-age, which may deviate in either direction from your chronological age, depending on the various risk factors in your life. It is another idea based on the concept of life insurance.

For every life insurance applicant, the question which the insurance company faces is how to fix the premium in relation not only to the age and sex of the applicant, but also to the various exceptional risk factors which may be present in the individual's life: high blood pressure, obesity, diabetes, cigarette smoking, motorcycle riding, hang-gliding, and so forth. There are different methods to determine the necessary premium adjustment for exceptional risk. One always starts with the standard premium for the person's age and sex and then adds extras to the premium according to the method chosen. One method consists of adding to the chronological age a certain number of extra years to adjust for risks in the individual's life that exceed those characteristic of his or her age and sex. This is possible because, as we shall see shortly, standard life insurance tables show a steady increase in risk with each year of additional age from your early adult years until the end of life. Table 2 shows the interrelations between risk multiples, SDU, and the years which are added to one's chronological age.

TABLE 2

YEARS TO BE ADDED TO CHRONOLOGICAL AGE TO DETERMINE RISK-AGE, RELATED TO INCREASED RISK

Increased Risk		*years added to*
risk multiple	*SDU change*	*chronological age*
1.25	−0.1	3
1.5	−0.2	5
2.0	−0.3	7
2.5	−0.4	9
3.0	−0.5	11
4.0	−0.6	14
5.0*	−0.7	16

Source: Brackenridge, R.D.C., *Medical Selection of Life Risks*, Table 9, p. 39

* The life insurer rarely ventures beyond a 5X multiple, so the table stops here.

An example will perhaps clarify this idea. As we shall discuss in more detail later, the life-shortening effect of smoking one cigarette is one minute. This figure may not impress the cigarette smoker who sees any diminution of life expectancy as being subtracted from the end of life. If you are, for example, 33 years old and smoke cigarettes, the fact of your smoking decreases your overall degree of safety by 0.3 SDU, which corresponds to a doubling of your normal, age-related death risk. In terms of the standard life insurance premium table, you are not 33 anymore, but 40, which is the age at which mortality is double that at age 33. In a certain sense, the act of smoking ages you by seven years. A similar "aging" occurs, for example, in a 25-year-old male with a serum cholesterol level of 330 mg%, or one who has managed to hang 280 pounds on a 6-foot frame.

Another example is that of a healthy 35-year-old woman who does not smoke but who uses tampons. As is well-known, super-absorbent tampons have been associated with the toxic shock syndrome, an infrequently occurring, sometimes fatal infection. The risk of death associated with the use of tampons—if indeed their use plays a causative role in toxic shock syndrome—is 1 in about 100,000 per year, i.e. 5.0 SDU.[5] This risk is simply too small to cause any change in risk-age, and, returning to the little device for computing insurance premiums, you can see that the premium for a $1 million policy against death from this cause would be $10. The fact that this risk is so dilute does not prevent people from getting toxic shock syndrome or from dying of it if they get it; rather, it means only that the additional risk is so small that the person's overall risk is affected to so miniscule an amount that it does not change the risk-age. The logical consequence should be to analyze those hazards of our lives which are able to increase our risk-age by a significant amount. Considering all measures which you **might** take to reduce risks in your life, this is a logical first step.

A useful rule of thumb is to direct your attention to things which increase your overall risk of death by 25% or more, and to ignore activities with a smaller death risk. Activities or behavior which increase overall death risk by 25% correspond to a loss of 0.1 SDU.

It seems rather obvious that it is not sensible to have a risk-age which is greater than your chronological age. It is already bad enough to age, year after year, and to have to face an increasing risk of death with each passing year. One should therefore attempt to maintain one's risk-age as close as possible to one's chronological age—or below, if one knew how.

Finally, we present in Table 3 the complete breakdown of overall death risk for each five-year step in age, together with the corresponding unicohort sizes, SDU values, and annual premiums for $1 million in insurance (in the same kind of hypothetical insurance cooperative described earlier, where the premiums are fully paid out as claims, without any reserves, profits, or overhead). There is a separate listing for males and females, since there is a consistent difference between the sexes in the risk of death in every year of life. These numbers are juxtaposed with data from standard actuarial tables from the life insurance industry, showing the risk basis for calculating life insurance premiums for each sex, at each five-year point. The complete actuarial tables, of course, go year by year, but, for our purposes, it suffices to see the data at five-year points, knowing that there is a steady, year-by-year progression in the intervening years.

The right-hand column for each sex shows the idealized annual premium for $1 million in life insurance. This is a useful figure against which to compare the risk added by specific hazards in your life. We can illustrate the point with two examples already mentioned. The cigarette smoker, with a doubled risk of death, should have to pay double the normal premium in our hypothetical insurance cooperative. (What happens in the real world is described in Chapter 5.) The 35-year-old woman who opts to use super-absorbent tampons, should, as noted above, have to pay a $10 premium to insure herself against this added risk. As Table 3 shows, however, her basic, overall risk is such that her annual premium is $630, to which we add the $10 for the added risk of death due to toxic shock syndrome—reflecting a 1.6% increase in her overall risk of death. That risk increment may be a basis for her abandoning tampon use, but it is hardly the stuff of national crisis, as the news media made it out to be when toxic shock syndrome was big news.

From Table 3, you can see that the standard risk for insurance purposes is more dilute than the yearly death risk determined from vital statistics. This difference occurs because the standard risk for insurance purposes is based on data from people who purchase life insurance and thus are demonstrably healthy when insurance is taken out—often because passing a doctor's exam is a precondition for obtaining insurance. The death rates determined from vital statistics include people who would have been too sick or infirm to be accepted for life insurance. Ten-year-old females are an exception in the table, because their current annual death rate (column B) is lower than the standard risk (column E), whereas it is the other way around for all other ages. This tiny difference probably relates to the fact that the insurance data come from 1970–75, while the vital statistics data come from 1978, and the steady progress in reducing death-risk at each age of life probably sufficed to drop the 1978 value for the entire population below the 1970–75 values for the select group of insured.

There are several other notable features about the data in Table 3, which gives a broad overview of how all risks sum up to whittle away at life. For both sexes, the lowest death risk occurs at age ten, and females show a steady, year-by-year increase thereafter. In males, death risk increases from age ten until the early twenties, after which it turns downward for a few years until age 30, after which it rises steadily with each passing year. The miniature peak in mortality in the early twenties for males is probably due to the clustering of accidental deaths in that age group—a process in which automobiles and alcohol play a considerable role, as discussed in Chapter 5.

Conclusion

In this Appendix, we have sought to elucidate a comprehensible scale for giving quantitative expression to risks. We have also shown how the Safety-degree Scale relates to the basic cost of insuring oneself against becoming victim to a risk. That device can be used as a simple way to understand how much risk a particular hazard adds to your overall, age-related risk, reflected by the insurance premiums listed in Table 3. Also, we have shown how risk changes with age and differs considerably between the two sexes. Also, we have presented the concept of risk-age, and how it can differ from chronological age. In Chapters 4–8 we discuss specific hazards and use these concepts to make clear how the addition or exclusion of such risks changes our general, overall risk of death. Armed with such information, you can identify the most important hazards in your life and decide what to do about them, besides merely worrying. Should you decide only

TABLE 3

CHANGES IN OVERALL LIFE RISK AND SAFETY DEGREE WITH ADVANCING AGE

Males

A	B	C	D	E	F	G
Age (years)	Current annual death rate (deaths per thousand)	Unicohort for 1 death per year	Overall life Safety-degree (SDU) per year	Standard risk for insuring lives of healthy males (death claims per year per thousand policies)	SDU for standard risk, per year (life Safety-degree for insurance)	Idealized annual pre-mium for $1 million life insurance policy ($)
0	13.37	75	1.9	3.70	2.4	3700
5	0.43	2326	3.4	0.41	3.4	410
10	0.24	4167	3.6	0.21	3.7	210
15	1.06	943	3.0	0.77	3.1	770
20	1.85	541	2.7	1.28	2.9	1280
25	1.79	559	2.7	1.08	3.0	1080
30	1.60	625	2.8	0.94	3.0	940
35	1.86	538	2.7	1.18	2.9	1180
40	2.68	373	2.6	1.91	2.7	1910
45	4.44	225	2.4	3.19	2.5	3190
50	7.46	134	2.1	5.01	2.3	5010
55	11.53	87	1.9	8.28	2.1	8280
60	19.07	52	1.7	13.20	1.9	13200
65	28.75	35	1.5	21.52	1.7	21520
70	42.64	23	1.4	34.07	1.5	34070
75	65.28	15	1.2	56.35	1.2	56350
80	98.30	10	1.0	87.28	1.1	87280

Females

A Age (years)	B Current annual death rate (deaths per thousand)	C Unicohort for 1 death per year	D Overall life Safety- degree (SDU) per year	E Standard risk for insuring lives of healthy females (death claims per year per thousand policies)	F SDU for standard risk, per year (life Safety- degree for insurance)	G Idealized annual pre- mium for $1 million life insurance policy ($)
0	10.58	95	2.0	2.45	2.6	2450
5	0.33	3030	3.5	0.30	3.5	300
10	0.19	5263	3.7	0.20	3.7	200
15	0.44	2273	3.4	0.33	3.5	330
20	0.61	1639	3.2	0.48	3.3	480
25	0.62	1613	3.2	0.53	3.3	530
30	0.69	1449	3.2	0.63	3.2	630
35	0.90	1111	3.0	0.82	3.1	820
40	1.49	671	2.8	1.44	2.8	1440
45	2.52	397	2.6	2.37	2.6	2370
50	3.98	251	2.4	3.50	2.5	3500
55	5.94	168	2.2	5.26	2.3	5260
60	9.58	104	2.0	7.11	2.1	7110
65	13.84	72	1.9	11.45	1.9	11450
70	20.92	48	1.7	17.79	1.7	17790
75	36.03	28	1.4	31.99	1.5	31990
80	60.22	17	1.2	56.56	1.2	56560

Sources: U.S. Bureau of the Census, *Statistical Abstract of the United States, 1980,* Table 108; Education and Examination Committee of the Society of Actuaries, Part 10 (LB), Study Notes, 10 LB-507-81, Chicago, July 1979.

to worry, however, then at least oblige us by worrying most about the biggest risks, and least about the smallest.

NOTES TO APPENDIX A

1. Kletz, T.A. "Hazard analysis, its application to risks to the public at large." *Occupational Safety and Health* (U.K.), Part 1, vol. 7, no. 9, (1977): 12; Part II, Vol. 7, no. 10, (1977): 12; Kletz, T.A. "What risks should we run?" *New Scientist* (May 12, 1977): 320–22.

2. Pochin, E.E. "Occupation and other fatality rates." *Comm. Health* 6 (1974): 2–13.

3. Reissland, J., and V. Harries. "A scale for measuring risks." *New Scientist* 83 (September 13, 1979): 809–11.

4. Brackenridge, R.D.C. *Medical Selection of Life Risks.* London: Undershaft, 1977, Chapter 4.

5. U.S. Center for Disease Control. *Morbidity and Mortality Weekly Report.* February 3, 1984.

Appendix B

American Cancer Society Questionnaire

| AMERICAN CANCER SOCIETY **CANCER PREVENTION STUDY II** CPS II **QUESTIONNAIRE FOR WOMEN** | Division No. | Unit No. | Group No. |
| | Researcher No. | Family No. | Person No. |

Date: _____

1. Name: _____
2. Date of birth: Month _____ Year _____
3. How old are you now? _____
4. Current weight with indoor clothing: _____ lbs.
5. Weight 1 year ago: _____ lbs.
6. Height (without shoes): _____ ft. _____ in.

7. ☐ White ☐ Black ☐ Hispanic
   ☐ Oriental ☐ Other _____ (specify)
8. Marital status:
   ☐ Single ☐ Separated ☐ Widowed
   ☐ Married ☐ Divorced
9. If ever married, age at first marriage: _____
10. Number of times married: _____
11. Social Security No.: _____ (optional)

FAMILY HISTORY (IN RELATION TO CANCER):

1. Fill in the following table as completely as possible for parents, brothers and sisters.

LIST ONE BLOOD RELATIVE PER LINE: (Circle Brother **or** Sister)	IS THIS PERSON? (Circle One)	IF ALIVE, GIVE AGE	IF DEAD, GIVE AGE AT DEATH	DID THIS PERSON **EVER** HAVE CANCER? (Circle One)	IF "YES," SPECIFY TYPE OF CANCER	AT WHAT AGE?
Father	Alive Dead			Yes No		
Mother	Alive Dead			Yes No		
Brother or Sister	Alive Dead			Yes No		
Brother or Sister	Alive Dead			Yes No		
Brother or Sister	Alive Dead			Yes No		
Brother or Sister	Alive Dead			Yes No		
Brother or Sister	Alive Dead			Yes No		
Brother or Sister	Alive Dead			Yes No		

2. When you were born, a) How old was your mother? _____ b) How old was your father? _____

HISTORY OF DISEASES:

1. Have you ever had cancer? ☐ Yes ☐ No. If "yes,"
   a) What type? _____
   b) Date of first treatment: _____
2. Place a check-mark by the following diseases or conditions for which you have ever been diagnosed by a doctor:

☐ High Blood Pressure ☐ Hay Fever
☐ Heart Disease ☐ Asthma
☐ Stroke ☐ Stomach Ulcer
☐ Diabetes ☐ Duodenal Ulcer
☐ Gall Stones ☐ Diverticulosis
☐ Chronic Indigestion ☐ Rectal Polyps
☐ Kidney Disease ☐ Colon Polyps
☐ Kidney Stones ☐ Thyroid Condition
☐ Bladder Disease ☐ Arthritis
☐ Cirrhosis of the Liver ☐ Breast Cysts
☐ Tuberculosis ☐ Gynecological
☐ Chronic Bronchitis   Problems
☐ Emphysema ☐ Hepatitis
☐ Any other serious disease (specify) _____
_____

3. Have you ever had an operation? ☐ Yes ☐ No
   If "yes," specify type and date(s) of operation(s):
   _____
   _____
   _____
   _____

4. How **many** x-ray or fluoroscopic **examinations** (GI series, barium enema, etc.) have you **ever** had of:

| | 6 or | | | 6 or |
	0 1-5 More			0 1-5 More
Stomach	☐ ☐ ☐	Chest		☐ ☐ ☐
Intestine	☐ ☐ ☐	Breast		☐ ☐ ☐
Back	☐ ☐ ☐	Head/Neck		☐ ☐ ☐

5. Have you ever been **treated** with radium, x-rays, or radioactive isotopes? ☐ Yes ☐ No
   If "yes," when? _____
   For what disease? _____
   _____
   What part of your body? _____

6. How many times have you had colds or flu in the past twelve months? _____

CURRENT PHYSICAL CONDITION:

1. How much exercise do you get (work or play)?
   ☐ None ☐ Slight ☐ Moderate ☐ Heavy
2. On the average, how many hours do you sleep each night? _____
3. On the average, how many times a month do you have insomnia? _____ ☐ None
4. Within the last twelve months, have you noticed:
   a) A lump or thickening in your breast?
      ☐ Yes ☐ No
   b) An unusual discharge from your breast?
      ☐ Yes ☐ No
5. Do you notice pains in your legs when you walk which go away when you rest? ☐ Yes ☐ No
   If "yes," how many years have you had these pains? _____
6. Are you sick at the present time? ☐ Yes ☐ No
   If "yes," with what disease or condition? _____
   _____
   _____

MENSTRUAL AND REPRODUCTIVE HISTORY:

1. How old were you when menstruation began? _____
2. What is your current menopausal status?
   ☐ Still regularly menstruating
   ☐ In menopause ☐ Past menopause
3. During your menstrual history:
   a) Are (were) your periods: ☐ Regular ☐ Irregular
   b) What is (was) the usual number of days of flow? _____
4. **If past menopause:**
   a) Was your menopause: ☐ Natural ☐ Artificial
   b) Age when periods stopped completely? _____
   c) Did you have excessive bleeding during menopause? ☐ Yes ☐ No
5. Have you ever had or tried to have children?
   ☐ Yes ☐ No
   If "no," skip to question 9.
6. Have you ever had difficulty becoming pregnant?
   ☐ Yes ☐ No
   If "yes," what was the reason? _____
   _____
7. How many times have you been pregnant? _____
   a) Your age at your first pregnancy? _____
   b) Your age at your first live birth? _____
   c) Number of children born alive? _____
   d) Number of stillbirths (carried 5 months or more)? _____
   e) Number of miscarriages (carried less than 5 months)? _____
8. Were you ever given DES (Diethylstilbestrol) to prevent miscarriage? ☐ Yes ☐ No
   If "yes,"
   a) At what age did you take it? _____
   b) For how many months did you take it? _____

9. Birth control methods: Indicate your age when **first used** and number of years of use.

Method Used	Age	Years
Rhythm		
Diaphragm		
Cream/Foam/Jelly		
Tubal Ligation		
Intrauterine Device (IUD)		
Condom (partner)		
Vasectomy (partner)		
NONE OF THE ABOVE ☐		

10. Have you **ever** taken oral contraceptives (birth control pills)? ☐ Yes ☐ No
    If "no," skip to question 11.
    a) Age when you first took them? _____
    b) How many years did you take them? _____
    c) What brand(s) do (did) you take? _____
    d) If you stopped taking them, what was the reason? _____
    e) Did you have irregular or painful periods when you stopped? ☐ Yes ☐ No
11. Have you **ever** used female hormones (estrogens) other than oral contraceptives? ☐ Yes ☐ No
    a) Why do (did) you take estrogens?
       ☐ Menopausal symptoms ☐ Hysterectomy
       ☐ Bone problems ☐ Cancer
       ☐ Other (specify) _____
    b) Age first took estrogens? _____
    c) For how many years did you take them? _____
    d) How did you take them? ☐ Injection ☐ Cream
       ☐ Pill (brand): _____

HABITS:

1. **Whether or not you smoke,** on the average, how many **hours a day** are you exposed to cigarette smoke of others:
   At home _____, At work _____, In other areas _____.
2. Do you now or have you ever smoked cigarettes, at least one a day for one year's time? ☐ Yes ☐ No

Smoking History	Current Smokers	Ex-Smokers
Number smoked a day		
Age began smoking		
Age quit smoking	▨▨▨▨	
Most recent (last) brand		
Years smoked **this** brand		
Total years smoked **filtered** cigarettes		
Total years smoked **non-filtered** cigarettes		
Total years of smoking (filtered + non-filtered)		

3. Current **and** ex-smokers:
   a) Do (did) you inhale? ☐ No, never
      ☐ Slightly ☐ Moderately ☐ Deeply
   b) Fill in the following information for:
      1) The **first** brand smoked regularly; and
      2) The brand of cigarette smoked for the **longest** period of time.

Brand Name	Size	Filter Yes	Filter No	Menthol Yes	Menthol No	Number Per Day	Years
1.							
2.							

DIET:

1. On the average, how many days per week do you eat the following foods? (If less than once a week, but at least twice a month, write 1/2.)

   Beef_____   Raw vegetables_____
   Pork_____   Carrots_____
   Chicken_____   Squash/Corn_____
   Liver_____   Citrus fruits/Juices____
   Ham_____   Spaghetti/Macaroni/
   Fish_____   White rice_____
   Smoked meats_____   White bread/Rolls/
   Frankfurters/   Biscuits_____
      Sausage_____   Brown rice/Whole
   Butter_____   wheat/Barley_____
   Margarine_____   Bran/Corn muffins____
   Cheese_____   Potatoes_____
   Eggs_____   Oatmeal/Shredded
   Green leafy   wheat/Bran
      vegetables_____   cereals_____
   Tomatoes_____   Cold (Dry) cereals____
   Cabbage/Broccoli/   Ice cream_____
      Brussels sprouts____   Chocolate_____

2. How many days a week do you eat the following **fried** foods?
   Fried eggs_____   Fried hamburgers
   Fried bacon_____   or beef_____
   Fried chicken/fish____   Other fried foods_____
   French fries_____
   DO NOT EAT FRIED FOODS ☐

3. Do you eat a vegetarian diet?   ☐ Yes ☐ No
   If "yes," what type and for how many years?_____

4. Has there been a major change in your diet in the last 10 years?   ☐ Yes ☐ No
   If "yes," what was the change?_____

5. a) Do you now or have you ever added artificial sweeteners (saccharin or cyclamates) to coffee, tea, or other drinks or food?
      ☐ Yes, currently ☐ Formerly ☐ Never
   b) If **ever** used artificial sweeteners, indicate amount per day and for how long.
   Packets: No. per day____ ____ Years_____
   Drops: No. per day_____ Years_____
   Tablets: No. per day_____ Years_____

6. Do you get your drinking water from: ☐ City supply
   ☐ Private well ☐ Other (specify)_____

7. Do you add any substances to soften your drinking water?   ☐ Yes ☐ No

8. How many cups, glasses, or drinks of these beverages do you usually drink a day, and for how many years? (If you no longer drink a listed beverage, or your pattern has changed in the last ten years, indicate previous and current amounts. If less than once a day, but at least three times a week, write 1/2).

Beverages	Currently Amount	Currently Years	Previously Amount	Previously Years
Whole milk (not skim milk)				
Caffeinated coffee				
Decaffeinated coffee				
Tea				
Diet soda or diet iced tea				
Non-diet colas				
Other non-diet soft drinks				
Beer				
Wine				
Hard liquor				

MEDICATIONS AND VITAMINS:

1. How many times in the last month have you used the following and how long have you used them? (If none, write 0; if used only occasionally, write 1/2.)

Medications and Vitamins	Times	Years
Aspirin, Bufferin, Anacin		
Tylenol		
Vitamin A		
Vitamin C		
Vitamin E		
Multi-Vitamins		
Blood Pressure pills		
Diuretics (water pills)		
Thyroid medications		
Heart medications		
Anti-Acid medications		
Valium		
Librium		
Prescription sleeping pills		
Tagamet (for ulcers)		
Other: _____		
_____		

OCCUPATIONS:

1. What is your current occupation and what are your duties?_____
_____ How many years: _____
2. If retired, what was your last occupation? _____
_____
_____ Year retired: _____
3. What other job have you held for the longest period of time?_____
_____ How many years: _____
4. What time of day do you start working? _____
Do you work rotating shifts? ☐ Yes ☐ No
5. How many hours a week do you work on:
paid jobs _____, volunteer work _____,
housework _____.
6. In your work or daily life, are (were) you **regularly** exposed to any of the following? If "yes," indicate the number of years exposed.

Exposure to:	Check One Yes	No	Number of Years
Asbestos			
Chemicals/Acids/Solvents			
Coal or Stone Dusts			
Coal Tar/Pitch/Asphalt			
Diesel Engine Exhaust			
Dyes			
Formaldehyde			
Gasoline Exhaust			
Pesticides/Herbicides			
Textile Fibers/Dusts			
Wood Dust			
X-rays/Radioactive Materials			

REMARKS:

MISCELLANEOUS:

1. Where were you born? _____
  city state/country
2. Where were your parents born?
Father: _____
Mother: _____
3. Religion: ☐ Protestant ☐ Catholic ☐ Jewish
☐ LDS ☐ Other _____ ☐ None
If Protestant, what denomination? _____
4. Education:
☐ 8th Grade or Less ☐ Some College
☐ Some High School ☐ College Graduate
☐ High School Graduate ☐ Graduate School
☐ Vocational/Trade School
5. How many years have you lived in your present neighborhood? _____
6. How many friends or relatives do you feel close to? _____
7. How many times a month do you:
a) Go to church or temple? _____
b) Attend club meetings? _____
c) Participate in group activities? _____
8. What is the most upsetting event that happened to you in about the last five years? _____
_____ ☐ None
9. How many people do you take care of in your household? (Include yourself) _____
10. Do you now or have you ever used a **permanent** hair dye? ☐ Yes ☐ No
If "yes,"
a) What brand? _____
b) What color? _____
c) How often applied? _____
d) How many years have you used it? _____
11. Do you now or have you ever used mouthwash? ☐ Yes ☐ No
If "yes,"
a) What brand? _____
b) How many times a week is it used? _____
c) For how many years have you used it? _____

Index